Convergence Media History

Convergence Media History explores the ways that digital convergence has radically changed the field of media history. Writing media history is no longer a matter of charting the historical development of an individual medium such as film or television. Instead, now that various media from blockbuster films to everyday computer use intersect regularly via convergence, scholars must find new ways to write media history across multiple media formats.

This collection of eighteen new essays by leading media historians and scholars examines the issues today in writing media history and histories. Each essay addresses a single medium—including film, television, advertising, sound recording, new media, and more—and connects that specific medium's history to larger issues for the field in writing multimedia or convergent histories. Among the volume's topics are new media technologies and their impact on traditional approaches to media history; alternative accounts of film production and exhibition, with a special emphasis on film across multiple media platforms; the changing relationships between audiences, fans, and consumers within media culture; and the globalization of our media culture.

Contributors:

Megan Sapnar Ankerson

Kyle S. Barnett

Richard Butsch

Chris Cagle

Marsha F. Cassidy

Sue Collins

Harper Cossar

Ken Feil

Kathryn H. Fuller-Seeley

Derek Johnson

Dan Leopard

Elana Levine

Hamid Naficy

Alisa Perren

Karl Schoonover

Laura Isabel Serna

Mark Williams

Pamela Wilson

Janet Staiger is William P. Hobby Centennial Professor of Communication in the Department of Radio-Television-Film at the University of Texas at Austin. The author of many books, her most recent include *Media Reception Studies*, *Blockbuster TV: Must-See Sitcoms in the Network Era*, and *Perverse Spectators: The Practices of Film Reception*.

Sabine Hake is Professor and Texas Chair of German Literature and Culture at the University of Texas at Austin. She is the author of *Topographies of Class: Urban Architecture and Mass Utopia in Weimar Berlin*, *German National Cinema*, and *Popular Cinema of the Third Reich*, and is currently working on a book on the fascist imaginary in postfascist cinema.

Convergence Media History

Edited by
Janet Staiger and Sabine Hake

Routledge
Taylor & Francis Group

NEW YORK AND LONDON

First published 2009
by Routledge
270 Madison Ave, New York, NY 10016

Simultaneously published in the UK
by Routledge
2 Park Square, Milton Park, Abingdon, Oxon OX14 4RN

Routledge is an imprint of the Taylor & Francis Group, an informa business

© 2009 Taylor & Francis

Typeset in Perpetua by Wearset Ltd, Boldon, Tyne and Wear
Printed and bound in the United States of America on acid-
free paper by Edwards Brothers, Inc.

Library of Congress Cataloging in Publication Data
Staiger, Janet.
Convergence, media, history/Janet Staiger and Sabine Hake.—
1st ed.
p. cm.
Includes bibliographical references and index.
1. Mass media–Social aspects. I. Hake, Sabine, 1956– II. Title.
HM1206.S72 2009
302.23–dc22   2008046079

ISBN10: 0-415-99661-9 (hbk)
ISBN10: 0-415-99662-7 (pbk)
ISBN10: 0-203-88343-8 (ebk)

ISBN13: 978-0-415-99661-7 (hbk)
ISBN13: 978-0-415-99662-4 (pbk)
ISBN13: 978-0-203-88343-3 (ebk)

Contents

Figures

Preface

Twenty-first century analysis of the production and reception of media recognizes the convergence of both media and approaches to studying the history of media. While likely print, movies, radio, television, and new media should never have been thought of as separate histories, the insistence of context now forces media historians to note relations among and between the various sites of information and entertainment. In a conference held at the University of Texas, October 11–13, 2007, established and emerging media historians were asked to tackle the issues of convergence: Where are we now? What are the issues today in writing media history and histories? What have we accomplished? Where might we go? For whom and why? The essays in this collection offer some initial answers to these questions based on reflections over those conversations.

Some of these essays deal with cross-media situations, with information showing up on multiple platforms for viewers. Other essays address lessons to be learned from other media to apply to new situations. Some reflect on the problems of finding evidence or considering texts not initially realized as worthy of study.

More significantly, "convergence media history" attacks the assumption that people can be solely a "film" or "television" scholar; competency across the media is beneficial in understanding the breadth of media influencing the particular object of study. People may watch a theatrically released film on the comfort of their home entertainment system. Is that a "film" or "television"? When a serial television program's clues to resolving the plot appear in television ads or via freeze-frame analysis and discussion on fan web pages, is that a television program, print, or new media?

In accordance with the anthology's critical agenda, we have organized the individual chapters into four parts: New Methods, New Subjects, New Approaches, and Research Issues. "Part I: New Methods" brings together five case studies that offer new models for doing film and media history. Hamid Nacify traces the contribution, as both spectators and producers of movies, of large displaced populations—exilic, diasporic, ethnic, transnational, cosmo-politan—to the continued revitalization of cinema in the age of globalization, creating what he, in expanding the notion of accented cinema, calls multiplex cinema. In his case study on *X-Men* and its marketing from the 1960s to the 1990s, Derek Johnson uses the practice of franchising to uncover the multiple media contexts that sustain an intra-industrial and inter-industrial process of multiplication and thus can serve as a privileged model of media convergence. Similarly Chris Cagle, in his revisionist account of 1940s leftist Hollywood cinema and the social problem film, uses Bourdieu's notion of social field to argue for the importance of the producer—in this case Dore Schary for RKO—and, in so doing, complicates the relationship between industry and ideology. Pushing the boundaries even further, Marsha Cassidy introduces such elusive categories as synaesthesia and sense memory into the writing of media histories, in this case by looking at the corporeal appeal of 1970s ciga-rette commercials on television. Finally, Mark Williams analyzes the 1949 Kathy Fiscus incident and its resonances in two 1951 productions, Billy Wild-er's *Ace in the Hole* and the independent film *The Well*, to reflect both on the intermedial borders separating film and television and on the dynamic relation-ships among media as a constitutive part of media history.

"Part II: New Subjects" shifts the focus to topics in film and media history that have not yet received sufficient attention. In her analysis of the 1907 Jamestown Exposition, Kathryn Fuller-Seeley examines the relationship between early cinema and what she calls provincial modernity, thus adding a new perspective to the dominant model of cinema and urbanism. Through her survey of film exhibition in Mexico of the early 1920s, Laura Isabel Serna shows in what ways cinema as a social practice served to challenge the interna-tional hegemony of the Hollywood film industry and turned local cinema culture into an instrument of Mexican nationalism rather than a mere agent of Americanization. Kyle Barnett examines the complex interactions among musicians, journalists, sound engineers, record salespeople, and consumers in the case of Gennett Records during the 1920s and, in so doing, sheds new light on the early recording industry and its multi-faceted history. Similarly, Richard Butsch revisits the social construction, via federal laws and regula-tions, of broadcasting from the 1920s to the 1940s, and considers its contribu-tion to the making of a deliberative public sphere and informed citizenry. The role of programming practices and short films as an integral part of media history and its underlying cycles of technical and aesthetic innovation is brought home by Harper Cossar's case study on the highly successful golf instruction films by Bobby Jones Jr.

The authors presented in Part III offer new approaches to established topics. Sue Collins adds a new perspective to the study of stardom in silent cinema by emphasizing the importance of liveness in the making of star personas and the political authority of celebrities, as evidenced by Mary Pickford's appearances during the 1917 to 1919 Liberty Loan Bond Drives. Karl Schoonover revisits the reception of Italian neorealism in the United States by complementing the familiar perspective of European art cinema with the voyeuristic gaze of exploitation cinema, a combination found to be crucial to the making of the political and cultural aspirations of the mid-century American moviegoer. The reception of *What's New Pussycat?* (1965) allows Ken Feil to move beyond the standard equation of camp, cult, and bad taste with marginal sensibilities and minority groups and to stress instead the embeddedness of such categories within mainstream culture. Dan Leopard revisits the myth of autonomous art practice and the conceptual binaries sustained by it by tracing its discursive and institutional permutations from the films of Stan Brakhage and Andy Warhol to the video practices of the Bay Area Video Coalition. And Alisa Perren revisits the complexities of television history by focusing on the popular movie-of-the-week, its connection to specific taste cultures and network cultures, and its nearly complete disappearance during the mid-2000s.

Part IV, finally, emphasizes research issues, including the more practical aspects of archival research. Rejecting universalist models in the study of soap operas (and genres as a whole), Elana Levine insists on a historical approach and enumerates the many difficulties of doing soap opera history in the absence of proper archives and complete records. Casting her net even further, Pamela Wilson compares media history to a hunting expedition as she surveys the difficulties of archiving new electronic and digital media and identifies the often competing objectives of media producers and consumers. Finally, Megan Sapnar Ankerson turns her attention to the most recent medium discussed in this anthology, the worldwide web, to highlight the difficulties of writing a history of web design and reconstructing the complex economic, social, and cultural dynamics that have influenced the look and style of web design.

Acknowledgments

For supporting the original University of Texas conference, we would like to thank the William P. Hobby Centennial Professorship in Communication, the College of Communication, the Swedish Endowment (College of Liberal Arts), the Department of Radio-Television-Film, the Texas Chair of German Literature and Culture, the Amon G. Carter Centennial Professorship in Communication, the Leslie Waggener Professorship in the College of Fine Arts, and the Harry Ransom Center. We would also like to thank Jennifer Bahr, Bo Baker, Sam Cooke, and Michelle Ty for their assistance with the bibliography. And we appreciate Matthew Byrnie's willingness at Routledge to take on our project and help it to reach completion.

Part I

New Methods

Chapter 1

From Accented Cinema to Multiplex Cinema

Hamid Naficy

As an industry, an institution, and a set of practices cinema has evolved, adjusted, adapted, adopted, assimilated, and grown vertically and horizontally. It has taken over, has been taken over, and has been privatized, nationalized, divested, diversified, and synergistically converged in myriad ways. In what might be considered as a great operational example of Gramsci's theorization of hegemony, it has changed in order to remain the same—cinema. And as a medium, film has remained not only relevant but has also proliferated widely and deeply by a process that Marshall McLuhan astutely identified decades ago. He said that old media survived by becoming the contents of newer media: "The 'content' of any medium is always another medium" (1964, 23). Today we are apt to talk about this under the rubric of remediation (Bolter and Grusin 2000). Since 1958 when John Tuky coined the word "software" and the Ampex color videotape recorder and 3M videotape came on to the market, turning television from a live and ephemeral medium into a recorded and lasting medium, and since other technological developments which transformed it from an analog medium into a digital one, film has become the indispensable software feeding all the newer electronic media and delivery systems.

An important source of its continual revitalization has been this adaptability and shape-shifting capacity of cinema and its product. This chapter explores the emergence of a new mainstream cinema in the USA and Europe in our current moment of post-diasporic, post-internet, postmodern neoliberal globalization, a cinema I call multiplex cinema. I appropriate the concept of "multiplex" from the site of film exhibition where multiple movies are screened in one complex and apply it to the films which are increasingly imbued with multiplicities of various sorts. This nomenclature is based on an analogy with electronics, in which multiplexing refers to a process whereby multiple analog signals or digital data streams are combined into one signal.

Two seemingly contradictory global movements intersecting each other are driving this textual multiplexing. One involves the increasing national fragmentation and physical displacement of peoples across the globe, while the other conversely entails a consolidation of the global media, involving "media convergence, participatory culture, and collective intelligence" (Jenkins 2006, 2). The presence of large numbers of displaced and globalized populations— asylee, exilic, diasporic, ethnic, transnational, and cosmopolitan—as both spectators and producers of movies is an important additional factor in the emergence of this multiplex cinema as well as this cinema's historical debt to "accented cinema," produced by them. Media convergence studies, however, tend to discount contributions of such populations.

Although physically displaced, accented filmmakers are not without a place. In fact, they are "situated but universal" figures working in the interstices of social formations and cinematic practices, which are highly potent places of creativity and criticism (Naficy 2001). By and large they operate independently, outside the studio system or mainstream film industries, using alternative production modes—interstitial and collective—that critique those systems and industries and are partly responsible for their films' peculiar accent. These filmmakers form a transnational, cosmopolitan, and multicultural population whose members often have more in common with each other than with their national compatriots. It is from this group that creators of both accented films and multiplex films have arisen.

While they share displacement and modes of production, the very existence of tensions and differences among them prevents accented filmmakers from becoming a homogeneous bloc or a film movement, and their films from becoming enslaved to linear narratives and traditional genres. Nevertheless, their films share certain stylistic attributes in terms of patterned uses of mise-en-scène, filming, narration, themes, characters, and structures of feeling. These common attributes also contribute to the accent, which signifies deterritorialization at the same time that they serve to reterritorialize them as auteur filmmakers. Specifically, mise-en-scène and filming are alternately claustrophobic or immense; time is fragmented and retrospective; space and place are split among a lost home, an uncertain elsewhere, and transitional places in between; narrative is broken up by journey, memory, nostalgia, and past; characters are not whole, they are haunted, absent, doubled, or divided; the intrusion of other languages threatens the integrity of language. In short, multiplicity and fragmentation are dominant in accented films.

The adoption of some of these strategies has led to the emergence of multiplex films, helping to rejuvenate mainstream cinema and giving it a multiplex accent. This is not to claim a cause-and-effect relationship between accented cinema and multiplex cinema, but to say that their textual similarities are products of the same exigencies of displacement, media convergence, and globalization.

Such multiplexing as described here in all its industrial, technological, authorial, linguistic, textual, and spectatorial formations has major consequences for film and media scholarship. One of these involves cultural and linguistic competencies needed for such scholarship. Would studying multilingual, multicultural, and multisited movies require multilingual and multicultural media scholars, or will it encourage increasingly atomized and narrowly defined "niche studies"? Alternatively, will it encourage collaboration among media scholars with specialized cultural and linguistic knowledge, the kind of collaboration not customary in humanities and film and TV studies but *de rigueur* in film and media productions and in sciences and medical fields? The various minority caucuses within Society for Cinema and Media Studies point to the cultural multiplexing that is already at work within our discipline.

A second major consequence involves the technical competencies needed to study multidevice, multimedia, multiplatform productions and receptions of multiplex movies, competencies that far exceed both single device familiarity and traditional separation of film production from film studies. As each of us has personally realized, increasingly film and media studies and production areas are also merging, paralleling the structural convergence within the global media industries. Increasingly job descriptions for new hires in film and media include preference for scholars competent in both critical studies and production, but this brings its own problems of focus and rigor. Finally, digitization is facilitating "device agnosticism" and competency across media (Denby 2007, 55), providing a lingua franca at the technical level that will not be duplicated for actual human languages, which will fortunately remain multitudinous. Our discipline is already responding to this situation too.

Multiplexing Resulting from Dispersion of People

Because they are made under conditions of displacement and often deal with the stories of dispersed people, multiplicity is overdetermined in accented films. Multiplicity is manifested in the films' multilingual dialogues, multicultural characters, and multisited diegeses, and the many languages of the filmmakers and their crews and the stories about which they make films drive it. Multiplicity feeds into and off of the horizontality of our globalized world, where compatriot diaspora and transnational communities and individuals are in touch with each other laterally across the globe, instead of being focused on an exclusive, binary, and vertical exilic relation between a former home country and the current homeland. The metaphor is more of rhizome than root. This sensitivity toward multiplicity is picked up in multiplex Hollywood movies, some of which are made by transnational and accented directors.

The multiplicity often results in the abandonment of the classic cinema's realist, linear, invisible style, which requires coherence of time, space, and causality. One of the greatest deprivations of displacement is the gradual deterioration in, and the potential loss of, one's original language. This is because language serves to shape not only individual subjectivity, but also personal and national identities prior to displacement. Threatened by this catastrophic loss, many accented filmmakers doggedly insist on writing the dialogues of at least their initial movies in their home languages—to the detriment of their films' wider distribution. Naturally, multilinguality makes intelligibility more complex, contributing to the film's accent. In addition, most accented films are bilingual, even multilingual, and multiaccented, such as *Calendar* (1993), directed by Egyptian-born Armenian-Canadian filmmaker Atom Egoyan, which is not only bilingual throughout in Armenian and English but also contains a series of telephonic monologues in a dozen other languages that are not translated or subtitled. Or *On Top of the Whale* (*Dak van de Walvis, Het*, 1981), directed by Chilean director Raúl Ruiz, whose dialogue is spoken in more than half a dozen languages, one of them invented by Ruiz himself. In these films, language is never taken for granted; in fact, it is often part of the plot and the reflexive agent of narration and identity.

Multilinguality permeates all aspects of accented films, not only on the screen but also in the multinational composition of the production crew behind cameras. The dialogue of Chantal Akerman's *A Couch in New York* (*Un divan à New York*, 1996), a romantic comedy filmed in Paris and New York City, is bilingual (English and French), but its camera crew was multilingual and multinational, consisting of a German cinematographer, a French camera operator, and a US focus puller (Bear 1995). Multilinguality may also, and ironically, be a result of the dominance of one language, such as English in this case, which facilitated cross-cultural communication among a sizable, diverse crew of sixty people.

Multilinguality impacts the films' reception, too, as different languages serve different communities of address, often privileging one over another, despite the film's subtitles. The more languages spectators know the more privileged they feel, for it appears that the global film is treating them as local insiders.

As far as multiplicity of characters in accented films is concerned, a good example is *Tangos, Exile of Gardel* (*Tangos, l'exil de Gardel*, 1985). In this sensuous and operatic work about exile by Argentine director Fernando Solanas, two characters seem tethered to each other across the national divide: Juan Uno in Buenos Aires, Argentina, and Juan Dos in exile in Paris, France. Uno is the authentic self, while Dos is secondary and half-finished, needing nourishment from home in the form of memories, ideas, and tango lyrics. Interestingly, by necessity, Juan Dos entirely imagines the original, authentic Juan Uno to channel inspirations from his homeland. In this film multiplicity means that not only the film's dialogue is in Spanish and French throughout but also that at least one character is split by the disruption of exile. Further, three other characters in the film literally fall apart, deflate, and disintegrate. As such, character splitting and disintegration emphasize subtraction and loss—a feature of political exile. A few years later, Polish director Krzysztof Kieslowski, who made many of his films in France, issued *The Double Life of Veronique* (*La Double vie de Véronique*, 1991), which centered on the life of two people, Veronika in Poland and Véronique in Paris, who seemed to be doubles of each other or somehow connected to each other without knowing how. Here multiplicity was configured as doubling—an additive process, which is characteristic of transnationalism.

Now, doubles, doubling, and splitting have been a staple of horror and science fiction movies from the beginning, but their increased frequency in other genres and the kinds of national, ethnic, and personal haunting that surround the doubled, the split, the multiple, the fragmented, the disappeared, the renditioned, the lost, and the ghosts point to new sources of instability and fragmentation that are driven by physical dispersions, political violence, and media and economic convergence.

In addition, linear and realistic storytelling is increasingly abandoned in multiplex films and replaced by fragmentation and circularity of time, space, and plot. Milcho Manchevski's terrific trilingual film (Macedonian, English, and Albanian) *Before the Rain* (*Pred dozhdot*, 1994) centers on the fragmentation and circularity of plots and character destinations in a post-Soviet Macedonia caught up in vicious nationalist and ethnic wars. Three interlocking stories are deftly woven into a tragic tapestry. An Iranian interlocking narrative film is Pourya Azarbayjani's *Unfinished Stories* (*Ravayat ha-ye Natamam*, 2006), in which three women abandoned to their fate by those they love spend one terrible night together in the streets of Tehran. The three films by Mexican director Alejandro González Iñárritu and writer Guillermo Arriaga—*Amores Perros* (*Life is a Bitch*, 2000), *21 Grams* (2003), and *Babel* (2006)—all consist of multiple interlocking stories, occurring in different times and spaces, involving multiple protagonists who speak in a variety of languages. For example, *Babel* is a Hollywood multiplex movie, a tripartite co-production (France, Mexico, and USA) that is distributed in a complex fashion for various types of screenings (theatrical, TV) and formats (DVD, all media) across the globe by over a dozen national and international companies. The film itself is no less multiplex, as its story takes places in five major sites across the globe, in Japan, the United States, Mexico, Africa, and Morocco, and it involves not only foreigners but also natives in prominent roles. This dispersion of story sites necessitates multilingual communication. The film's dialogue is in six spoken languages and is a further nod to the idea of multiplexity in one sign language (the Japanese Sign Language).

This necessitated what has been unusual in Hollywood cinema, namely subtitling of the entire film. For decades Hollywood studios avoided either making films in foreign languages—except for some foreign-edition movies—or subtitling foreign movies on the grounds that people would not want to read in the cinemas. But now both Hollywood and its audiences have changed; they have become more multicultural and multilingual. What higher homage to the emergence of foreign languages in Hollywood can there be than the Oscar-winning Clint Eastwood film *Letters from Iwo Jima* (2006), which is almost entirely in Japanese requiring subtitling throughout? In 2006 to 2007, both the Broadcast Film Critics Association of America and the Chicago Film Critics Association recognized it as the best "foreign language movie" (ironically, the Japanese Academy, too, awarded it the Best Foreign Language Film in 2008!).

Nowhere is this multiplexing ethos more readily visible than in Todd Haynes's *I'm Not There* (2007), a biographic picture about Bob Dylan's enigmatic and mercurial personality who through talent, chutzpah, and a series of identity camouflages and radical transformations evolved to remain the poetic and musical voice of several generations. To showcase his life and work, Haynes "hurls a Molotov cocktail through the façade of Hollywood biopic factory" (Scott 2007), exploding the traditional literal and linear narratives of the genre. In addition to creating fragmented and palimpsestic narratives each with its own style, the subject of the film, Dylan, remains unnamed and six different actors from different countries (with different accents), races (one is black), and sexes (one is a woman) play his part. Nevertheless, all these centrifugal multiplications converge into a passionate rumination on Dylan's life and times.

Another interesting dimension of multiplexing is the emergence of anthology films (also omnibus or portmanteau films), consisting of several short films by different directors, which have something in common—an organizing idea, a city, an event, a product. These are multiplex films as they offer multiple perspectives on a single topic. For example, the US war in Vietnam resulted in *Far From Vietnam* (*Loin du Vietnam*, 1967), containing short films by six distinguished leftist European auteurs: Godard, Marker, Lelouch, Ivens, Renais, and Varda, who critiqued US involvement in Vietnam and sympathized with the North Vietnamese. For the centennial of cinema in 1997 the British Film Institute commissioned many world-class filmmakers to shoot short films using the Lumière camera. The Island of Kish in the Persian Gulf is the subject of half-a-dozen Iranian art-house filmmakers in *Tales of an Island* (2000); likewise, *Persian Carpet* (*Farsh-e Irani*, 2007) consists of contributions by fifteen acclaimed Iranian directors ruminating on the meaning and the making of this iconic textile.

To this anthology format should be added the "multipart movies" in which a director's movie consists of several shorter films that may or may not be interconnected. These are different from the interlocking films, as their plots and characters do not conjoin. Examples are a pair of tripartite movies by husband and wife filmmakers from Iran: Mohsen Makhmalbaf's *The Peddler* (*Dastforush*, 1987) and Marziyeh Meshkini's *The Day I Became a Woman* (*Ruzi keh Zan Shodam*, 2000). The terrorist attack on the World Trade Center towers resulted in at least two omnibus films. *11'09'01—September 11* (2002) consists of eleven shorts by well-known directors from eleven countries while *Underground Zero* (2002) contains short films by fifteen independent filmmakers. The individual shorts in these multipart films essentially follow the logic of short stories involving strong singularities of various sorts—of character, location, time, and plot. The entire film often functions like a short story collection, whose logic is based on accumulation of disparate parts.

Multiplexing is also surfacing in the expanding lengths of films by accented and art cinema filmmakers. For example, many of Jonas Mekas's diary films, such as *Lost, Lost, Lost* (1949–1976), are three hours long or more, as are Sohrab Shahid Saless's dystopian exilic movies made in Germany, *Utopia* (1983) and *Roses for Africa* (*Rosen für Afrika*, 1992), which are 198 minutes and 183 minutes, respectively. Some filmmakers find that even extending the movie beyond the customary length is not sufficient to accommodate the range and complexity of their topic, resulting in "serial films" or "episodic films." Claude Lanzmann's nine-and-a-half-hour *Shoah* (1985) about the Nazi-inflicted Holocaust (spoken in English, German, Hebrew, Polish, Yiddish, and French) is a prime example of the serial genre in the documentary field. Jennifer Fox's *Flying: Confessions of a Free Woman* (2007) is a six-hour episodic documentary about her travels to more than a dozen countries to solicit advice from friends and specialists. Multiplicity of form and multiplicity of locations and characters are integral to this film, as is the use of the innovative technique of "passing the camera" to her subjects to create a shared point of view. Such multiplication of point-of-view filming and serialization counter the usual auteur conceptions of cinema, which are based on the singularity, authority, and authoritativeness of an auteur who is often conceived to be male and his product fiction movie. This is how Fox describes her film technique and counters such conceptions:

> Honestly, I can't explore what I want to explore in 90 minutes. And the older I get, the more the feature form seems almost male—very conclusive, very "here it is," all summed up. The serial is more like life, with multiple stories, multiple conclusions. It's a fabric, or a layered cake. The serial is more female.

> (quoted in Anderson 2007)

Multiplexing Resulting from Technological and Financial Convergence of Media and Digitization

With financial consolidation, media convergence, digitization, and the Internet we have entered the multidevice, multiplatform, and multichannel media world to whose multiplex creations multiple users flung far and wide contribute. This is clearly a vast, complex, and rapidly evolving topic; suffice it to say that it will give new meaning to the ideas of collective production and reception. It will also raise serious questions about the nature of authorship, which has traditionally been tied to singularity and uniqueness. What would authorship in a multiauthored, user-generated, multiplatform, and multidevice environment consist of? Will it lead to the rise of egalitarian, democratic, amateurs, and citizens, or community journalists, self-taught filmmakers, dorm-room musicians, and unpublished writers who, empowered by the Internet and artisanal do-it-yourself strategies, can crash through the traditional gatekeepers of ideas and cultural products; or will it lead, as Andrew Keen claims, to a cult of parasitic amateurs producing shallow, repetitious, mediocre art—a bunch of rumor mongers, idea spinners, and intellectual property kleptomaniacs who copy and paste other people's works (2008)? Will the considered opinions of the experts be replaced by the wisdom of the crowd (Surowiecki 2005)? The jury is out on this debate.

The fact remains, however, that citizen or community journalists and amateur mediamakers are creating their work collectively and uploading their homemade narratives to video-sharing sites such as YouTube, MySpace, and Facebook, contributing to the creation of what is called the post-Google participatory "Web 2.0" (O'Reilly 2006). Politically oriented mediamakers continue to form collectives, among them Independent Media Center (aka Indymedia), a global participatory network of journalists and filmmakers, who create "collectively-made videos aimed at affecting political change" (Stringer 2006). Originally formed during anti-WTO protests in Seattle in 1999, it champions global justice causes and democratic media by practicing "open web based publishing" and "non-hierarchical and anti-authoritarian relationships" (http://docs.indymedia.org/view/Global/PrinciplesOfUnity). In addition, Indymedia provides "copyleft" content, which means it allows free use of its content as long it is for non-commercial purposes. Alternatively, corporate news media, always looking for new venues to deliver more eyeballs to advertisers, are tapping into community journalists and amateurs. For example, in the USA, the cable news network CNN regularly solicits eyewitness videos of the day's events from passersby for inclusion in program segments it calls "i Report" and "News to Me." Much of the programming and advertising of Current TV, a global cable and satellite TV network whose motto is "You make the news we put it on television," is user generated (former Vice President Al Gore is the channel's chairman and chief evangelist). To emphasize its collective intelligence, the channel's website calls itself "crowdsourced TV" (http://current.com/).

Now, it may be argued that while the accented filmmakers' multiplex tendencies are genuine and emanate from their own lived experiences of deterritorialization, interstitiality, and production practices, mainstream cinema's multiplexity—typified by Hollywood multiplex cinema and television—is driven by a new form of cultural tourism and imperialism, which tends to coopt the experiences of otherness and their aesthetics in the service of reaching multiple micro markets and higher profits. In the process, by *diffusing commercially* the aesthetics of alternative cinemas, Hollywood multiplex cinema *defuses them politically*. The particular dynamism of our current moment of globalization, however, is such that the flow of influence is not unidirectional, for the alternative, accented, decentered, collective, crowd-sourced film and video practices are having a reciprocal impact on the mainstream and centered production modes. As the cases of Mexican filmmakers Alejandro González Iñárritu and Guillermo del Toro (*Pan's Labyrinth / El Laberinto del fauno*, 2006), Indian directors Mira Nair (*The Namesake*, 2006) and Manoj Night Shyamalan (*Lady in the Water*, 2006), Taiwanese director Ang Lee (*Brokeback Mountain*, 2005), Ukranian director Vadim Perelman (*House of Sand and Fog*, 2003), and many other foreign directors currently working in Hollywood show, by employing not just exilic and émigré directors as before but also diasporic and transnational directors, who make movies in their own and others' languages, Hollywood has changed and rejuvenated itself in order to remain the same—on top of the game of cinema.

Not just the cinematic texts and the film industry, but also the institutions that bestow value on films are recognizing the increasing multiplexity in their midst. In 2006, for the first time the Academy of Motion Pictures Arts and Sciences changed its rules for the Oscars to allow a foreign language entry to be in a different language from its country of origin, as long as the "creative talent of that country exercised artistic concern." This allowed *Water*, directed by Indian-born Canadian director Deepa Mehta, filmed in Sri Lanka, to be designated as a Canadian product, since Mehta and the film's producer David Hamilton are both Canadian (Amdur 2007). In 2008, the Oscar statue became an export item, since four of the five awards for best actor/actress went to foreigners as well as the Oscars for art direction, makeup, costume design, and best song.

Television, too, has authenticated the multiplex by creating multicultural ensemble shows, such as *Lost* and *Heroes*, which are supported by multicultural writers, some of whom are hired through the studios' "diversity programs"

(Knolle 2006). Hollywood does not believe in ethnic essentialism, but it has realized the value of ethnic authenticity to the believability and freshness of its products, given that a sizable proportion of its creators and spectators are now multiethnic and multicultural. The hiring of above-the-line personnel of color, gays, and women for these shows has led to a wider repertoire of representations. Even the presence of one key character, like Lt. Col. Sarah "Mac" MacKenzie played by Iranian-British-American actor Catherine Bell in the series *JAG* (1995–2005), seemed to result in more nuanced stories, realistic situations, and accurate representations of Arabs and Iranians.

Dominance of one lingua franca, which facilitates communication among constituents, undergirds multiplexity. This lingua franca is not only the English language, which dominates the entertainment industry worldwide and the Internet in particular, but also the new visual vocabulary created through computer-generated and manipulated imagery as well as the terminologies, technologies, procedures, and software of the production, all of which are becoming streamlined and standardized thanks to US dominance and digitization. Today it is impossible to think of film pre-production, production, post-production, distribution, exhibition, and reception without some form of digital technology leading the process. The mouse click is perhaps the most ubiquitous sound in the industry. It is the personification of the mouse that roared adage!

Works Cited

Amdur, Neil. 2007. "Indian Film with Roots so Deep that it Defies Borders." *New York Times*, 24 February: A17.

Anderson, John. 2007. "Women's Stories, Including Her Own." *New York Times*, 1 July: 8.

Bear, Liza. 1995. "Berlin to Paris, With an All-Important Stopover in Brooklyn." *New York Times*, 9 July: H16.

Bolter, Jay David and Richard Grusin. 2000. *Remediation: Understanding New Media*. Cambridge, MA: MIT Press.

Denby, David. 2007. "Big Pictures: Hollywood Looks for a Future." *The New Yorker*, 8 January: 55–63.

Jenkins, Henry. 2006. *Convergence Culture: Where Old and New Media Collide*. New York: New York University Press.

Keen, Andrew. 2008. *The Cult of the Amateur: How Blogs, Myspace, Youtube, and the Rest of Today's User-Generated Media Are Destroying Our Economy, Our Culture, and Our Values*. New York: Doubleday Business.

Knolle, Sharon. 2006. "Multi-Authentic." *Daily Variety*, 28 September: A1, A5.

McLuhan, Marshall. 1964. *Understanding Media: The Extension of Man*. New York: Signet.

Naficy, Hamid. 2001. *An Accented Cinema: Exilic and Diasporic Filmmaking*. Princeton: Princeton University Press.

O'Reilly, Tim. 2006. "Web 2.0 Compact Definition: Trying Again." http://radar.oreilly.com/2006/12/web-20-compact-definition-tryi.html.

Scott, A.O. 2007. "Another Side of Bob Dylan and Another and Another . . ." *New York Times*, 21 November: B1,7.

Stringer, Tish. 2006. *Move. Guerrilla Films, Collaborative Modes, and the Tactics of Radical Media Making*. Ph.D. Dissertation, Rice University.

Surowiecki, James. 2005. *The Wisdom of Crowds*. New York: Anchor.

Chapter 2

Franchise Histories

Marvel, *X-Men*, and the Negotiated Process of Expansion

Derek Johnson

In the first decade of the twenty-first century, the intellectual property *X-Men* has supported multiple sites of content production across the comic, film, television, video game, and toy industries, much to the commercial satisfaction of Marvel Comics and its licensed partners. As a result of this flurry of industrial activity, *X-Men* may be recognized as an entertainment franchise—a perennially extensible network of content in the service of several wide-reaching culture industries. To focus on that result and not on the process that has produced it, however, obscures not only the historical struggles and negotiations by which franchises like *X-Men* have been established but also the nature of franchises themselves. Given ongoing interest in these properties by culture industries, franchises demand an historical approach that can grasp the various contexts and institutional formations they cut across over time. As enduring cultural products, franchises have been enduring cultural *processes* with their own historicity.

To write the history of the media franchise, therefore, historians must account not for the singular result of its expansiveness but instead for the multiplicity of contexts and permutations contained within it. The historical development of a franchise like *X-Men* was a process of multiplication: *intra-industrially*, as the original comic book spun-off satellite titles, and *inter-industrially*, as the property came to support production in several other markets. Franchises thus act as sites through which many diverse media contexts converge. The historiographic challenge that results, however, is to uncover the tensions within that convergence. Rather than considering the media franchise as the product of convergence (Jenkins 2006) or in terms of a defined set of production practices (Thompson 2007), media historians must conceptualize it as a process of convergence wherein a multiplicity of texts, institutions, practices, and historical contexts collide, leading to uneven experimentation, challenge, and failure.

To actualize this historiographic approach, this chapter considers the fraught processes through which Marvel pitched *X-Men* as a franchise prior to 1995, exploring how entry into a variety of contexts both enabled and stymied the multiplication of the property, leading to successively distinct forms of franchising. Drawing from Michele Hilmes's examination of the contentious interactions between various culture industries in shaping broadcast forms, practices, and institutions, this investigation adopts a historiographic model that conceptualizes the entertainment franchise not as a site of consensus within and between media industries but instead as an embattled process of "conflict, compromise, and accommodation" (Hilmes 1990, 1). Rather than uniformly demonstrating how franchising has worked over time, this model "focuses on process rather than outcome, on conflict rather than consensus" (5) to consider just as frequently how the franchise *has not worked*. From this perspective, I first examine the period between 1963 and 1989, asking how imbalanced, incompatible exigencies in different industries lead to asymmetrical intra- and inter-industrial extensions of *X-Men*. Second, by examining the boom period between 1990 and 1995, I explore how Marvel responded at a corporate level to the collision of so many media systems within *X-Men*, reconfiguring the institutional infrastructure of franchise as a result. Perhaps more than anything, the ultimate failure of this reorientation demonstrates the conflicted, contingent, processual character of the franchise rather than its ideal realization.

In its variable, uneven form, *X-Men* evinces the imperfect negotiation through which culture industries have managed collisions of institution and context through content. Through this process, many overlapping configurations of media franchising have emerged, a multiplicity for which media historians must take account. While this approach will provide detailed analysis of a single property based in the comic book industry, it will also provide insights applicable to the culture industries at large by demonstrating that cultural products extend between media contexts neither naturally nor without resistance.

Uneven Expansion

Even if the term had been in play to describe media culture prior to the late 1980s, "franchise" would inaccurately describe *X-Men* as first published in 1963. Two years earlier, Marvel Comics had reinvigorated the superhero genre with *The Fantastic Four* and inaugurated the "Marvel Age of Comics." Given such declarations, branding played no small role in Marvel's success: as chief editor Stan Lee later recalled, "I treated the whole thing like a big advertising campaign. I wanted to give the product . . . a certain personality" (Allen 1984, 12). To reproduce that winning personality, *X-Men* mimicked the team-based superheroics of *Fantastic Four*, attributing the fantastic abilities of

Cyclops, Beast, Angel, Iceman, and Jean Grey to genetic mutation instead of cosmic rays. While the idea of mutation supported themes of persecution based in social difference and thus civil-rights-era topicality, *X-Men* would be judged "only a moderate success" in this original context (Murray 1984a, 68; Thompson 1986, 18). Given unremarkable sales, Marvel halted production in 1969 in favor of reprint issues. Thus, as Marvel began to pursue external media licensing agreements, it disregarded the mediocre *X-Men*. In 1966, the Canadian-made *Marvel Superheroes* debuted in US television syndication, rotating weekdays between Captain America, Hulk, Iron Man, Thor, and Sub-mariner stories. Only when animators hoping to team Sub-mariner with the Fantastic Four learned that they lacked rights to Marvel's most popular team did they include the less iconic X-Men, renamed "The Allies for Peace." Serving ironically as the generic Brand X of the Marvel universe, the *X-Men* brand defied recognition as an extensible intellectual property.

In 1975, however, Marvel Comics resumed production of original *X-Men* stories. With sales of *Fantastic Four* declining at that time (Murray 1984b, 29), Marvel had increased interest in revisiting its lesser superhero teams. *X-Men* had the benefit of malleability; since its characters had never become so iconic, the established *X-Men* name could be used to introduce entirely new superheroes like Wolverine, Storm, and Colossus that might fare better with readers. *X-Men* thus resumed production but in an iteration distinguishable from the original title. While the "All-New, All-Different" *X-Men* would generate massive comic sales, however, this did not assure the subsequent extension of the property across media industries. Although *X-Men* became one of Marvel's hottest comics by 1980, it still lacked the cross-media success of *Spider-Man*, a property that supported three television series between 1978 and 1981. Even after purchasing DaPatie-Freleng animation to form Marvel Productions, Marvel made little progress in extending *X-Men* to television. Although integral to media franchising in the 1980s as the animation studio hired to bring Hasbro toys like *G.I. Joe* to television and comics, Marvel Productions failed to capitalize similarly on its own intellectual properties. Marvel actively developed *X-Men* for television, but in 1984 NBC rejected its proposal (McNeill 1984, 22). While *X-Men* may have been hot within the comics industry, network gatekeepers saw a non-starter.

Although obstructed inter-industrially, distinct conditions within the comics business enabled *X-Men* to adopt a parallel, intra-industrial franchise configuration. In 1981, Marvel underwent "a complete reorganization of the editorial department" in which all its comics (approximately thirty-five titles) were assigned to one of five group editors ("Marvel News" 1981, 5). These new conditions, however, did not systematically support content management based on shared intellectual property franchises. While one editor did handle two *Spider-Man* books, the related *Spider-Woman* and *Spidey Super Stories* each fell under different editorial groups. The group to which *X-Men* was assigned, however, held less ambivalent promise for a strategy of coordinated franchise management; while it unified both *Conan the Barbarian* titles under a single editor, it also instituted editorial liaisons between *X-Men* and newer titles *Dazzler* and *Ka-Zar* (both centered on characters first introduced in the mutant book). This infrastructural support for an extended *X-Men* network advanced further in 1982, when Marvel officially expanded the property beyond a single title into a group of books, beginning with *Wolverine*, Marvel's first mini-series (Main 1983, 16–17). In 1983 *New Mutants* was added, the first ongoing title spun-off from *X-Men* in what would soon become a family of related X products—a franchise.

Crucially, this intra-industrial manifestation was not the natural development of any successful intellectual property but a response to the specific economic context negotiated by Marvel at the time. Comic distribution in the 1980s had shifted away from mass-market drug stores and newsstands towards the "direct" market, where specialty retailers gauged audience demand and ordered products directly from the publisher on a no-returns basis. With retailers eating the cost of unsold titles, the market for content contracted, with only those titles which retailers felt confident they could sell reaching the shelves. Although Marvel dominated this market, competition from DC Comics as well as a number of upstart independent publishers created the perception of a zero-sum game where every competitor comic sold meant one less Marvel sale. Thus, analyst Robert Overstreet called 1983

> the year that Marvel made a determined effort to hold or even increase its market share ... "flood"[ing] the market with Marvel product so the consumer who wanted to keep up with his Marvel collection would have little money left over to spend on other publishers.
>
> (1984, A21)

By launching *New Mutants* but also several additional mini-series like *X-Men and the Micronauts* and *Illyana and Storm* that drew upon the *X-Men* name and characters (Main 1983), Marvel forced a choice upon its readers: obtain the full *X-Men* experience by buying multiple titles, or spend that money on the competition and miss out. This franchise strategy of expansion, therefore, emerged as a negotiation of direct market conflicts.

Yet despite this direct market focus, the mass market limped on—creating a parallel context for the *X-Men* franchise to negotiate. According to industry figures shared with comic book readers, for example, the overall bestselling comic title in 1981 was *Amazing Spiderman*, moving 298,000 copies monthly.

While *X-Men* outperformed all of DC's competing titles with 192,000 copies, it was only Marvel's tenth bestseller—behind *Star Wars*, *Hulk*, *Fantastic Four*, *Avengers*, *Conan*, and others ("TCR Mailboat" 1981, 19). Surveys of direct market retailers told a different story, however, with *X-Men* in the top spot and *Spider-Man* a distant eighth place ("TCR Top 100" 1981, 48). This divergence reveals that what sold well in the specialty direct market did not necessarily have as much mass-market appeal. Although Hollywood clearly maintained interest in Marvel properties, optioning *Thor*, *Ghost-Rider*, *Daredevil*, *Man-Wolf*, and even *Howard the Duck* ("Marvel News" 1981, 6), the mass-market appeal of a property like *X-Men* remained unproven. While *X-Men* captured the niche direct market and topped reader polls in fanzines like *Comics Collector*, this did little to interest film and television institutions courting much larger audiences. Without the mass-market resonance of something like *Spider-Man*, the television development of *X-Men* enjoyed no more success in the latter half of the 1980s than it had with NBC in 1984. Although eight-year-old *Spiderman and His Amazing Friends* reruns were still viable as part of the syndicated *Marvel Action Universe* hour in 1989, even giving Marvel a continued foothold in television, the *X-Men* pilot produced for incorporation into that program failed to garner support to go to series.

So while *X-Men* conquered the comics industry and Ronald Perelman's MacAndrews & Forbes purchased Marvel in 1989 to enter into "the business of the creation and marketing of characters" (Raviv 2002, 12), they found few buyers outside that industry interested in their *X-Men* wares. Incompatibilities among media institutions led to distinct, multiple franchising prospects, causing Marvel to struggle as much as thrive across these contexts in its attempts to manage and extend its intellectual property.

Boom and Bust

Shifts in those media systems, however, would once again enable new configurations of franchising to emerge, and new corporate responses to the multiple contexts brought into collision through content. While inter-industrial mobilizations of the property had been thwarted prior to the 1990s, *X-Men* comics persevered in the direct market. In 1991, to strengthen its intra-industrial brand further, Marvel discontinued *The New Mutants*, also at a sales peak, and relaunched it in June as *X-Force*. Given "the name change to include X at the beginning," one analyst predicted that direct market retailers could "expect to see some meteoric rise in that sales column" (Brooks 1991, 10). Now more overtly branded as part of the *X-Men* behemoth, *X-Force* #1 sold 3.9 million copies, obliterating the 2.65 million record set by mass-market favorite *Spider-Man* in 1990. In August 1991, Marvel issued a second *X-Men* series to run alongside the original, selling 7.5 million copies of the first issue (Biggers 1992, 46). An entire order of magnitude larger than typical 1980s sales, these numbers resulted from the increased market presence of speculators hoarding multiple copies in hopes of monetary appreciation. Nevertheless, such strong sales attracted much-needed popular attention to the X brand, and the cool reception which *X-Men* received from external media institutions began to reverse—particularly as the needs of those institutions themselves changed.

A case in point was the upstart Fox television network. Interested in seizing less competitive Saturday morning market share from the Big Three networks, it now saw Marvel and the niche (but increasingly visible) *X-Men* as potential allies in its differentiation strategies. Partnered with Saban Entertainment, Marvel Productions received a green light for an animated *X-Men* series, ultimately debuting in October 1992 to No. 1 Saturday morning ratings. This would not be the first success *X-Men* had outside the comic book world, already licensed to a 1992 Konami arcade game and a line of low-end action figures. But for analysts, the cartoon added the most value to the property, increasing the popular appeal and sales of *X-Men* comics (Colabuono 1994, 30; Markley 1994, 67). Overall industry newsstand sales increased from $21.4 million to $33.4 million between 1992 and 1993, "driven no doubt by the mass market exposure of the *X-Men*" (Flinn 1994c, 37). So although the 1980s had presented two distinct industrial contexts for Marvel to negotiate in its management of *X-Men*, those institutional spheres began to collide more forcefully in the 1990s, with the comic and television markets intersecting.

Although the success of inter-industrial expansion parallel to intra-industrial success surely pleased Marvel, this collision simultaneously presented a new set of economic relationships and conflicts to manage. With *X-Men* producing increasingly higher dividends outside the comics industry, Marvel was forced to share those rewards with its licensed partners in those external markets. Thus, in late 1992 Marvel executives launched a process of expansion to redefine its franchise strategies around ideals of horizontal integration that could fully recapture licensed markets. After buying the Fleer trading card business for $286 million, Marvel immediately announced its intention to self-publish the next set of *X-Men* cards (Anderson 1993, 18). Similarly, in 1993 Marvel granted toymaker Toy Biz a no-fee license for properties like *X-Men* but in exchange gained controlling interest over that licensee and direct access to all its profits (rather than just a royalty) (Raviv 2002, 41). Marvel even used *X-Men* to launch Marvel Made, a line of merchandise of the sort typically handled by licensees—including phone cards, Christmas ornaments, character busts, and so on. Rejecting the logic of licensing, Marvel's retailer solicitations promised that customers could "count on much more high-quality merchandise from Marvel Made—because who can make Marvel products better than Marvel?" ("You've Got It" 1994, M27).

The long-pursued expansion of *X-Men* across inter-industrial contexts therefore pressured Marvel to expand horizontally and modulate its franchise strategies to leverage more effectively its lucrative property. By 1994, Marvel reported that only 37.3 percent of its revenues still came from comics, down from 90 percent in 1988 (Flinn 1994c, 37). However, with overall sales for Marvel comics peaking at seventy million units a month in January (up from fifty million in May 1993 and twenty million in January 1991) (Market Watch 1995, M40), Marvel also reorganized its *vertical* management of franchises like *X-Men*. To sell more comics, Marvel introduced not only its Marvel Mart mail-order catalog but also plans for a chain of Marvel stores across the country, much to the dismay of independent dealers fearing direct retail competition with Marvel (Biggers 1994, 10; Flinn 1994b, 3). In July, Marvel also implored retailers to stop shelving comics alphabetically, and instead to group comics by family, so that the entire *X-Men* franchise could be shelved together, which helps "create brand identity and can serve as an easy magnet in merchandising your product" ("Shop" 1994, M37).

Codifying this notion of a comic book family, the direct market trade journal *Internal Correspondence* in fact began ranking comic book sales by family group in August. Over the following year, the aggregate *X-Men* franchise— between twenty and thirty titles each month—would capture between 13 and 19 percent of the entire comic book market. Thus, as Marvel worked to develop new infrastructures to support inter-industrial franchising, it simultaneously did so at the intra-industrial level.

In the 1990s, therefore, *X-Men* became a franchise in ways that were incredibly distinct from the 1980s, now positioned by Marvel as heir apparent to the waning *Teenage Mutant Ninja Turtles* craze. As one 1993 advertisement for *X-Men* trading cards boasted, "It's a good bet the kid's favorite mutants ain't turtles" (Advertisement 1993, 41). With *X-Men* notably gracing the August cover of *New York Times Magazine*, 1994 arguably represents a peak for the franchise's expansion and thus, by implication, Marvel's attempts to accommodate its growth. Most significantly, Marvel's reorganization of its entire publishing division in November spoke not just to the company's desire to leverage success but simultaneously to the challenges imposed by that expansion of content.

In this new model, dubbed "Marvelution" by COO Terry Stewart, properties would be distributed among four executive editors who would "run their particular family of titles as a separate publishing entity under the Marvel umbrella," each with its own brand logo (Flinn 1994a, 7). The move sought to accommodate the 100 percent increase in publishing output since the beginning of the decade by making the management of franchise families more decentralized and responsive to the market. *X-Men* literally became a functioning corporate division within Marvel, alongside one focused on *Spider-Man*, one on the Marvel Universe, and one on General Entertainment publishing. According to Marvel executive Mike Martin,

> Everyone knows that the *X-Men* and *Spider-Man* franchises are two of the most successful ones in comics. *X-Men* alone dwarfs entire comic book companies in market share ... Marvelution is a way to apply the principles that distinguished *X-Men* and *Spider-Man* to the entire Marvel enterprise.
>
> (1995, 39)

Marvel may have looked to *X-Men* as the future, but in the present its expansion and circulation throughout a multiplicity of institutional contexts presented a challenge to be negotiated at the same time. Explaining that one could "change the course of a Coast Guard cutter a heck of a lot faster than you can an aircraft carrier," Martin signaled the difficulty of steering a massive enterprise like *X-Men* and the corporate challenges of managing it (39).

The real corporate struggles and conflicts incurred by franchising came to a head in 1995, as the speculative bubble burst in both the comics market and the trading card business, cutting heavily into sales. Many retail analysts had already questioned the wisdom of Marvel's family structures and the glut of content they produced: "some collectors must devote their entire budget to keep up with one or two of these franchises ... The danger is that publishers will prop up failing titles after they are no longer viable" (Davis 1994, 59). With the comics market in a tailspin, the family footprint supported by franchises like *X-Men* had become a potential liability: multiple chances of failure instead of one. With many of the markets into which Marvel had expanded—both in terms of content like *X-Men* and in terms of its own corporate infrastructure—suddenly in freefall, the company's stock price fell in late 1995 from a high of $34 to $15. Toy Biz remained the only division to turn a profit, and Marvel posted an overall loss of $48 million, which would balloon to $464 million by 1996 (Raviv 2002, 39). Mired in debt from its attempts to accommodate the multiplication of intellectual properties like *X-Men* through corporate expansion, Marvel filed for bankruptcy and naturally retreated from the franchise strategies that had failed it. In those particular configurations, the franchise has proven untenable for Marvel.

A Negotiated Process

If we consider the history of media franchise in terms of results, we are likely to perceive a set of coherent strategies designed to produce and exploit vast content networks. If we adopt a historiographic model based in *process*, however, franchises like *X-Men* alternatively become comprehensible as an overlapping, imperfect series of historical negotiations contextually configured and reconfigured to accommodate variable, colliding media systems and historical moments. In the case of *X-Men* in the 1980s, intra-industrial multiplication provided Marvel with a competitive edge within a newly contracted niche marketplace, whereas the mass-market orientation of external media institutions thwarted attempts at similar inter-industrial multiplication. When shifting conditions in those markets permitted distinct media systems to interface more effectively through the *X-Men* property in the early 1990s, however, Marvel reconfigured its approach to the franchise once more—a fraught process that pursued greater economic leverage but posed obstacles that sunk the company. Marvel's eventual triumph in extending *X-Men* across media did not so much realize a final, long-term franchise strategy as establish new points of conflict, compromise, and accommodation to negotiate in the ongoing management of the property. Thus, instead of considering the media franchise as the result or embodiment of success, we might alternatively view it as an ongoing historical process through which success has been negotiated and fought for within the culture industries—but not always won.

Works Cited

"A Marvelous Showing." 1985. *Comics Collector* Fall: 30–34.

Advertisement: Sky-Box X-Men Trading Cards, Series 11. 1993. *Comic Buyers Guide Price Guide* March–April: 41.

Allen, David. 1984. "Stan Lee Speaks." *The Comics Buyers Guide*, 6 July: 12.

Anderson, Dick. 1993. "Project X Launches Marvel-Fleer Marriage." *Comic Buyers Guide Price Guide* January–February: 18–19.

Biggers, Cliff. 1992. "X Makes it Hot!" *Comic Buyers Guide Price Guide* January–February: 46–47.

———. "An Industry Break-Down: Steady as She Goes." *Comic Buyers Guide Price Guide* March–April: 10, 106.

Brooks, Brett. 1991. "Return of the Mutants." *Comic Buyers Guide Price Guide* April–June: 10, 12.

Colabuono, Gary. 1994. "What Will Be Hot!" *Comic Buyers Guide Price Guide* January–February: 30, 32.

Davis, John. 1994. "Monthly Market Wrap: Too Much of a Good Thing?" *Internal Correspondence: The Newsmagazine for Specialty Retailing* October: 59.

Flinn, Tom. 1994a. "Marvel Announces Reorganization." *Internal Correspondence: The Newsmagazine for Specialty Retailing* November: 7–8.

———. 1994b. "Marvel Under Fire." *Internal Correspondence: The Newsmagazine for Specialty Retailing* May: 3–5.

———. 1994c. "Random Notes from Marvel's Annual Report." *Internal Correspondence: The Newsmagazine for Specialty Retailing* June: 37–38.

Hilmes, Michele. 1990. *Hollywood and Broadcasting: From Radio to Cable*. Champaign: University of Illinois Press.

Jenkins, Henry. 2006. *Convergence Culture: Where New and Old Media Collide*. New York: New York University Press.

McNeill, Darrel. 1984. "Animation News: GI Joe II, Transformers Mini-Series to Air This Fall." *The Comics Buyers Guide* 1 June: 22.

Main, J.R. 1983. "The Mini Series Market." *Comics Collector* Spring: 16–17.

"Market Watch: December 1994." 1995. *Sales to Astonish* 76: M40.

Markley, Wayne. 1994. "1993 Market Wrap." *Internal Correspondence: The Newsmagazine for Specialty Retailing* January: 67.

Martin, Mike. 1995. "A View from the Field: You Say You Want a Revolution." *Sales to Astonish* 74: M38–39.

"Marvel News." 1981. *The Comic Reader* 189: 5–6. Wisconsin State Historical Society Pamphlet Collection, 75–1655.

Murray, Will. 1984a. "The First X-Man." *The Comics Buyers Guide* 8 June: 68.

———. 1984b. "Return of the Fantastic Four." *Comics Collector* Fall: 18–29.

Overstreet, Robert M. 1984. *The Comic Book Price Guide*. Harmony: Overstreet Publications.

Raviv, Dan. 2002. *Comic Wars: How Two Tycoons Battled over the Marvel Comics Empire—And Both Lost*. New York: Broadway Books.

"Shop 'Til You Drop." 1994. *Sales to Astonish* 67: M37.

"TCR Mailboat." 1981. *The Comic Reader* 189: 48. Wisconsin State Historical Society Pamphlet Collection, 75–1655.

"TCR Top 100 Comic Books." 1981. *The Comic Reader* 189: 48. Wisconsin State Historical Society Pamphlet Collection, 75–1655.

Thompson, Kristin. 2007. *The Frodo Franchise: The Lord of the Rings and Modern Hollywood*. Berkeley: University of California Press.

Thompson, Maggie. 1986. "X-Men into X-Factor." *Comics Collector* Winter: 18.

"You've Got It Made with Marvel Made." 1994. *Sales to Astonish* 68: M27.

Chapter 3

When Pierre Bourdieu Meets the Political Economists

RKO and the Leftists-in-Hollywood Problematic

Chris Cagle

If any issue in American film historiography seems fully explored, it is the experience of leftist writers and directors in the producer-oriented milieu of mid-twentieth-century Hollywood. Film-as-history historians have tackled the occasional trends toward social problem and political filmmaking, while social and oral historians have chronicled the blacklist and its effect on a generation of artists. Where other areas of film historiography suffer from a paucity of empirical details (or access to these details) with the left-leaning artists, historians have amassed a collection of interviews, archival material, and production histories.

However, the scholastic thoroughness of Brian Neve's *Film and Politics* (1992) or Paul Buhle and Dave Wagner's *Radical Hollywood* (2003) has blinded the field to a central explanatory problematic: why, exactly, did the major studios hire leftist artists and finance projects with left-leaning content? The historiography on the period tends to take the perspective of individuals who, understandably, bristled at the constraints on their work and their politics. However, this focus on the artist exposes only one half of the social game; instead of seeing producers and the studios as mostly an obstacle to the writers and directors for hire, one can ask under what conditions each came to share goals. From this explanatory perspective, media history explains not only individual agency, institutional structure, or economic environment but also the coordination or divergence of social interests.

The social problem features that RKO produced in the late 1940s provide a useful case study for revisiting the leftists in Hollywood problematic. The number of features is finite: *Crossfire* (Edward Dmytryk, 1947), *Boy with the Green Hair* (Joseph Losey, 1949), and a couple of secondary examples like *The Farmer's Daughter* (H.C. Potter, 1947) or *So Well Remembered* (Dmytryk, 1947). Key figures who faced HUAC and eventually the blacklist worked on these films, and for this reason the RKO problem films point to key contributing roles of leftist talent. Yet the studio underwent a rapid succession of owners and production heads and a similarly abrupt evolution of studio direction. As such it can also present the case for a studio- and producer-centric understanding of liberal-left content. The studio's social problem dramas, I hypothesize, came about in part because of the industry's changing economics and in part because of the studio's place in what Pierre Bourdieu calls the field of cultural production (1992). This dual explanation helps make sense of certain stubborn empirical details—why, for instance, the social problem film continues well after the HUAC trials—at the same time as it provides a new agenda for film and media historians trying to connect the practices of culture industries to larger ideologies.

Both postwar observers and subsequent film historians use the term the "social problem film" for entertainment narrative features that contained strong, often didactic themes about conflicts larger than the character or story. While film scholars have become adept at understanding all entertainment cinema as in some nature political and socially meaningful, problem films laid explicit claim on the public sphere and contained some formal markers of didactic address. To take as an example *Crossfire*, RKO's polemic against anti-Semitism, the third-person *noir* narration of the story frame and flashbacks gives way in the film's turning point to a lengthy monologue from Detective Finlay (Robert Young), who talks about the "real American history" of bigotry in a long take, nearly two minutes long and conspicuously absent of reverse shots. Whatever the formal means of achieving it, this strategy of didactic address cuts across much of the genre, from Twentieth-Century Fox's cycle (*Gentleman's Agreement* (Elia Kazan, 1947) or *Pinky* (Kazan, 1949)) to Stanley Kramer's independent production *Home of the Brave* (1949).

Figure 3.1 Frontality as didactic address in *Crossfire*.

RKO's experience with the problem film was brief, but it quickly became the studio most associated with the cycle after Twentieth-Century Fox. The cycle had its rumblings in the immediate postwar years with the anti-fascist Edward Dmytryk films *Cornered* (1945) and *So Well Remembered*, and the Dore Schary joint productions with RKO and Vanguard *Till the End of Time* (Dmytryk, 1946) and *The Farmer's Daughter*. *Crossfire*, though, was the film that signaled the start of the two-year Schary reign as production chief at RKO. A *noir* thriller, it used a flashback structure and expressionistic style as a frame for a narrative about an anti-Semitic hate crime. Since the success of *Murder My Sweet* (Dmytryk, 1944), an informal production unit had formed around producer Adrian Scott, director Dmytryk, and writer John Paxton. *Crossfire*'s success in urban markets—it was held over for weeks at the Rivoli Theater in New York—inspired the studio to make *Boy with the Green Hair*, an allegory about racial intolerance, directed by Joseph Losey. As the film entered postproduction, RKO's controlling shares were sold to Howard Hughes, and the studio entered a distinctly new phase in its management. Consequently it abandoned the social problem film; Hughes even held up *Boy with the Green Hair*, hoping to revise the content.

The historical scholarship on these films has tended toward two directions. The first approach has been to follow the individual history of leftist artists in Hollywood. Losey, for instance, had a background as a director in leftist theater, including a stage production of *Waiting for Lefty* in Moscow (where he met Bertolt Brecht) and work for the Federal Theatre Project (along with eventual Fox problem-film director Elia Kazan) (Neve, 1992, 13). Dmytryk and Scott lacked ties to the New York left-literary circles, but their differing experiences with the Communist Party led to their inclusion in the Hollywood Ten. Paxton was by Brian Neve's assessment (95) more liberal than left in his politics, but his papers show both his friendship and political sympathy with Scott (Paxton collection). In sum, RKO's unit had several left-leaning individuals whose influence could shift the films' ideology. A social history of the industry usefully connects the experience of directors and writers to New York's theatrical milieu of the 1930s.

The other direction in scholarship has been a reflectionist history that sees films as expressing a broader culture. The problem film, that is, represented a wider tone of both liberalism and pessimism in postwar America. The best articulated versions of this approach are in Richard Maltby's reading of liberal consensus in the problem picture (1983) or Charles Maland's reading of pessimism in the *film gris* (2002). In the case of RKO, one can read the message of *Crossfire* or *Boy with the Green Hair* as tapping into the cultural zeitgeist of a nation grappling with racial inequality after a war against a fascist state.

Each of these approaches provides part of the historical puzzle, yet it is worth finding an explanation that makes sense of the specificity of the film industry. One start is to recognize the importance of management and the production head. If in the 1940s the emphasis on quality, high-A products led to unit production and in-house independents and thereby weakened the central producer's role (Schatz, 1999), the production chief still held control in initiating and supervising projects. John Paxton has challenged accounts of Schary's importance in *Crossfire*'s genesis, and rightly so: the film was Scott's pet project and was likely begun under interim production heads Peter Rathvon and William Dozier (Paxton). But Schary at least proved instrumental in clearing the project for production and in putting every RKO resource at its disposal, within the $500,000 budget, to allow the feature to beat the *Gentleman's Agreement* release by a month. Moreover, *Crossfire* fit the liberal, message-picture model that Schary gravitated toward before his role as RKO production chief (*Farmer's Daughter*) and after (*Go For Broke!* (Robert Pirosh, 1951)). If an auteur's hand is at play, the head producer seems as logical a choice as the writer or director.

So, too, does Scott, whose producer role potentially explains RKO's problem film cycle. Jennifer Langdon-Teclaw (2007) documents how Scott's unique role as "progressive producer" meant that the former writer straddled competing demands (he was economizing and managerial on one hand, pro-union and radical on the other) and that by negotiating these competing interests he wielded considerable influence on RKO's pre-blacklist leftism.

Yet neither Scott nor Schary were alone in gravitating toward the message picture, which served as a privileged genre for a new type of prestige film in postwar Hollywood. Given the finite duration of RKO's socially relevant phase, a political economy approach can help explain why the studio took to making problem films in 1947.[1] The move to social relevance in the late 1940s owed much to the new economic conditions in which the studios were operating. The Paramount ruling divorced exhibition arms from the studios and destabilized the A–B film distinction by curtailing, then prohibiting, block booking. High attendance since the war years had shifted the major studios toward mostly A production only to face a retrenchment of domestic and foreign revenues in 1947 and 1948. Finally, favorable tax laws and the market gap left by A-oriented studios encouraged independents. In this climate, studios had a particular incentive to make B product function as A and to make mid-budget A films function as prestige films. Studios adopted different strategies in this environment, but one clear option was the use of socially relevant content as a way of culturally upgrading. Producers saw that inexpensive films could "punch above their weight" in either box-office or critical prestige. Schary, in fact, established his reputation on the ability to make near-A product sell in the top half of the double bill (Schatz, 1999, 188–189). *Crossfire* was the quintessential ambitious high-B film whose strong first run crossed it over into a well-performing A picture.

Still, where political economy explains the structure underpinning the individual actions, it does not explain what the blacklist historiography or the zeitgeist readings hone in on: why, given the industrial constraints, social relevance worked as an upgrading strategy. Industrial explanations, that is, are insufficient for the opposite reason ideological explanations are. They provide specificity but fail to capture the general. Schary's decisions and the microeconomic climate in which RKO operated are clearly important, but they alone cannot capture the larger political legitimation at stake. At best they are the conditions of film-historical change—or the fulcrum for its effects—but not the source of change itself. As Paul Kerr argues in his study of the industrial determinants of *film noir* style:

> An analysis of *film noir* as nothing more than an attempt to make a stylistic virtue out of economic necessity—the equation, at its crudest, of low budgets with low-key lighting—is inadequate: budgetary constraints and the relative autonomy of many B units in comparison with As were a necessary but by no means sufficient condition for its formation . . . It was determined not only economically but also ideologically.
>
> (1986, 232)

Other film historians have offered this explanatory model of "economics plus ideology," where the one explanation looks to industrial organization, profits, and markets, the other to broad cultural notions like "progress" or "quality." David Bordwell and Janet Staiger argue of deep focus cinematography that an ideology of "progress" guided cinematographers' increasing preference for using technology to show the pro-filmic reality with more fidelity (1985, 250). However, if in the eyes of Bordwell and Staiger Jean-Louis Comolli "makes the concept of 'ideology' do too much work" (244), the "industry plus ideology" historians make the concept of ideology do too little work. Reading them, one does not always have a sense of any precise political stakes or meaning in what leads cinematographers toward realist style. Similarly, Kerr adopts the hypothesis that an actual formal subculture existed among the Poverty Row studios, without suggesting how that subculture was ideological in the ordinary sense of the term.

Between these two levels, industry and ideology, however, is room for a third: what Bourdieu calls the social field. While film historians usually draw on Bourdieu simply for a notion of taste differentiation, his related concept of the social field is equally useful.[2] The social field refers to a range of objective social relations that structure the disposition of individuals who inhabit or traverse it—and is in turn structured by them. A journalistic field, for example, is the universe of those practicing journalism within a society, but it is not simply an aggregate of those individuals and institutions.

> Today, invisible but objective relations connect people and parties who may never meet—say, the very serious monthly *Le Monde diplomatique*, at one extreme, and the TF1 television channel, at the other. Nevertheless, in everything these entities do, they are led, consciously or unconsciously, to take into account the same pressures and effects, because they belong to the same world. In other words, if I want to find out what one or another journalist is going to say or write, or will find obvious or unthink-able, normal or worthless, I have to know the position that journalist occupies in this space ... This impact can be measured by indicators such as the economic weight it pulls, that is its share of the market. But its symbolic weight also comes into play.
>
> (Bourdieu, 1996, 41)

Just as the journalistic field structures social agents according to, on the one hand, economic or political capital and, on the other hand, cultural capital, so, too, does an educational field, a literary field, or any artistic field that Bourdieu calls a field of cultural production. Furthermore, Bourdieu uses the concept of habitus to posit a process of internalization, a matching between objective circumstance and subjective experience. Aesthetic sensibility is one locus for this internalization.

While the cinema too functions as a field of cultural production, the operations of this field are not nearly as autonomous from pure marketplace considerations as the literary and artistic fields are, nor as consecrated or intimate with the field of power. Still, once the oligopoly of the marketplace was established, Hollywood began to seek broader prestige for its products and for itself. Thus battles in the cultural marketplace, internally and externally, grew in importance alongside competition in the economic marketplace. In the long run, the postwar years witnessed a stark elevation in the status of the cinema, but in practice this shift was experienced as a series of conflicts, changes, and give-and-take among agents in the fields of both production and reception.

Seen in this light, RKO in the 1940s was the site of struggle and shift in this cultural field. We can posit three levels on which this struggle worked. First, the struggle was a battle between artists and studio, a labor struggle that doubled for an aesthetic struggle. Scott certainly believed that RKO and the PCA hindered political and artistic expression in the films. Moreover, the excitement at RKO around *Crossfire*'s production suggests that the Scott unit did function as an artistic and political subculture defined against the studio management and the MPDAA in particular. Second, the struggle was a competitive battle between the studios. The oligopolistic structure minimized the direct economic competition but maximized the battle for prestige among studios, producers, and artists. Third, Hollywood studios and artists defined their products against both established and lower cultural forms. For both internal and external reasons, Hollywood's position in the cultural hierarchy was changing, and in tandem, Hollywood's films began, at the margins, to align themselves with established literary and artistic fields in new ways, while film critics and social betterment organizations took up the cause of a new, "serious" Hollywood.

To take the first level, the subjective experience of leftist artists should not blind us to the ways artists' interests converged with producers in the problem film. When we look more closely, we see that producers and studios had different reasons for their championed causes than those they employed; nonetheless, they shared the causes. Republican Darryl Zanuck shared a sense of *Pinky*'s importance with liberal writer Dudley Nichols (and his ultimate inspiration, Gunnar Myrdal). Liberal Schary shared with more radical filmmakers like Dmytryk and Losey a commitment to social problem filmmaking. This convergence begs historical explanation.

One part of the explanation is that different players saw something different in the films. Remarkably enough, the social problem film leads observers to explain away either the leftism or the liberalism of the film. That is, sometimes they see problem films to embody a leftist perspective of the writers that goes beyond liberal acceptance of the political system, while at other times problem films are seen to reflect liberal inability to see deeper social causation. For instance, where Robert Warshow complained that *Best Years of Our Lives* treated political problems as personal problems (1970), Siegfried Kracauer claimed that, while

> Wyler's characters are no less individuals than Capra's . . . they reflect the inner workings of the society to which they belong. The bankers in this film behave as typical bankers would—no better, no worse; and Frederic March as the ex-sergeant, himself no paragon of virtue, accuses them not so much of irregular villainy as of a stubborn insistence on regular practices that are apt to harm veterans.
>
> (1948, 568)

Rather than adjudicate who is correct, Warshow or Kracauer, it is more productive to understand the problem film as straddling two different conceptions of social overdetermination. The Marxian version, which Kracauer describes, views social problems as matters of structural economics and thereby promises a left ideological analysis. The Durkheimian conception, a vision shared with the postwar functionalist sociologists, understood social problems as emerging from anomie (social normlessness). RKO's problem films combined both by layering Marxian allegorical elements on top of Durkheimian themes. In *Crossfire*, for instance, an extreme version of anomie (bigotry is a pathology) is also a mild version of social and class conflict (fascism starts at home, an implicit rallying cry against the Fair Deal's opponents). Schary privileged the former, while the Scott unit privileged the latter.

The mutual misrecognition likely sprang from parallel social trajectories within the Hollywood studio. About the literary field, Bourdieu "postulate[s] the existence of a pretty rigorous correspondence, a homology, between the space of works considered in their differences ... and the space of producers and institutions of production, reviews, publishing houses, etc" (1990, 147). The studio system managed the first level of social struggle (artist-studio) by sublimating it into the second (inter-studio). Even more than Fox, RKO was an aspiring major studio, without the tradition of quality that either MGM or Paramount represented. It was predisposed to champion a newer version of prestige cinema that discounted the effects of money alone. "Frequent turnover in high-level personnel and constant tinkering with management structures and strategies kept the production system at RKO unusually fluid, preventing the emergence of a clear 'house style'" (Langdon-Teclaw, 2007, 154). Moreover producers could value the left-leaning artists' sense of independence and social critique if it rebuked the genre production of the entrenched majors. That is, the financial success of the Scott unit's films helped, but so did its charting of a possible new direction for a studio in need of social and product differentiation. For a studio on the cusp of renewed profitability, the studio's objective position in the field of cinematic production corresponded to the studio's aesthetic (and political) choices.

Finally, the social field model suggests the third level of struggle over aesthetic differentiation. This is a model most familiar to film scholars, but it is worth signaling that the social field allows us to picture a continuity of aesthetic differentiation among consumers and producers. Schary was aware of, and caught up in, the legitimization gambits that Bosley Crowther of the *New York Times* or *Time* magazine applied to the problem film. The industry as a whole did not immediately share the broader cultural legitimization; rather, "context" exercised a greater force over some agents because of their place in the industry's internal social struggles.

Stepping back from the particulars of 1947, we can ask why we as media historians should bother with a framework combining political economy and Bourdieu's notion of a social field. In part, it is an explanatory model that makes sense of the empirical: in this case, later problem films or producers' input. In addition, the model allows us to connect arenas too often kept conceptually separate: industry economics and cultural context, artist biography and house style, or artists' class positions and cinematic ideology. Film historians still lack adequate vocabulary to talk about demand-side causes that avoid the "box-office feedback mechanism." In practice, media history sees a division of labor between materialist approaches that ascribe specificity and causal primacy to the industry and cultural studies-inflected approaches that look for use value, negotiation, or resistance. It would be useful to describe the particularity of industrial economics and producers' decision-making without discounting the variable tendency for consumers to influence cultural products. The work on media convergence, after all, starts from political economy fact (media corporations' synergy) and moves to cultural use value. Where political economy necessarily outlines the constraints of supply of culture, habitus understands how producers are social agents as susceptible to outside forces as consumers. The synthesis will require more detailed historical work, but as a start the model of structural homology shows one route around the impasse between supply-side and demand-side—or between industry critique and consumer populism—by demonstrating how taste differentiation played a structuring role for both producer and consumer. Perhaps this is the lesson that the preachy, didactic problem dramas can best teach us.

Notes

1. For a fuller political economy explanation of the postwar problem film, see Cagle (2007).
2. Some film historians have begun more sustained application of Bourdieu's work (see Lastra 2000, Tudor 2005).

Works Cited

Bordwell, David and Janet Staiger. 1985. "Technology, Style, and Mode of Production." *Classical Hollywood Cinema*, David Bordwell, Janet Staiger, and Kristin Thompson. New York: Columbia University Press, 243–261.

Bourdieu, Pierre. 1990. *In Other Words: Essays Toward a Reflexive Sociology.* Stanford: Stanford University Press.

———. 1992. *The Rules of Art: Genesis and Structure of the Literary Field*, trans. Susan Emanuel. Stanford: Stanford University Press.

———. 1996. *On Television.* New York: The New Press.

Buhle, Paul and Dave Wagner. 2003. *Radical Hollywood: The Untold Story Behind America's Favorite Movies.* New York: The New Press.

Cagle, Chris. 2007. "Two Modes of Prestige Film." *Screen* 38.3 (Autumn): 291–311.

Kerr, Paul. 1986. "Out of What Past? Notes on the B film noir." *Screen Education* 32–33

(Autumn/Winter 1979–1980): 45–65. Rpt. in *The Hollywood Film Industry: A Reader*, ed. Paul Kerr. London: Routledge & Kegan Paul; British Film Institute, 220–244.

Kracauer, Siegfried. 1948. "Those Movies with a Message." *Harper's* June, 567–572.

Langdon-Teclaw, Jennifer. 2007. "The Progressive Producer in the Studio System." *"Un-American" Hollywood: Politics and Film in the Blacklist Era*, ed. Frank Krutnik, Steve Neale, Brian Neve, and Peter Stanfield. New Brunswick: Rutgers University Press, 152–168.

Lastra, James. 2000. *Sound Technology and the American Cinema: Perception, Representation, Modernity*. New York: Columbia University Press.

Maland, Charles. 2002. "*Film Gris*: Crime, Critique and Cold War Culture in 1951." *Film Criticism* 23 (Spring): 1–26.

Maltby, Richard. 1983. *Harmless Entertainment: Hollywood and the Ideology of Liberal Consensus*. London: Scarecrow Press.

Neve, Brian. 1992. *Film and Politics in America: A Social Tradition*. London and New York: Routledge.

Paxton, John. Correspondence. John Paxton manuscript collection. Los Angeles: Margaret Herrick Library.

Schatz, Thomas. 1999. *Boom and Bust: American Cinema in the 1940s*. Berkeley: University of California Press.

Tudor, Andrew. 2005. "The Rise and Fall of the Art (House) Movie." *The Sociology of Art: Ways of Seeing*, ed. David Inglis and John Hughson. London: Palgrave, 125–138.

Warshow, Robert. 1970. *The Immediate Experience: Movies, Comics, Theatre, and Other Aspects of Popular Culture*. New York: Atheneum.

Chapter 4

Touch, Taste, Breath

Synaesthesia, Sense Memory, and the Selling of Cigarettes on Television, 1948–1971

Marsha F. Cassidy

At the stroke of midnight on January 1, 1971, more than two decades of ciga-rette advertising on television came to an end. With it vanished almost $230 million in advertising revenue (Brandt 2007, 271) and the daily specter of men and women puffing away on the small screen. During these decades of "satu-rated" television promotion, viewers witnessed tens of thousands of cigarettes caressed, savored, and inhaled (Pollay 1994), and the percentage of US smokers reached record highs (Brandt 2007, 309).[1] In a promotion that appeared in *Advertising Age* in 1962, the CBS network touted television as the "greatest ciga-rette vending machine ever devised" (quoted in Pollay 1994, 130).

This chapter investigates the corporeal appeals in TV's cigarette commer-cials, drawing upon theories of "synaesthesia" and "sense memory" from the field of phenomenology and, in so doing, demonstrating how television history can be re-evaluated beyond the audiovisual. Although my emphasis is on tactil-ity, taste, and somatic sensation, this approach does not preclude theories of gender. As Vivian Sobchack reminds us, the body is "always also a lived body—immersed in, making, and responding to social as well as somatic meaning" (2004, 139). While feminist scholars have pondered the theoretical links and discontinuities between phenomenology and feminism (Fisher 2000, 1–38), my analysis acknowledges the body as "materially acculturated," in Susan Bordo's words, conforming to "social norms and habitual practices" of femininity and masculinity (1993, 288).[2] Analyzing historical television texts with the gendered body in mind provides access to the lived experience of men and women from the past—in the case of advertising, expressed as an ideal. As Bordo explains, "[h]omogenized images *normalize* . . . [T]hey function as models" for the self (1993, 25). Moreover, attention to the somatic can serve to mark social stagnation or social change. The gendered body is always historically situated,[3] and the comportment and sensual range of televised bodies can demarcate cultural shifts.

Theories of synaesthesia and sense memory newly gaining currency in film studies are particularly useful in understanding the full force of cigarette advertising. While clinical synaesthesia describes a patient's literal cross-modal perception of stimuli—the sound of laughter registering as a golden-brown color, for example—Sobchack argues that all of us are synaesthetes in our ability to readily experience films across the full range of our senses (2004, 68, 71): "Our fingers, our skin and nose and lips and tongue and stomach and all the other parts of us understand what we see" (84). In Laura Marks's work on synaesthesia, she explores the evocation of "sense memories" in cinema viewing (148)—"All sense perceptions allow for, and indeed require, the mediation of memory" (2000, 202)—and she suggests that viewing an image with the eye activates the full circuit of sense memory, including the "tactile, kinesthetic, and proprioceptive functions" (162). Just as Marks devotes her study to the ways cinema "can appeal to senses that it cannot technically represent" (129), the study that follows reconsiders the full circuit of sense memories awakened by cigarette advertising's overdetermined aural and visual stimuli, agreeing with Sobchack that synaesthetic perception "*is* the rule" (2004, 70). I will discuss tactility as centered on hands and lips; the "taste" of cigarettes—"rich," "fresh," "mild," "smooth," and "cool"; and, finally, the kinesthetic, proprioceptive, and interoceptive sensations of inhalation, exhalation, and the accompanying kick of a nicotine high.

How the film and television media differ is a crucial question, particularly regarding the past emphasis on the distracted nature of television viewing. Yet cigarette commercials were costly film productions, and, as John Caldwell suggests, the stylistic impact of film techniques cannot be minimized (1995, 50). While Caldwell notes that in the 1950s the importation of cinematic style was "muted and constrained" (51), by the late 1960s and 1970s filmed commercials had learned to engage viewers "through the lower sensory channels," exploiting "nonverbal mechanisms" (94).

Regarding distracted reception, since television commercials are characteristically overcoded and repetitive, they may be potentially more powerful in stimulating the full sensorium. Anecdotal evidence suggests that the entire range of corporeal sensation may be more readily triggered in a distracted state through the kind of repetition TV ads depend upon, as the total experience seeps into our bodily memory little by little. (An example would be when we learn an ad jingle "by heart" without making any effort to memorize it.) As Steve Shaviro says, television "colonizes us obliquely, by distraction. It allures us, willy-nilly, into getting connected" (2003, 6).

A marketing research study conducted in 1970 appears to confirm somatic over cognitive recollection. In a day-after recall survey, only 4 percent of respondents could remember that a Kent commercial talked about the cigarette's filter, the cognitive message of the ad. But in "verbatim" responses, viewers did recall a "girl and fellow . . . running with a kite" on a beach, a "lady" taking a cigarette "out of a man's hand," and phrases about "refreshing," "mild" and "smoother" taste, each example a trigger for sense memory ("Beach" 1970).

A 1967 commercial for Newport cigarettes even directly confronts the distracted nature of television viewing. As a middle-aged man watches a Western on television, he appears to doze off, then sees on the screen an attractive couple waving at him from the beach. The young figures in beach clothes jump out of the television set into the man's living-room. The beautiful blonde sits on the arm of his armchair and sings the praises of Newport's taste, while the young man lights his cigarette. At the climax of the narrative, the armchair viewer delights in deep inhalation. This ad makes literal the way in which the cigarette commercial on television was strategically designed to leap off the screen and activate the sense of touch, taste, and breath in the viewer's body, even in a groggy, semi-distracted state (YT).[4]

The Act of Smoking

Early on, advertising agencies recognized television's remarkable capacity to highlight the act of smoking and its pleasures. At the advent of television in 1948, three of TV's biggest advertisers were tobacco companies, each selling a single brand of cigarettes: Camel, Lucky Strike, and Chesterfield ("Tele's" 1948, 23). By the Fall of 1963, cigarette makers sponsored fifty-five network TV programs, totaling 62.5 hours of airtime per week (Pollay 1994, 131–132).

Agencies quickly grasped the advantages of television advertising over print. In 1950, Thomas Whiteside, writing for the *New Yorker*, talked with BBDO advertising executive Jack Denove who oversaw the Lucky Strike account. "You don't show people smoking in still ads because the cigarette would hide the face," Denove explained, "but smoking looks wonderful on television." Denove then lit up a Lucky and demonstrated the TV formula to Whiteside. "Look," said Denove, "You put your cigarette up to your face. You take the puff in the normal manner ... and you blow out the smoke ... Then you see the person's face again. What could be more natural?" (Whiteside 1971, 2–3).

While modified by cultural shifts, this formulaic depiction persisted across the decades. In my survey of some 300 cigarette commercials that aired between 1948 and 1971, almost every one featured the act of smoking as its centerpiece. In 1968, Dr. Daniel Horn, director of the National Clearinghouse on Smoking and Health, even verified the visceral power of television smoking. According to Whiteside, Horn's studies showed that "viewing this act had an unhinging effect on the resolution of people" who were trying to quit (92). Advertisers hardly needed this confirmation. As Whiteside concluded, television gave tobacco companies a "remarkable tool for persuading people to smoke . . . It showed young people puffing away, inhaling deeply and blowing smoke around with obvious pleasure and always in settings that made the habit seem attractive" (47).

Gendered Smoking

While space does not permit a complete discussion of the gendered subjectivity of TV smokers, a dominant depiction of men featured what Chesterfield labeled the "Men of America"—like virile sailors and policemen (TVCC 86, 87).[5] The male smoker was first and foremost a version of "the Marlboro Man" (Brandt 2007, 263–264): a rugged man of action, a man "who thinks for himself" (CTCC 37). Whether he smoked alone, with other men, or with a woman, he consumed cigarettes with a decidedly masculine flair.

Against this masculine backdrop, representations of women shifted more noticeably. During the early 1950s, fewer women than men actually smoked in TV ads (Whiteside 1971, 20), but a version of the pretty "cigarette girl" was commonplace as women were shown graciously offering a cigarette to their companions without smoking themselves. In this role, Lucy Ricardo in *I Love Lucy* fetches a pack of Philip Morris for Ricky and lights his cigarette. As he inhales with pleasure, she says to the camera, "See how easy it is to keep a man happy" (TVCC 58).

By the mid-1950s, the vision of a woman lighting up and inhaling had become universal, however, and tobacco companies soon demanded that female models learn how to inhale "properly" (Whiteside 1971, 20). Commercials often portrayed couples smoking together, an efficient way to target both sexes at once. Whiteside quotes a storyboard for Parliament from the late 1960s that illustrates this dual gender appeal. The Parliament couple is riding in a jeep on the sand dunes:

> THEY LAUGH AS THEY SMOKE, CUT TO HER REACTING: LAUGHS AS SHE TAKES IN DEEP, DELICIOUS DRAG ON CIGARETTE STAY ON HER AS SHE REMOVES CIGARETTE . . . LOOKS AT FILTER WITH QUIET APPROVAL. CUT TO HIM FAST HE BLOWS OUT SMOKE SO YOU KNOW HE THINKS PARLIAMENTS ARE GREAT.
>
> (21)

As second-wave feminism gained momentum in the United States, Leo Burnett's ad campaign for Virginia Slims in 1968 marked an important shift in the promotion of independent females smoking (Kluger 1996, 315–317). This approach was not new in the sale of cigarettes to women—the earliest ad campaigns of the late 1920s took a similar tack (Schudson 1984, 192–198)—but it did significantly alter representations of the woman smoker that had up until then dominated television, freeing women to smoke alone and with aplomb (Toll and Ling 2005).

Over time, women as well as men were allowed to experience the full pleasure of smoking, but the social practices associated with the habit divided along a familiar binary of masculine/feminine, most notably in the realm of touch and taste.

Different Touches

The sense of touch is strongly evoked for hands and lips as the act of smoking commences on television. Hands caress the cigarette pack in close-up; fingers touch the desired object, described in one commercial as "so round, so firm, so fully packed"; the cigarette is then pulled from the pack and lifted to the lips, where it lingers momentarily. Its firmness, says Chesterfield, is "pleasing to the lips" (CCC v.1 61). Yet in this ritual, men and women touch cigarettes differently. Women are often shown posing with cigarette in hand as an elegant accessory before or after they inhale. Their fingernails are beautifully manicured, their hand and fingers gracefully positioned near the mouth, elbow bent. Virginia Slims, although noted for its "feminist" rhetoric, capitalized especially on this familiar convention, declaring that its cigarettes were "tailored slim for your hands—for your lips ... slimmer than the fat cigarettes men smoke."[6]

Gender differences are most apparent when couples smoke together. The man always extends the pack to her (a new pack, with three or four cigarettes artfully stacked at the opening); she withdraws the longest cigarette in a refined sweep and carries it to her lips. His touch shifts to the lighter as he clicks the flame against the tip of her cigarette. She may or may not touch his hand briefly (and intimately) to steady it (CTCC 30). She inhales. Looking radiant, she continues to hold the cigarette delicately between the V of her first two fingers as he takes one for himself and lights up. He can either duplicate her V with his fingers or assert his masculinity, as Steve McQueen does, by holding the cigarette instead with the thumb and forefinger, a gesture denied women across all the ads surveyed (CCC v.1 22). Alternately, he can remove the cigarette from the pack with his lips, another male prerogative. In the most macho commercials, the man can also be found puffing on a cigarette as it dangles from his mouth—while he is repairing his car engine, for example (TVCC 5), or driving cattle (CT 35 8). This light-up ceremony does much more than teach smoking etiquette. In its visual explicitness, it imposes a gen-

Figure 4.1 Touching Kent cigarettes with hands and lips was a gendered act.

dered tactility upon the hands and mouth of the smoker. By means of aural and visual cues, smoking ads *feel* different for men and women. They sense in their arms, hands, fingers, and lips the rite of smoking as a gendered act.

That smoking becomes a way to perform gender is underscored in a 1970s ad campaign for Kool Filter Longs, which revolves around the jingle, "Lady Be Kool."[7] These ads feature an especially tall, slim model sauntering along the beach, riding a bicycle, strolling in a garden, walking her dogs, or sailing. A male voiceover exults, "Everything about her is stylishly long, from the clothes she wears to her flowing hair. And tastefully cool. Excitingly cool. And her cigarette is as stylishly long and tastefully cool as she is." Here, the aesthetically pleasing longer look and feel of the cigarette in a woman's hand is magnified to encompass the grace and attractiveness required of her entire body.

"Winston Tastes Good, Like a (clap-clap) Cigarette Should"

The pleasure of touch evoked in the act of lighting up shifts immediately to the pleasure of taste in the mouth. An early Chesterfield ad expresses this transition exactly: "Yes, to the touch. To the taste. Chesterfield packs more pleasure"

(TVCC 69). Claims about cigarette taste were especially overemphasized during a period Robert Sobel calls an age of "experimentation" when king-size, filter tip, and mentholated brands were introduced (1978, 158). After government and industry restrictions clamped down on cigarette advertising's misleading health claims (Kluger 1996, 185), ad agencies mastered the art of equivocal language to imply a safer smoke by promising a gentler taste. The sensate watchwords were "mildness," "freshness," "coolness," and "smoothness." Tareyton was "the real thing in mildness," while Pall Mall's "natural mildness" was "downright smokable" (TVCC 21, 25).

As the "tar derby" emerged in the late 1950s, tobacco companies battled to reassure smokers, however deceptively, that filter tips removed harmful toxins (Brandt 2007, 244–247; Kluger 1996, 183–191). Yet the slogans continued to stress the sensate pleasure of taste: Marlboros were "the filter cigarette with the unfiltered taste," while Kent offered "the best combination of filter and good taste," according to Dick Van Dyke (TVCC 39). Liggett and Myers drove the message home in a jingle: "They said it couldn't be done/They said nobody could to it/But L&M is low in tar with more taste to it" (TVCC 57).

Gender preference was a factor in the battle of new brands. Men clung to their desire for a rich taste (CCC v.1, 7) but could be persuaded by other men (or their wives, TVCC 16) to enjoy filtered products. Menthol cigarettes were particularly appealing to women (Kluger 1996, 187), although men convinced other men to smoke them too (CCC v.2 8),[8] and TV was awash with cross-sensory memory prompts that associated these brands with fresh air and coolness. Salem, which ranked fifth in the market by 1961 (Sobel 1978, 184), transported its smokers into a country setting each time they lit up, underscoring its jingle, "You can take Salem out of the country, but . . . you can't take the country out of Salem." Kool connected images of water fountains with its "menthol magic" and featured animated penguins ice-skating (TVCC 4). In one ad, a man emerges from a cloud of irritating smoke to retrieve a pack of Kools from a refreshing cascade of water, accompanied by the soothing tones of the jingle—"Smoke cooool, cooool, cooool" (TVCC 84).

The great outdoors provided a collection of visual metaphors that appealed to synaesthetic memory. Smoking Newport, couples frolicked on beaches, in mountains, on lake fronts, and along country roads. In a Kent ad, a man and woman rise in a ski lift to romp in fresh snow, and the announcer exclaims, "It's fun to be active/To feel all your senses alert, including your sense of taste" (CCC v.2 61). These ads crossed the sensorium, manipulating words, music, visual imagery, and olfactory memories to elicit the gratification of a pleasing taste. Sixty seconds of cross-modal stimuli all converged on the mouth.

Breathing Easy

The sensation of breathing was the ultimate somatic experience of the TV ad. Inhaling and exhaling served as a narrative climax that promised full-body pleasure and satisfaction to both sexes. Michael Schudson has noted that a new smoker at first experiences a discomfort and disgust when breathing in cigarette smoke, so advertisers were challenged to overcome this initial "physical threshold" until the effects of nicotine pleasure—and addiction—took hold (1984, 186–187).

For smokers, television images of inhalation and exhalation retrieved the full memory of dragging on a cigarette, an experience that references not merely the muscular control of the diaphragm in deep breathing (proprioceptive awareness) but also the interoceptive sensations in brain and body as the nicotine enters the bloodstream seven seconds later ("Effects" 2007). For would-be smokers, the respiratory act served to instruct viewers about the art of puffing and its gratifications, calling to mind the primal pleasure of breathing itself.

Here the artful tools of the television ad come together with full force. Synaesthesia is achieved through multilayered sensory transference. Close-up shots detail the sucking action of the mouth as inhaling begins; the woman's eyes drift closed in pleasure; she holds the smoke momentarily in her lungs; her lips purse to exhale; the smoke streams from her mouth in an arc; she smiles contentedly, often glancing with admiration at the cigarette.

Medical studies have found that individual smokers exhibit a "wide degree . . . of variability . . . in the number of puffs, puff volume," and their inhalation patterns ("Pattern" 2007; Tobin et al. 1982). Cigarette commercials, too, demonstrated this variability, recognizing that nicotine can both stimulate and sedate ("Nicotine Addiction" 1989; "Nicotine and Mood" 1994).

Some ads associated smoking with a blur of activity, often accompanied by shallower puffing. Studies show that initial puffs activate nicotine's stimulation affect, raising the heart rate and adrenalin levels. An early Lucky Strike ad finds a young woman lighting up at the edge of a swimming pool as her boyfriend swims over to join her. As they inhale together, the announcer explains, "How good that smoke is after a swim" (YT). With a fast-moving camera and set to rapid theme music, a much later ad for Winston depicts a couple in high spirits at an amusement park, dipping and diving on the roller coaster before they race off the platform and light up (CCC v.2 26). And an ad for Oasis even follows a couple smoking while waterskiing (CCC v.1 9)!

The ad campaign for Virginia Slims is another notable case in point. To illustrate the now legendary slogan, "You've come a long way, baby," clever vignettes contrasted women smokers from the 1910s with a 1960s beauty

Figure 4.2 Water skiing in the great outdoors evoked the taste of "mildness" and nicotine's stimulation effect.

boldly striding toward the camera, cigarette in hand (Kluger 1996, 315–317).
In a sassy gesture, this active, energetic, and "liberated" woman inhales but
briefly and then teasingly blows smoke directly into the camera. She then
sashays away.

The recurring theme in many other ads, however, was the slow, drawn-out
pleasure of smoking for relaxation and contentment when nicotine's stimulation of dopamine in the brain took hold. In one ad, a Chesterfield couple lights
up while lounging aboard a boat as the announcer describes a bodily transcend-
ence: "You're relaxed/Really enjoying life/Completely satisfied" (TVCC 69).
In another ad, a woman lies in a hammock, leisurely inhaling the new BelAir,
eyelids descended in bliss. The jingle instructs, "Breathe easy . . . Think pleas-
ant thoughts. Forget every care" (CCC v.1 10). These ads duplicate the sensation of well-being produced by the visceral and neurological afterglow of a
nicotine high. While the masculine/feminine binary dictated how cigarettes
were to be handled and savored, the corporeal thrill of inhalation was shown
to captivate the male and female body alike, momentarily bypassing gender
difference.

For over two decades, a bombardment of stimuli, many cross-modal, celebrated the somatic pleasures of smoking, even as Americans began to confront

Figure 4.3 With BelAir cigarettes, smokers could "breathe easy" and experience the satisfying release of dopamine in the body.

the knowledge that cigarettes were lethal.[9] Because TV smokers also performed a "stylized repetition of acts" that expressed gender as a "historical situation" (Butler 1997, 402–403), retheorizing cigarette commercials introduces the lived body, ideally gendered, into the discussion of history.

Just as Sobchack has postulated a "cinesthetic subject," approaches to television history that include synaesthesia and sense memory raise the possibility of the "telesthetic subject" and the "telesthetic historian." If Sobchack is right that we experience the reciprocity and intercommunication of the senses *without a thought* (2004, 71), then the task of the telesthetic historian is to bring the full sensorium back to critical consciousness.

Notes

1. By 1959, the number of US men who smoked had reached an astonishing all-time peak of 60 percent. Between 1949 and 1965, the percentage of women who took up the habit rose from approximately 21 percent to almost 35 percent, hovering around 30 percent until 1971.
2. See also Butler's (1997) discussion of the connection to Simone de Beauvoir's work.
3. See the contrast between feminine motility as described by Young (2005) and Chisholm's (2008) response thirty years later.

4. "YT" indicates ads viewed on YouTube.
5. The number refers to ad's position on the DVD.
6. Six Virginia Slims commercials were accessible on YouTube on June 5, 2007. Philip Morris registered a copyright complaint in July 2007 and the ads were pulled.
7. Seven such commercials were available on YouTube in July 2007.
8. African Americans of both sexes were associated with mentholated brands and later targeted by advertisers. See Brandt 2007, 310–313.
9. This occurs especially after 1964, when the Surgeon General's report led to decisive restrictions by Congress, the FTC, and the FCC.

Videography

Classic Cigarette Commercials (CCC), v 1 and 2, tvdays.com.
Classic Television, Cigarette Commercials (CTCC), Hollywood's Attic.
Classic Television (CT), Video Scrapbook nos 35 and 36, Hollywood's Attic.
TV Cigarette Commercials: The Classics (TVCC), earthstation1.com.
YouTube (YT).

Works Cited

"Beach." 1970. April 28. http://ltdlimages.library.ucsf.edu/imagesv/v/k/e/vke91e00/Svke91e00.pdf.
Bordo, Susan. 1993. *Unbearable Weight: Feminism, Western Culture, and the Body.* Berkeley: University of California Press.
Brandt, Allan M. 2007. *The Cigarette Century: The Rise, Fall, and Deadly Persistence of the Product That Defined America.* New York: Basic Books.
Butler, Judith. 1997. "Performative Acts and Gender Constitution: An Essay in Phenomenology and Feminist Theory." *Writing on the Body: Female Embodiment and Feminist Theory*, ed. Katie Conboy, Nadia Medina, and Sarah Stanbury. New York: Columbia University Press, 401–417.
Caldwell, John. 1995. *Televisuality: Style, Crisis and Authority in American Television.* New Brunswick, NJ: Rutgers University Press.
Chisholm, Dianne. 2008. "Climbing Like a Girl: An Exemplary Adventure in Feminist Phenomenology." *Hypatia* 23.1 (January–March 2008): 9–40.
"Effects of Nicotine on the Body." 2007. NicotineGuide.com, July 15. www.nicotineguide.com/effects-of-nicotine.php. Accessed July 15, 2007.
Fisher, Linda. 2000. "Introduction" and "Phenomenology and Feminism: Perspectives on their Relation." *Feminist Phenomenology*, ed. Linda Fisher and Lester Embree. Boston: Kluwer Academic, 1–38.
Kluger, Richard. 1996. *Ashes to Ashes: America's Hundred-Year Cigarette War, the Public Health, and the Unabashed Triumph of Philip Morris.* New York: Alfred A. Knopf.
Marks, Laura. 2000. *The Skin of the Film: Intercultural Cinema, Embodiment, and the Senses.* Durham, NC: Duke University Press.
"Nicotine Addiction and Cigarettes." 1989. *American Lung Association Pamphlet.* http://

findarticles.com/p/articles/mi_m0602/is_1989_August/ai_n18605911. Accessed August 22, 2007.

"Nicotine and Mood." 1994. TobaccoDocuments.org, July 14. http://tobaccodocuments.org/product_design/2025988295–8300.html. Accessed August 22, 2007.

"Pattern of Inhalation," "Chart 3," and "Summary." 2007. profiles.nlm.nih.gov/NN/B/C/D/M/_/nnbcdm.pdf. Accessed June 25, 2008.

Pollay, R. W. 1994. "Exposure of US Youth to Cigarette Television Advertising in the 1960s." *Tobacco Control* 3: 130–133.

Schudson, Michael. 1984. *Advertising, The Uneasy Persuasion: Its Dubious Impact on American Society.* New York: Basic Books.

Shaviro, Steve. 2003. *Connected: Or What It Means to Live in the Network Society.* Minneapolis: University of Minnesota Press.

Sobchack, Vivian. 2004. *Carnal Thoughts: Embodiment and Moving Image Culture.* Berkeley: University of California Press.

Sobel, Robert. 1978. *They Satisfy: The Cigarette in American Life.* New York: Anchor Books.

"Tele's Top 10 Bankrollers: Camels' 800G as No1 Client." 1948. *Variety*, October 27: 23.

Tobin, M.J., G. Jenouri, and M.A. Sackner. 1982. "Subjective and Objective Measurement of Smoke Inhalation." *Chest* 82: 696–700.

Toll, B.A. and P.M. Ling. 2005. "The Virginia Slims Identity Crisis: An Inside Look at Tobacco Industry Marketing to Women." *Tobacco Control* 14: 172–180.

Whiteside, Thomas. 1971. *Selling Death: Cigarette Advertising and Public Health.* New York: Liveright.

Young, Iris Marion. 2005. *On Female Body Experience: "Throwing Like a Girl" and Other Essays.* New York: Oxford University Press.

Chapter 5

Rewiring Media History
Intermedial Borders

Mark Williams

> History is the subject of a structure whose site is not homogenous, empty time, but time filled by the presence of the now.
>
> (Walter Benjamin, in "Theses")

The contemporary media environment has on occasion been promoted to be unprecedented: in its tendencies toward and dynamics of convergence, in its scale of socio-economic impact, in its capacity to rerender and reimagine the worlds of representation and mediated expression. Considering such a dramatic purchase on the present, but also on our anxious/awed imagination of the future, media history and historiography are crucially important to produce a capacity for critical distance from these phenomena and the hyperdiscourse about them. The rise of digital culture may be seen to have afforded pressure toward the pursuit of a new series of critical and historiographic lenses by which to reunderstand the history of media and media culture. There is an emerging historiographic emphasis on challenging a merely linear continuity of media history, in accord with Foucault's historiographic interventions, to emphasize fissures, occlusions, discontinuities, and synecdoche which complicate and multiply the threads of this history.

This chapter will call for new work in media history that features a purchase on the archaeology and genealogy of intermedial studies: examinations of relations between and across specific media at significant historical junctures. Intermedial studies can especially bring into relief significant but often overlooked visions and determinants of media history. The recognition of these dynamics suggests both opportunities and imperatives for work in media history and historiography.

The attention to intermedial issues is also in part a historiographic response to the contemporary media environment of convergence. If we are to understand the many and continuous changes in our media environment and ecology, studies that afford a better reckoning of the scale and complexity of prior relations between and across "media" (understood in as complex and multiple a sense as required) will be important in media history. I am not proposing one definition or methodology of intermedial studies, since I find the term functionally valuable in its polysemy, its messiness.

As Wendy Chun has suggested, the very term "media" illustrates in its etymology a legacy of conflicting and non-identical meanings such that media signify "an important discontinuity that calls into question fluid histories . . . to the present" (Chun 2006, 2–3). But this does not suggest that no overarching arguments are possible: any such argument must grapple with the ways in which media have changed rather than concentrating on the remarkable yet overdetermined similarities between entities now considered media.

Mary Ann Doane suggests that the rise of digital media has enforced a return to issues of indexicality in media theory, especially as a site to assess media specificity. Nevertheless, Doane recognizes that "despite its essentialist connotations, medium specificity is a resolutely historical notion, its definition incessantly mutating in various sociohistorical contexts" (Doane 2007, 129). For Doane, it is impossible to reduce the concept of media specificity to materiality alone but also impossible to disengage media specificity from materiality—an important claim in a digital age that often portends a symptomatic immateriality. Media specificity arises in part from both the "positive" capacities of a medium and also, crucially, from the limitations, gaps, and incompletions of a medium, which are determined largely in relation to the forms and modes of aesthetics generated and conditioned by the "matter" of the medium (Doane 2007, 130–131). Intermediality, then, is utilized as an umbrella term that includes a wide variety of media singularity, accumulation, synthesis, regeneration, including dramas of media identity and even the haunting of media by its forbears (Doane 2007, 148).

In this case study, I mobilize the term "intermediality" toward an investigation of a series of borders that exist at the levels of technology/industry/mode of address, borders that appear to have inspired or enabled an attention to spatial/social/historical borders in the texts to be considered. This mobilization complements the sense of the term intermediality as deployed by Fluxus artist and theorist Dick Higgins: as a means of recognizing and challenging media in their normative uses so as to reconfigure awareness about them and to promote both aesthetic and social criticism (Busse, Friedman, and Spielmann in Breder and Busse 2005). In this way, I hope to promote intermedial studies that direct attention not only to what might be termed interobject issues but to issues of intersubjectivity as well.

One emphasis of this case study will be an insistence on the significance of television and television history to such intermedial considerations. This is in part a response to a perceived tendency to overlook or leapfrog television as a key electronic medium in the movement(s) toward digital culture. Indeed, as Chun has pointed out, early new media discourse posited a decidedly simple grasp of media specificity: they resolutely disidentified with television (Chun 2006, 1). Television's electronic capacity for liveness, for example, is central to the intermedial issues of my case study. Doane suggests in her study of media specificity and indexicality that in image culture—and therefore in ways that Charles Sanders Peirce himself did not anticipate—the conviction of the index is produced by a dialectic that exists between Peirce's two understandings of the index: the trace (the "once" or pastness), and deixis (the now or presence) (Doane 2007, 140). The historical specificity of the effect/affect of televisual liveness, and the borders of representational practices related to them, may be seen to be drawn emphatically from this dialectic and therefore to suggest new historicized and historiographic threads to pursue in media history. In this way, this case study will contribute to what might be conceived of as archaeologies and genealogies of the "live" in the age of Real Time (Williams 2003).

I will initiate an analysis of two films from 1951: Billy Wilder's *Ace in the Hole/The Big Carnival* and the independent film *The Well*, written by Russell Rouse and Clarence Greene and directed by Rouse and Leo Popkin. I argue that the representations of the US Southwest in these films, including representations of racial and ethnic difference, may best be understood in relation not only to the broad cultural and sociopolitical context of that time but also as rerenderings/transpositions of the impact of the April 1949 rescue attempt in Los Angeles of Kathy Fiscus, a three-year-old child who had fallen into an abandoned water well, an incident that was televised locally but surprisingly attracted national and even international attention. From this intermedial perspective, the two 1951 films—produced within an industry that was undergoing a period of "crisis" not unrelated to the rise in popularity of television—posit distinctive adaptations of, and anxious projections related to, the Fiscus incident. The films illustrate different responses to emergent intermedial "pressures" of representation that arose in relation to the televisual capacity for immediate "live" coverage, creating a series of borders (both temporal and figurative/thematic) that the present analysis will describe and unpack.

In the Wake of the Kathy Fiscus Telecast

Due to space limitations, I will present only a brief précis of the impact of the Kathy Fiscus events. The telecast of the unsuccessful rescue attempt of Fiscus is perhaps the most famous early remote telecast in US history. Station KTLA was on the air for nearly twenty-eight hours of continuous coverage, an unprecedented technical achievement, which proved to make a widespread, indelible impression, virtually pivoting the valuation of the still new TV apparatus in the Los Angeles public imagination and jump-starting its promise to access the real. In many ways television was making news by covering the news. The overwhelming public interest and concern for Kathy's rescue, which by many accounts virtually brought the city to a standstill, merged in a silent way with an adjacent topicality—that of television, still new to most as an apparatus, and especially new as a primary source of "live" news coverage. The Fiscus telecast may therefore be seen to be a pivotal episode in forging a public awareness and experience of television in relation to emotional identification and social mobility.

Both at the rescue site and citywide, popular and practical conceptions of TV were being significantly altered. The most striking example of this kind of transformation occurred near the end of the telecast: the sheriff in charge of the operation approached television reporter Bill Welsh and asked him to break the news of the child's confirmed death to the Fiscus family, who had been watching the coverage but had turned off their set when the outlook became too bleak and depressing. The family felt they "knew" Welsh from his television proximity, and he consented to break the news to them.

Figure 5.1 The Fiscus rescue attempt: arrow shows location of the well. (Note various newsmen and rescue workers.)

Even though the rescue attempt was televised only in Los Angeles, the intensity of interest in the rescue effort was national and even international. Newspaper coverage in New York, Washington DC, and Chicago reveals detailed and timely front-page attention to the Fiscus story, typically well illustrated with photos from the scene and diagrams of the complex rescue strategies ("Miners Go Down to Rescue Kathy"). The acuity of interest is suggested in the attention to specific times that news was reported before deadline, and especially in the culminating headlines that refer to the child by her first name ("FIND KATHY DEAD IN WELL!").

As a symbolic locus in the public imagination, the Fiscus incident may be seen to have literally represented and brought into view repressed and dreaded possibilities of post-World War Two America, engaging a complex fantasy regarding the buried body of the child in relation to shifting boundaries of social and mediated subjectivity. This fantasy is especially marked in relation to attendant social anxieties, which a fundamental interruption to a presumed sense of normality has the potential to roil, a process that I refer to as an avant-garde of the real. Such a scenario opens up a gap in our socialized, rational experience of the "everyday," necessarily introducing the dread of anarchy, which our introduction to the Symbolic insists upon, but also a fantasy longing for origins and resolutions.

The Well

Independently produced, and a minor hit for distributor United Artists, *The Well* garnered mixed reviews but predominantly a reputation as an "important" film to be seen (United Artists press book, *The Well*). Part utopian fable, part exploitation film, the premise is literally based on a simple transposition of the Fiscus event: what if the little girl was black? (Hill 1951). The degree of dramatic escalation that is reverse-engineered from this simple question speaks directly to the issues attendant to an intermedial analysis of this film. Here, the interval between the child's accident and the discovery of her predicament is expanded, to produce the conditions for a melodramatic crescendo of social panic, soon to be quelled by the communal rescue effort.

The Well refigures the "threat" to the everyday attendant to the Fiscus event in terms of racial difference, a sign of how close to consciousness "race" was figured as contiguous to "threat." Set in an unspecific "nowhere" of the postwar middle class, the film is accepted as a fable about desires for racial harmony through mutual efforts but may also be read as ultimately justifying the segregation of new housing developments at the core of postwar "white flight" to the suburbs, in the name of preserving a "safe" distance between incendiary social differences.

Part of what justifies such a reading is the relation between "law," in the figure of the police, and the attempt to render "objectivity" in the film. Presented at first as a kind of police procedural, the film opens with the revelation of the little girl's "actual" situation (she falls into a well) and then the realization of her disappearance in the public sphere. Sheriff Kellogg soberly assesses all the information as it comes to him, following leads and advising members of the public. A key moment of revelation, from which much of the rest of the film derives its melodramatic potential, is a detail of racial difference that is sufficient to rupture procedures of the everyday: the little girl had last been seen talking to a white man. (Dmitri Tiomkins's score and Kellogg's facial expression speak an unmistakable shock.)

What follows is a process of unauthorized face-to-face news dissemination which is cast as prone to be inauthentic, outside of sober police deliberations. The film's own discursive border is provisionally set when a black male relative of the missing girl asserts to the Sheriff that the stranger in town has not been located because he is white, and then asks for a description of the man. The Sheriff advises him in no uncertain terms that the police "had better take care of this," clearly disallowing any question of the integrity of his department. The film does work to "balance" its depictions of the race-based escalation of suspicion and rancor (in one interesting reversal of common practice,

Figure 5.2 A radio technician lowers a microphone into the well; watching are the girl's parents, the Sheriff, and the first members of a growing crowd.

the police are seen to monitor briefly all the white men in public), though this includes several problematic casual uses of the "N" word by various whites.

The tone soon becomes increasingly less sober, however, raising border issues between socially responsible fare and exploitation films. Eventually, as the racial tensions begin rapidly to escalate toward physical violence, the Sheriff's assessment of his own officers is shown to be at issue. But the knowledge of the child's true whereabouts creates for the audience a different, related melodramatic temporality concerning integrity and the law. Because we know she has not in fact been kidnapped or assaulted, part of our melodramatic investment in "justice" revolves around the innocence of falsely accused Claude Packard, a relative of local construction magnate Sam Packard, an unexpected visitor in town. His interrogation by the police for what was casual and even generous behavior—among his wanderings he bought the little girl flowers and escorted her across the street—creates a central breach in the melodramatic potential for (white) justice in the film. This breach is sustained across the quasi-race riots that ensue, even across the discovery that the girl is alive in the well. It is finally filled only by Claude's deployment as a veteran mine worker to rescue the little girl. (He emerges from the well covered with grime and mud, temporarily "raced" in his expulsion of guilt and triumphant role as a savior.)

The most direct relationship between *The Well* and the Fiscus incident relates to the final forty minutes of the film, which comprises a roughly accurate depiction of many of the techniques and events of the attempted Fiscus rescue. In this, the film's peculiar fantasy of the temporality of social crisis becomes more complete. At one level, it presents a delayed visual representation of the Fiscus "rupture" to the everyday, coverage that only Los Angeles's resourceful television viewers had previously been able to witness in this detail (and likely enjoyed witnessing again in this form). At another level, it projects a kind of tinder-keg vision of a fear of the future, specifically repercussions of "past" and present race relations that the simplest misunderstanding at the right instance could trigger. Its construction of a "present" in the form of a melodramatic reclaiming of the "falsely" besmirched reputation of an industrious but itinerant white male laborer—the hero of the attendant rescue of the little girl and the society at large—appears to rectify the tensions running across these temporalities with an aspiring, can-do vision of finding that man a home, precisely the project of postwar suburbanization, and part of the original set of issues within patriarchy placed under crisis in the Fiscus event.

Ace in the Hole

An important aspect of the intermedial perspective toward *Ace in the Hole* is that KTLA, the station most acclaimed for and identified with the Fiscus coverage, was owned and operated in Los Angeles by Paramount, the studio in which this film was produced and the creative "home" of the film's director Billy Wilder. *Ace in the Hole* references different aspects of Wilder's personal life and career, not least of which was his experience as an exile in the *frontera*, awaiting clearance to enter the USA from Mexicali. The film configures its fantasy construction of the mediated public sphere via a historicized recognition of the lineage between media events such as the Fiscus and Floyd Collins incidents, yet transposed on to the Southwest—border country—which entails exile discourse as part of a consideration of the geography of race within the subjectivity of the US national imaginary.

If the Fiscus incident produced a fantasy about the body of the child, surprising in the scope and depth of its response, this film produces a series of fantasy constructions about the degree and extent of that response, a somewhat relentless jeremiad about willingness and culpability in the perceived corruption of the US public sphere. A kind of anomaly of the Cold War era, the film does not leave much room for a sense of satisfaction in the American way. It presents the kind of politicized critique that *film noir* was capable of even then, though it also reveals the limits to such a critique: the construction of its perverse media fantasy scenario, I will argue, evokes yet also covers over the border issues of race and ethnicity that the film appears to illuminate.

Protagonist Chuck Tatum is positioned in a key role as antihero audience surrogate: instigator of media fraud, seasoned instructor of its potentialities, and ultimately the only and ideal witness to the full range of its effects. He intentionally plans to prolong the rescue of a New Mexico roadside business owner, Leo Minoso, who is trapped in a cave that once served as a Native American burial ground. The central triad configuration is between Tatum, Leo Minoso, and Leo's wife Lorraine, a relation that Tatum literalizes by stating, "There's three of us buried in that cave." The goals they each perceive based on the initial situation exhibit a certain complementarity to one another, even as they ultimately contradict one another: Tatum wants to condition a sustained, successful rescue effort, with characters and plot points in place; Lorraine wants to escape a failed marriage and needs traveling money; and Leo enjoys the notion of his emergent notoriety since it may procure customers and a financial upturn, and hence save his marriage.

The film presents a troubled economy in negotiating certain social differences in relation to "others": a "difference" in the marking of difference that seems to delimit its social critique. Most Mexican American and Native American characters are rendered as nearly void of subjectivity: Leo's mother never speaks, fulfilling a stereotype as devoted in prayer to the exclusion of any other interaction; Leo's father is constantly placating whomever might help or show concern for his son; Leo himself may be seen to be passive to the point of being infantilized. None of these characters exhibits any emotion even close to anger; their collective agency is proscribed within the confines of enduring hardships. While they certainly evoke sympathy from the audience, they appear to be proper victims and nothing more, blind in their grief to the exploitations that surround them.

Leo's status eventually declines into a position as one of the mummies entombed in the holy mountain, which may be seen to "race" him in the classical US sense of producing a literally blackened complexion. In this way, the film seems to overwrite the trauma of Native American history twice—framing it as hype and also as mestizo guilt about impurity—even as it calls upon it as myth to propel the diegesis.

Nevertheless, this trauma is given some kind of representation that haunts the film's broader themes about "normative" subjectivity within contemporary capitalism. The more explicit concerns about capitalism in the film seem to revolve around the positions in a perverse triad regarding the audience/citizenry: the assumed Cold War model of a homogeneous and unified public, especially in a master binary versus "the Communists"; an emerging slippage within the postwar economy of nascent postmodern and transnational capitalism, concerning whether the definition of "choice" for the citizen-consumer is reducible to a function of the market; and (self?) contempt emerging in class

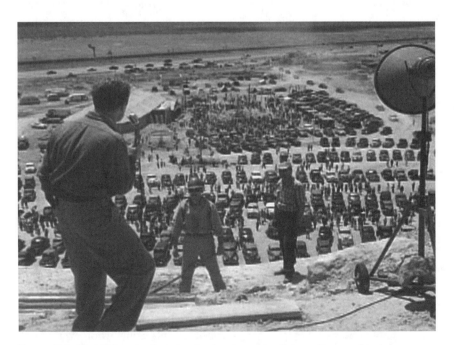

Figure 5.3 Tatum announces Leo's death to the "circus" crowd below.

distinctions embedded in the disdain for being identified with the "masses," especially as related to crowds, the notion of the common denominator, and so on.

These last two tropes are directly related to Tatum and Lorraine. Tatum, the journalist, may be seen as the original just-in-time worker, meeting deadlines and feeding circulation as needed, producing cultural capital that has a presumably short shelf life but long-term effects which are less than stable. Lorraine falls into the standard sexist assignation of "common" culture as "feminized," classed as a bad object especially in juxtaposition to Tatum, and punished by Tatum for being obviously avaricious and especially for not fulfilling Leo's idealization of her. Tatum acts out his self-contempt about Leo on Lorraine's person, choking her with Leo's spurned gift for her, and forcing Lorraine to strike back fatally. Tatum, who had variously revealed and masked to key participants and authorities what the nature of the rescue enterprise really was, experiences his own deathwatch in relation to disinterest in his "real" story about the construction of the media event.

The complex figural relations among these three contiguous texts indicate the potential for rewiring media history toward an attention to intermedial dynamics. In closing, I want to reiterate that despite the contradictions in the two films, I find that the figure of the subject trapped within them remains, as a still resonant metaphor of the catastrophic imaginary that underlies the American success ethic of this era. It brings into phase the charged social anxieties embedded in the Fiscus event and its mediation. The dynamic temporal configurations related to the missing (raced) body mobilize the anxious lure of representation that had emerged at the intermedial borders between newspapers, radio, television, and cinema, but also demonstrate an evident slippage toward figuring the historical trauma to the body politic performed under the sign of racial and ethnic difference—what Anne Anlin Cheng calls the melancholy of race (2001). What still remain are questions rather than resolutions: Whose raced imaginary/imagination of raced subjectivity is at stake in this configuration? What subject/citizen is imagined to be staring back from the void? Whose voice and cries echo there? Historical work at the intermedial borders can generate, in the best historiographic sense, new understandings of the past that produce progressive contexts by which to mobilize the future today.

Works Cited

Breder, Hans and Busse, Klaus-Peter. 2005. *Intermedia: Enacting the Liminal.* Norderstedt: Dormunder Schriften zur Kunst, 262–270.

Cheng, Anne Anlin. 2001. *The Melancholy of Race: Psychoanalysis, Assimilation, and Hidden Grief.* New York: Oxford University Press.

Chun, Wendy Hui Kyong. 2006. "Introduction: Did Somebody Say New Media?" *New Media, Old Media: A History and Theory Reader*, ed. Wendy Hui Kyong Chun and Thomas Keenan. New York: Routledge, 1–10.

Doane, Mary Ann. 2007. "Indexicality and the Concept of Medium Specificity." *Differences: A Journal of Feminist Cultural Studies* 18:1 (Spring): 128–152.

"FIND KATHY DEAD IN WELL!" 1949. *Chicago Daily Tribune*, April 11: 1ñ3.

Hill, Gladwin. "Human Tragedy Recreated in 'the Well'." 1951. *New York Times*, September 9: X6.

Williams, Mark. 2003. "Real-Time Fairy Tales: Cinema Pre-Figuring Digital Anxiety." *New Media: Theories and Practices of Digitextuality*, ed. Anna Everett and John T. Caldwell. New York: Routledge, 159–178.

Part II

New Subjects

Chapter 6

Provincial Modernity?

Film Exhibition at the 1907 Jamestown Exposition

Kathryn H. Fuller-Seeley

In what ways did motion pictures, which film scholars have associated with urban modernity, play an ideological role at a provincial event, 1907's Jamestown Tercentennial Exposition? The seven-month-long Exposition commemorated the 300th anniversary of the founding of English colonies in America with the establishment of the Jamestown, Virginia, settlement in April 1607. Unlike the era's other major expositions in Chicago, Buffalo, and St. Louis, this deliberately historical, provincially focused exposition, held outside the small Southern city of Norfolk, Virginia, explicitly did not promote ideologies of upcoming prospects such as industrial manufacturing, consumer product innovations, visions of the future, or solutions to the challenges of the urban metropolis (Love 1907; Rydell 1984). The rurally situated festival focused on everything that was the opposite of the fast-paced life of the Big City. It dwelt on white colonial heritage and celebrated a mythical past of pioneers conquering wilderness, eradicating Indians, and bringing civilization and American ideals to new lands. It celebrated military heritage and the exploits of the US Navy's Great White Fleet in the Pacific (as Norfolk was a naval and shipbuilding center). It danced uneasily around optimistic visions of the New South, focusing more on the dominance of agriculture in the Southern economy than on any promises of industrial growth or racial equality. The only Big City represented at the fair was destroyed daily (shaken and burned to the ground at the "San Francisco Earthquake and Fire" exhibit).

Nevertheless, the new technology of motion pictures was there. Entrepreneurs commissioned two one-reel films, *Pocahontas: Child of the Forest* (1907, Edwin S. Porter) and *Scenes in Colonial Virginia* (1907, Porter), to be produced by the Edison Company. These were shown in a small brick theater located in the fair's entertainment zone, the Warpath. The films were especially designed, as Hayden White (1978) reminds us all histories are, to represent America's founding myths in particular ways. While the Exposition's subjects reinforced traditional themes of the Anglo-Saxon foundation of American civilization, I will nevertheless argue that the film narratives opened up small spaces for readings that allowed modernity to be adapted to provincial tastes and some modern ideas to slip quietly in through the back door.

Aspects of these film narratives moved beyond the traditional male- and white-dominated history that most US Americans learned in school at that time. Instead, they emphasized family building by the pioneers over the exploits of individual male pioneers. Pocahontas, a woman, energetically rescued lovers and colonists, anticipating the movie serial heroines to come. "Great white men" triumphed not due to natural inevitability, but through trickery, the labor of African slaves, and with the partnership of spunky wives and Indian maidens. Such representations indicate different attitudes toward women and Native and African Americans than those held in the nineteenth century, ones more in line with women suffragette and civil rights themes to flourish in the 1910s and 1920s. Overtly labeling these "modern," however, is troublesome since suffragette movements often based their demands for women's votes on exceptionally traditional views of women and families as well as specters of racial others taking control of the United States (Staiger 1995, 29–53; Schuyler 2006). Still, centering narratives on strong, independent women and showing white men not at their best presented new images of the past.

This chapter asks us to re-evaluate exhibition and reception practices at the dawn of the "transitional era" of American cinema, when scenic tableau films coexisted and competed with narrative films, whose form was growing in complexity and length. At the same time in American society, nineteenth-century ideals coexisted and competed with twentieth-century ones (Fuller 1997; Fuller-Seeley 2008). As Ben Singer suggests, the transitional era of American cinema (and, I would argue, the interactions of cinema and modernity) were a "complex, dynamic process in which disparate forces—competing paradigms and practices—overlap and interact" (2004, 76). Film scholars contend that motion pictures embodied the idea of modernity produced by urban cultural change (Charney and Schwartz 1995). If so, then at the Exposition, this cinema intermingled change with cultural continuity, in a melding of new media form and cultural/ideological tradition. The films exhibited turned old stories into new ones, and linked the past with the speed, dislocations, and dangers of the present for the provincial middle-class audiences who viewed them.

The 1907 Jamestown Tercentennial Exposition did not emphasize commerce or consumer culture in the manner of most world fairs. In this unsettled time of rapid industrial growth, some were wary of the wholesale rush into the "modern" world of goods, and the Jamestown Fair was a moment to discuss it, as one commenter noted:

> The very best thing about it [Jamestown] perhaps is that it is not a "tomato can" exposition. By the tomato can exposition is meant the enormous

aggregations of canned fruits and other mercantile products, familiarly known as "exhibits", which have bordered miles and miles of aisles and aisles in previous fairs.

(Love 1907)

Here the spotlight was to be on linking the English founding of the settlement to the strengths of contemporary US American heritage and culture.

Not only the historical rather than commercial focus but also the geographic location and challenges of transportation and cost of attending the Exposition influenced the profile of Jamestown Fair attendees. Although aimed at a nation-wide audience, the fair was located more than 200 miles south of Washington, DC, which made travel difficult for any but the middle class and upper class. In comparison, St. Louis, site of the 1904 Louisiana Purchase Exposition, was a city of over 600,000, and fair organizers had invested $40,000,000; Norfolk's and Richmond's populations combined were 150,000, and Exposition particip-ants invested only $10,000,000, excluding the warships that the US and inter-national governments lent to the event (Jones 1907, 305). Making easy or repeated attendance even more difficult, the fairgrounds, six miles outside of Norfolk on several hundred acres of swampy riverside fields—the Jamestown settlement, fifty-two miles further up the James River, had been abandoned 200 years earlier—were accessible only by special railroad line or automobile (Jones 1907, 306). Construction delays meant that many exhibits, special attractions, and hotels were not ready on opening day, and drainage difficulties and hot weather brought outbreaks of disease. Early reviewers focused on the problems and deficiencies, nicknaming it the "Jamestown Imposition," further retarding attendance (Inglis 1907; Gleach 2003). The Jamestown Exposition achieved only modest success—it reported 2.75 million visitors, but 41 percent had been admitted free (Keiley 1909, 721). The majority of visitors were prob-ably from the upper South and mid-Atlantic states. It is doubtful that many Southern mill workers and sharecroppers could attend.

Despite the many factors that limited the exhibits at the Jamestown Exposition to ideas and modes of expression that were traditional and con-servative, nevertheless one recent technological innovation, cinema, was readily accepted at the Exposition. Movies were included without controversy (and largely without comment) as educational materials, representations of history, effective storytellers, and amusement fit for small-town families, women, and children. Several travelogs and factory-tour films shown at gov-ernment and consumer product manufacturers' booths joined the two histor-ical films. Movies were the equal of other spectacles at the Jamestown Exposition: fireworks, parades, flotillas, large-scale battle re-enactments, his-torical recreations, and Wild West shows.

Information about the genesis of *Pocahontas* and *Scenes in Colonial Virginia* is, however, scarce. In Spring 1907, a group called the Colonial Virginia Company commissioned the Edison Manufacturing Company, which produced numerous films for private organizations and industrial manufacturers, to create special films to exhibit at the Jamestown festival (Brownlow 1992, 232–233, 266–268; Fuller 1997, 78–82). Charles Musser located receipts in the Edison Company records documenting that director Edwin S. Porter produced 2,285 feet of film at a total cost of $1,866.24 for ten days of studio work (1991, 333, 424, 526). One newspaper article describing the upcoming Exposition noted,

> Colonial Virginia will be represented in a building which will be a copy of the old House of Burgesses in Williamsburg, as far as information about that structure is obtainable. This is a moving picture drama in which the old worthies will appear in characteristic costume, a reproduction of them, so far as is possible, as they walked in life in the olden times. Many dramatic incidents will be incorporated and the production, it is said, will be of genuine historic and artistic interest.
>
> ("Going" 1907)

Frustratingly for the historical researcher, these films received almost no attention in the motion picture trade press or in Exposition publicity materials in 1907 despite their substantial cost and the elaborate exhibition space in which they were shown. The 800-page *Official Blue Book* history of the Exposition devoted one small paragraph to the attraction. However, the Jamestown exhibitors' thriftiness ultimately extended the life of these two films; at the Exposition's conclusion, the Colonial Virginia Company sold the negatives back to the Edison Company for $150. The Edison studio commercially released the films in fall 1908, generating synopses, advertising copy, and reviews in the film trade press. As only small fragments of the films exist in archives, we must rely on the Edison publicity materials for descriptions of the films.

Pocahontas, Child of the Forest retold the legend of the meeting of Captain John Smith and an Indian princess in ways that reshaped traditional narratives ("Stories" 1908a). The film turned this story of the founding of British America into a one-reel melodramatic romance. In a plot which shared much in common with another Edison fictional history film released that year, *Daniel Boone, Or Pioneer Days in America* (1907, Porter), the power of white Anglo-Saxon males was not emphasized. Smith escapes execution not through physical might or superior weapons but through trickery and through Pocahontas's repeated intervention. She is an active heroine; her assertive sexual desire for John Smith and her centrality to the film's plot marked her as a far more complexly realized character than schoolbook histories owned. The eight-scene film, as described in the Edison Company synopsis, opens with a prologue that presents Captain John Smith as a heroic, honored figure, a "hardy adventurer, sailor, soldier and traveler, he founded Jamestown in 1607. Made friends of the Indians. This story tells of his meeting Pocahontas" ("Stories" 1908a). Next is "The Treaty of Peace," a scene in which a group of Indians, led by Chief Powhatan, arrives at Jamestown to sign an agreement with the British. His daughter Pocahontas takes the initiative to look over Captain Smith with a frankly admiring gaze, which immediately triggers jealousy in her Indian lover Kunder-Wacha, a character added by the film's scenario writer.

Smith is shown quelling mutiny among the English colonists, establishing order at Jamestown, and then mounting an expedition into the wilderness. Kunder-Wacha trails the company. The Indians capture the English, killing all but Smith, whom they take as captive to the Indian camp. Smith relies on his wits to avoid torture, fascinating the Indians with a compass. Imagining him to be a powerful Medicine Man, the Indians lead him to Powhatan, where their previous acquaintance is renewed. Pocahontas also welcomes him warmly, and her renewed attentions further inflame Kunder-Wacha's hatred. The spurned lover argues to the Indian Council that Smith must be killed, and as they prepare to execute the Captain Pocahontas demands that he be spared. While the film claims that Pocahontas's romantic feelings for Smith move her to save him, the synopsis also shows Powhatan citing her legal rights ("Indian Law in her favor") to enable Smith's release.

As the Captain returns to Jamestown, Kunder-Wacha shoots him, and Pocahontas appears to bind his wounds. Smith then sails for England, but soon afterward the Jamestown settlement turns chaotic and famine threatens. Pocahontas appears again with emergency food rations for the British settlement. There, a new character, John Rolfe, breaks the news that Smith is dead; she grieves and Rolfe comforts her, forming a new romantic relationship. This quickly leads to a climactic struggle in which Kunder-Wacha attacks the new lovers, but Rolfe finally dispatches the vengeful Indian.

The final scene depicts the historic wedding of Rolfe and Pocahontas, with all members of the English and Indian settlements joyfully celebrating. "Grand wedding. Colonists happy and prosperous," notes the final line of the synopsis, as the film's ending gives the impression that with this romantic union, the "Indian problem" is solved and the British could proceed to build their fortunes in Virginia.

The second film commissioned from the Edison studio by the Jamestown exhibitors was titled "Scenes in Colonial Virginia" ("Stories" 1908b). Unlike the Pocahontas film's attempt to tell a continuing narrative focusing on individual characters, this motion picture is a series of tableaux, a form that still characterized many films of 1907. The film consists of eight scenes visualizing historic events in the founding of the Jamestown settlement. Serious depictions of historical events are interspersed with humorous incidents that work to undercut the idea of unquestioned Anglo-Saxon male authority and allow brief moments to think about the roles of women and family building, and to question the history of race relations.

First, the English adventurers' three ships are shown arriving in Chesapeake Bay, carrying "a party of fortune seekers, including gentlemen and mechanics." A month later, the English arrive at the shore of what would become Jamestown, and they surprise a group of Indians enjoying an oyster roast. Scaring the natives away, the English hungrily appropriate the Indian feast, suggesting that theft accompanies the founding of the British settlement in Virginia.

The next three tableaux visualize moments in colonial history that also address then-current concerns in early twentieth-century Southern society. The first legislative assembly session is depicted as disorganized colonists struggling to create self-government, with officers having forcefully to eject several unruly delegates. This is an ironic, tongue-in-cheek portrayal of Virginia institutions and early settlers, instead of showing them to be brave, stoic Founding Fathers in the reverential manner that the Massachusetts Pilgrims were often represented. Second, a boatload of English women are shown landing at Jamestown, and the joyful men dance and flirt with the women; the establishment of a stable, permanent society is depicted not as mere economics but as a playful sexual encounter.

"Next we see an event of a different character," the synopsis continues, "with an ending, years later, but little foreseen by the Colonists. That is, the institution of the first American slave market" ("Stories" 1908b). This scene may have shocked viewers with its starkness after the two previous comic tableaux, and interestingly it is not mentioned in trade journal advertising for this film, which describes all the other scenes. The destruction of Jamestown by fire immediately follows. Could spectators possibly have read this juxtaposition of slavery and destruction as a comment on the impact of slavery on Southern society, or was it just an example of the "cinema of attractions" (Gunning 1990)? The penultimate vignette shows a Virginia Colonist who returns to England to introduce tobacco smoking to Sir Walter Raleigh. The end results of these pivotal moments are depicted in the final scene: a colonial ball with dancers in elegant dress, subtitled "many years later, when Virginia was a well established and successful colony."

The scenario writer's desire to tell complicated stories in a one-reel format limited the success of both films that only allow for twelve to fourteen minutes of action. When film trade journals reviewed the films in Fall 1908, critical reactions were mixed. In the spirit of uplifting the quality of motion pictures from low-class melodrama to appeal to an audience of educated middle-class viewers, critics applauded the historical and educational focus of both films. "It is not too much to say that such films as this [Scenes in Colonial Virginia] ought to be more numerous. They would attract a desirable class of patrons to the theater showing them and the profits would be immeasurably increased," noted the Moving Picture World reviewer ("Comments" 1908b). Indeed, films such as these and Daniel Boone were precursors of the serious, "quality" films drawing their plots from Shakespeare, literature, history, and the arts that studios such as Edison, Vitagraph, Thanhouser, and Biograph would begin featuring in their output (Gunning 1991; Musser 1991; Uricchio and Pearson 1993; Bowers 2001).

Moving Picture World editor Stephen Bush praised the excellent scenery and photography of Pocahontas, "The Indian canoe made of white birch decorated in the Indian fashion with fantastic figures, the scene of embarkment on the James River, and the journey to the white settlement, will thrill and delight every audience" (1908, 279). Bush found fault, however, with the telescoping of plot that failed to depict with more pathos the tragic personal aspects of what he understood of the Pocahontas legend, in which he included her deep love for Smith, the false report of his death, a forced trip with Rolfe to England, then her sorrow of meeting Smith in England and subsequent early death. ("To explain her marriage to Rolfe, an Indian rival has been forced into the story--not a happy thought," he noted.) Bush proposed a more psychological treatment focused on Pocahontas as an individual rather than the use of her to represent a fecund New Land wanting to welcome, protect, and offer the gift of herself to the new colonists.

Another reviewer expressed impatience with the scenic tableau form of Scenes in Colonial Virginia and found it lacking elements of more recent films that focused on narrative development. He noted that the film "was well received by the audience. It is a class of subject that is a welcome change from the usual thing, but needs to be presented with a lecture for the spectators to fully understand and appreciate the scenes that are presented" ("Comments" 1908a). Edison had advertised the film as part of the shared heritage of all Americans, "A graphic tracing of famous scenes and incidents connected with the founding of Jamestown and early life in Virginia. Scenes we have all pictured in our minds since school days, are made real in the film" (Edison 1908). Lecturers were now being used less frequently in theaters and perhaps the critic wondered how familiar this history might be to recent immigrant audienced. Other reviewers were critical of inaccurate details in the actors' costumes in Pocahontas, with the Dramatic Mirror reviewer questioning the use of Navaho blankets by Virginia Indians, and Sime Silverman of Variety sniping that the Indians looked more like Chinese ballet girls and the Colonists more like Hebrew impersonators (quoted in Musser 1991, 424–425).

During the course of the Jamestown Exposition in 1907, a Hale's Tours film exhibit with three train cars outfitted as theaters in which viewers watched scenes of foreign travel joined the Colonial Virginia Company attraction of these two films in the Warpath exhibition area (Keiley 1909, 686; "Warpath" 1907). Although motion pictures were becoming very popular in the nickelodeon theaters, which were rapidly springing up in large cities and small towns elsewhere across the nation, most Southerners still only encountered films as part of vaudeville shows in larger cities or through itinerant exhibitors' programs. Richmond and Atlanta only saw their first nickelodeon theaters in fall 1907. Atlanta film exhibitors noted the Jamestown precedent of a movie-theater district, dubbing their row of four nickelodeons on Viaduct Place "The Warpath" ("Real" 1907; Fuller-Seeley 2002).[1]

The highest grossing attractions on the Warpath were the large-scale re-creation of the Civil War naval battle between the Monitor and Merrimack ironclad ships ($138,366) and the 101 Ranch Wild West Show which featured nearly 1,000 human and animal performers ($67,081). The Destruction of San Francisco attraction earned $11,872 (Keiley 1909, 721). Ticket sales at the Hale's Tours exhibit totaled $5,539.10. Listed as "Virginia history and moving pictures," Colonial Virginia Company's movie attraction earned $3,936.50. Assuming that tickets cost 10 cents, nearly 40,000 visitors may have viewed the Jamestown historical fiction films (721).

Despite the efforts of Jamestown Exposition planners to keep the specter of modernity at bay by focusing on history, tradition, and the status quo, new ideas and alternative points of view would not stay shut out. Twentieth-century Indians, African-Americans, women, racial and gender equality, consumer products, industrialization, rapid social and cultural change: all kept intruding into the Exposition proceedings, insisting on making themselves visible. At a time when white racial prejudice ran high across the South, and Jim Crow segregation was ubiquitous, nevertheless black sculptor Meta Warrick filled the Exposition's Negro Building with plaster figures representing the trauma of slavery's introduction to Jamestown just as did the film *Scenes in Colonial Virginia* (Brundage 2003). While Virginia State Registrar Walter Plecker would soon work to erase Indians from the records by declaring "pure" Indian identity gone and classifying everyone of non-white blood "colored" (with a quiet exemption for the hundreds of whites claiming descent from Pocahontas), in 1907 Indians were all over the fairgrounds (Gleach 2006), and a band of real Powhatan Indians performed their own story live on the Warpath, along with the popular Plains Indians performing at the 101 Ranch show. Pocahontas was featured in a film and on thousands of postcards and souvenirs, and the founding of Jamestown involved sexual flirting. Despite plans to keep "tomato cans" away, visitors had voted with their feet to explore the offerings of consumer product manufacturers and amusement vendors. It is possible that even at as unlikely an event as the Jamestown Tercentennial 1907, modernity seeped through the cracks and fissures of the exhibits and films on display, presenting itself for consideration to the visitors.

Note

1. Motion pictures were also shown in several exhibitors' booths for educational purposes. The Post Office exhibit featured a row of twelve Mutoscope machines, which illustrated postal delivery services across the nation. The Department of the Interior exhibit included a 200-seat room in which daily lectures, illustrated with films and lantern slides, were given on Indian resettlement and education programs and conservation of parklands (Keiley 1909, 406, 500, 501). Consumer-product exhibits also included lectures with films and slides, presenting factory tours and programs on "social betterment among employees and their families" at National Cash Register, H. J. Heinz, Larkin soap manufacturers, and Ballard and Ballard flour company booths (455–456, 572). While not a "tomato can" exposition, the Food Building, which featured 100 consumer product manufacturers' exhibits, nevertheless drew the largest crowds of the Exposition. The Blue Book claimed that free samples of coffee, tea, and breakfast foods were the main draw, but motion pictures were also successfully used to promote integration of consumer products into visitors' lives (584–585, 650).

Filmography

Daniel Boone, Or Pioneer Days in America. Dir. Edwin S. Porter. Edison, 1907.
Pocahontas, Child of the Forest. Dir. Edwin S. Porter. Edison, 1907 (released 1908).
Scenes in Colonial Virginia. Dir. Edwin S. Porter. Edison, 1907 (released 1908).

Works Cited

Bowers, Q. David. 2001. *Thanhouser Films: An Encyclopedia and History*. CD-ROM. Thanhouser Film Company Preservation, 1997.

Brownlow, Kevin. 1992. *Behind the Mask of Innocence*. Berkeley: University of California Press.

Brundage, W. Fitzhugh. 2003. "Meta Warrick's 1907 'Negro Tableaux' and (Re) Presenting African American Historical Memory." *Journal of American History* 89.4: 1368–1400.

Bush, Stephen. 1908. "Comments on Film Subjects." *Moving Picture World*. October 10: 279.

Charney, Leo and Vanessa R. Schwartz, eds. 1995. *Cinema and the Invention of Modern Life*. Berkeley: University of California Press.

"Comments on Film Subjects." 1908a. *Moving Picture World*. November 21: 398.

———. 1908b. *Moving PictureWorld*. November 28: 422.

Edison Company. Advertisement. 1908. *Moving Picture World*. November 21: 405.

Fuller, Kathryn H. 1997. *At the Picture Show: Small Town Audiences and the Creation of Movie Fan Culture*. Washington, DC: Smithsonian Press.

Fuller-Seeley, Kathryn. 2002. *Celebrate Richmond Theater*. Richmond, VA.: Dietz Press.
———. ed. 2008. *Hollywood in the Neighborhood: Historical Case Studies of Local Moviegoing*. Berkeley: University of California Press.
Gleach, Frederic W. 2003. "Pocahontas at the Fair: Crafting Identities at the 1907 Jamestown Exposition." *Ethnohistory* 50.3: 419–445.
———. 2006. "The Ritual World of Pocahontas." *Natural History* November: 40–46.
"Going on the Warpath." 1907. *Perry [Iowa] Daily Chief*, 24 May. World's Fairs and Expositions: Defining America and the World, ed. Jim Zwick. Accessed June 1, 2007. www.boondocksnet.com/compos.index.html>.
Gunning, Tom. 1990. "The Cinema of Attractions: Early Film, Its Spectator and the Avant-Garde." In *Early Cinema: Space, Frame, Narrative*, ed. Thomas Elsaesser. London: British Film Institute, 56–62.
———. 1991. *D.W. Griffith and the Origins of American Narrative Film: The Early Years at Biograph*. Urbana: University of Illinois Press.
Inglis, William. 1907. "The Troubles at Jamestown." *Harpers Weekly* June 8: 834–837.
Jones, Plummer F. 1907. "The Jamestown Tercentennial Exposition." *American Review of Reviews* 35: 305–318.
Keiley, Charles Russell, ed. 1909. *Official Blue Book of the Jamestown Ter-Centennial Exposition*. Norfolk, VA: Colonial Publishing.
Love, Robertus. 1907. "An Exposition with a Warpath: What the Jamestown Fair Means and Why It is a Milepost in American History." *Newark [Ohio] Daily Advocate* April 23. *World's Fairs and Expositions: Defining America and the World*, ed. Jim Zwick. Accessed June 1, 2007. www.boondocksnet.com/compos.index.html.
Musser, Charles. 1991. *Before the Nickelodeon: Edwin S. Porter and the Edison Manufacturing Company*. Berkeley: University of California Press.
"Real 'Warpath' Planned by Moving Picture Men." 1907. *Atlanta Constitution* 11 (February): 8.
Rydell, Robert. 1984. *All the World's a Fair: Visions of Empire at American International Expositions, 1876–1916*. Chicago: University of Chicago Press.
Schuyler, Lorraine Gates. 2006. *The Weight of Their Votes: Southern Women and Political Leverage in the 1920s*. Chapel Hill: University of North Carolina Press.
Singer, Ben. 2004. "Feature Films, Variety Programs and the Crisis of the Small Exhibitor." *American Cinema's Transitional Era: Audiences, Institutions, Practices,* ed. Charlie Keil and Shelley Stamp. Berkeley: University of California Press, 76–100.
Staiger, Janet. 1995. *Bad Women: Regulating Sexuality in Early American Cinema*. Minneapolis: University of Minnesota Press.
"Stories of the Films." 1908a. *Moving Picture World*. October 10: 263.
"Stories of the Films." 1908b. *Moving Picture World*. November 21: 405.
Uricchio, William and Roberta Pearson. 1993. *Reframing Culture: The Case of the Vitagraph Quality Films*. Princeton: Princeton University Press.
"Warpath is Amusing; All Sorts of Eccentric Things to Be Found There." 1907. *Washington Post*. August 18: 12.
White, Hayden. 1978. *Tropics of Discourse: Essays in Cultural Criticism*. Baltimore: Johns Hopkins University Press.

Chapter 7

Exhibition in Mexico During the Early 1920s

Nationalist Discourse and Transnational Capital

Laura Isabel Serna

In the early 1920s, conservative and liberal observers alike agreed that Mexico seemed to be Americanizing at a frighteningly rapid pace. Many blamed this state of affairs on American motion pictures and the new models of gender, class relations, and consumer behavior they offered to Mexican audiences. The country had come under the sway, as one journalist phrased it, "of the characteristic North American film ... a docile and faithful instrument of tenacious and unbreakable propaganda" (Alvarez 1924). These concerns echoed those being raised in other countries as the increasingly consolidated US film industry went about selling America and itself to the world.

The notion that the consumption of American popular culture inexorably leads to ideological dominance, *pace* Ariel Dorfman and Armand Mattelart (2002), and inevitably displaces national or local culture continues to be central to debates about the globalization of media past and present. While scholars such as Toby Miller (2008) focus on the seemingly ever-growing power of the contemporary US film industry, others have questioned the Hollywood-as-hegemony thesis by focusing on the "activities of local agents" (Maltby 2004, 7) and examining the historical reception of Hollywood film in local contexts.[1]

The identification of Hollywood film as American film and agent of Americanization continues to influence the analysis of national cinemas. As Stephen Crofts points out, the very idea of a national cinema depends on the existence of an antithesis, Hollywood film (1993, 49). Scholarship on various national cinematic traditions thus typically privileges production *as* cinema, neglecting the equally important modalities of distribution and exhibition. The history of Mexican cinema is no exception. Indeed, in the 1920s when the influence of American films was a major concern, the development of a national cinema was an oft-proposed antidote. In writing the history of Mexican cinema, the years preceding the Golden Age of Mexican cinema, which began in the mid-1930s, appear as a period of anticipation.[2] The overwhelming popularity of first European and then North American films, when not glossed over, is skipped over as an embarrassing imperialist interregnum.[3]

In this chapter, I approach the question of the relationship between Mexican audiences' consumption of US cinema and Americanization by looking at exhibition. In order to expand upon Ana M. López's observation that the cinema's spread in Latin America "followed a pattern determined by ... the level of development of railroads and other modern infrastructures" (2000, 51), I examine discursive practices and the material conditions and structure of the industry. In doing so, I suggest that during this period the nationalist dimensions of Mexican cinema were far more likely to be found in the discursive space of film culture or the social space of the theater than on the screen, while also examining less obvious ways in which transnational culture and capital influenced the formation of mass spectatorship in Mexico.

Cinema Exhibition: A National Industry

In the 1920s, films produced in the United States flooded the Mexican market. Throughout the decade an average of 500 American titles were screened a year, leading some commentators to dub the phenomenon the "yanqui invasion" (Amador and Blanco 1993, 465–469; "El hijo de la loca" 1923). In contrast, between 1916 and 1929 the national industry produced an average of just six films per year (García Riera 1992, 11). Thus, while the postrevolutionary state focused its attention on the production of Mexican national identity through the fine arts, national histories, and the popularization of national types and celebrations, Mexican audiences consumed a steady diet of American productions in a growing number of venues across the country.

Although distribution would increasingly become the province of American film studios, exhibition outside of the capital continued to be the national industry's domain. In fact, despite being purveyors of imported cultural products and in the capital sometimes foreigners themselves, cinema owners were portrayed in public discourse as contributors to Mexico's economic growth and social advancement. In Mexico City the opening of new cinemas was announced with pride. For example, when the *Cine Majestic* reopened under new ownership in 1924, the newspaper *Excélsior* called the new owners, the Granat brothers, "truly progressive" for providing entertainment that was "perfectly moral, attractive, and entirely appropriate to the needs of the neighborhood" ("El Cine Majestic" 1924). The entertainment editor for another major daily *El Universal* waxed euphoric over the *Cine Capitolio*'s décor, projectors, screen—"the only one of its kind in Mexico"—seating, lighting, and two orchestras, one of which played the latest foxtrots "imported from New York." The newspaper praised the cinema's owners for "planning this new and important *business* in the cinema field ("Hoy" 1924). Whether these articles truly reflected the newspapers' editorial perspective or were a form of paid advertising,[4] their rhetoric urged the public to see both the buildings and the entertainment they offered as part of Mexico's progress.

Municipal authorities in the capital likewise saw the cinema as an important contributor to the city and the nation's modernization. In 1922 cinema inspector Alfonso de Icaza compared the new *Cine Odeón* with less well-appointed theaters, calling the former "proof of our [Mexico's] progress" (Special Municipal Inspector 1922). What is more, municipal government officials saw the act of movie-going, even if it meant watching American films they frequently described as completely lacking in artistic merit, as a more desirable alternative to other forms of popular entertainment. "In addition to the fact that they will be in places less immoral than the *pulquerías*," Inspector Hipólito Amor wrote, "they will spend less . . . in *cantinas* [bars], *fondas* [neighborhood restaurants], or *pulquerias*" (Amor 1922). The act of movie-going, these comments suggest, combined the values of morality and thrift the Mexican elite believed essential to the country's modernization (Knight 1990).

Figure 7.1 The Cine Odeón, Mexico City, Fototeca INAH Pachuca.

Cinema owners took every opportunity to reinforce the image of themselves as patriotic citizen-entrepreneurs. On national holidays, movie theaters offered functions at "popular" prices—often in hopes of currying favor with municipal authorities. They also sponsored special events that blended spectatorship and patriotism. For example, in September 1923 the *Cine Majestic* in Mexico City hosted a special event sponsored by the newspaper *Excélsior* in honor of young women from two local *colonias* [neighborhoods] who had been nominated for queen of the upcoming *Fiestas Patrias* [Mexican Independence Celebration] ("Advertisement" 1923). Two years earlier in addition to official

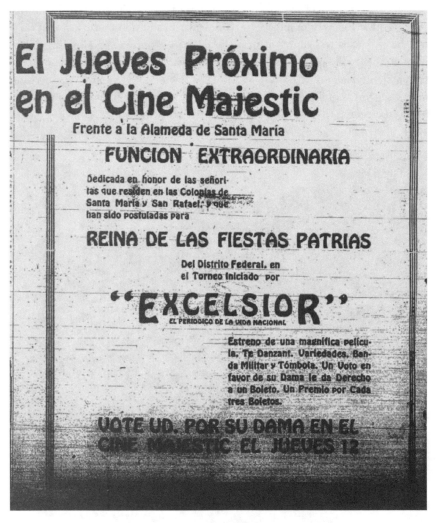

Figure 7.2 Advertisement, *Excélsior*, 10 July 1923.

fêtes, extensive press coverage, and the place of honor in the parade celebrating the country's centennial which Rick Anthony López describes, a series of special screenings at the Cines San Juan de Letrán, Venecia, Trianon, and Lux celebrated the winner of the *India Bonita* contest, Bibiana Uribe. Sponsored by Paramount films, the "select program" featured the Cecil B. DeMille film *Porque cambia de esposa* (*Why Change your Wife?*, 1920) and *Culpa de amor* (*Guilty of Love*, 1920) starring Dorothy Dalton ("Advertisements" 1921).

Valuing the social practice of movie-going as a nationalist gesture was not exclusive to the capital. In Matehuala, San Luis Potosí, when municipal authorities imposed new taxes that threatened to close the theater *Teatro E. Durand* and its rival the *Teatro Ocampo*, the editors of the local literary, political, and cultural review took the municipal government to task for endangering "the culture of the city" ("Los espectaculos" 1919). In 1927, the national weekly *México en Rotograbado* referred to the opening of the *Cine Alcázar* in Ciudad Juárez, Chihuahua, as a "patriotic act" ("La empresa Calderón" 1927). Thus, in the provinces as well as in the capital, the business of cinema was perceived as an important part of Mexico's post-revolutionary nation-building project.

Beyond publicity-generating gestures, cinema owners regularly employed nationalist rhetoric when lobbying the government on behalf of their business interests. When the federal government threatened to institute new censorship regulations in the *Distrito Federal* [Federal District] in 1919, cinema owners protested that complying with the regulations would crush an important industry ("Los empresarios" 1919). Likewise in 1931, when the government implemented a protective tariff measure in response to the introduction of sound films, cinema owners—mostly but not all Mexican nationals—argued that the duties would protect a "hypothetical industry"—production—leaving an existing and important industry in a tenuous position (Pezet 1931, 9).

Exhibitors were not alone in positioning themselves as patriots. Cinema workers also considered themselves participants in the nation's economic development. They mobilized the same nationalist rhetoric when pressing the government to promote the growth of the cinema industry or defend their interests as workers. For example, during the 1922 embargo on films from US studios, the employees of the *Circuito Olimpia*, Mexico City's largest movie theater chain, wrote to then President Alvaro Obreón to assure him, as "genuine representatives of *la raza*," that the films that had sparked the embargo were in no way offensive (Villegas 1924). As I have discussed elsewhere, workers perceived the embargo as preventing them from fulfilling their patriotic duty of being economically active citizens (Serna 2006).

Although, in the case of the embargo, *Circuito Olimpia* employees supported their employers, cinema workers more often sided with other Mexican laborers demanding better wages, safer working conditions, and job security.[5] As

Mexican film historian Aurelio de los Reyes recounts, the early 1920s saw increasing activism on the part of skilled cinema employees whose jobs were put in jeopardy due to shifts in ownership—the *Circuito Olimpia*'s sale to a group of American investors, for example—and the increasingly corporate organization of the exhibition industry (1993, 350–355).

A disparity between the generous wages paid to management staff, typically foreign-born, and Mexican runners, projectionists, doormen, ticket sellers, and janitors characterized the cinema industry, like other industries connected to transnational capital such as mining and oil. In the capital, unequal power relations infused the everyday interactions between American-owned or managed cinemas and their Mexican labor force. For example, both the employees and patrons of the *Cine San Hipólito* complained about the attitude of American manager Charles Rich. In his report to the chief of the municipal department of public diversions, a Mexican inspector noted that Rich "possesse[d] absolutely no grasp of the national language" and treated employees and patrons alike "despotically, insultingly, and in a denigrating manner" ("Jefe de sección" 1922). Reports of other clashes between American cinema representatives and the Mexican public surface periodically in municipal records, indicating that while Mexican audiences appreciated the quality of US films, expatriate managers' failure to treat their Mexican workers with respect grated on the public.

By the late 1920s and early 1930s cinema workers had become strong supporters of economic nationalism. In addition to rallying around the many musicians displaced by the introduction of sound films, workers petitioned the government to look out for the interests of "honorable Mexicans" by protecting the exhibition industry and supporting cultural nationalists' fight against sound films in English (Espinosa and Castillo 1931). Others feared that protectionist measures would once again put the exhibition industry in jeopardy as American film studios threatened to pack up shop and leave the country ("Desde hace" 1931). That fear pointed to an uncomfortable truth: the Mexican exhibition industry, characterized as it was as a *national* industry, relied on American films to meet the public's demand for entertainment.

The 1923 Censo Obrero: Transnational Capital and the Mexican Cinema Industry

The discourse on cinema and its social function shows how the consumption of an imported cultural product could be recast as part of Mexico's nation-building project. Looking at the structural aspects of the exhibition industry suggests other ways in which the movement of transnational capital affected the history of cinema and the development of national audiences. In 1923 the newly reorganized department of labor undertook a nationwide census of working conditions in the cinema industry, which in addition to its association with industrialization and modernization was becoming a growing source of employment. The census was part of a larger project to gather information about labor conditions in important employment sectors such as printing, bricklaying, and textile production. Surveys asked about salaries, employee literacy, nationality, and the prevalence of union membership. Collected data were published periodically in the department's monthly bulletin, alongside detailed information on the cost of living in each state of the Republic ("Promedio del salario" 1922). I have been unable to locate published results of the film exhibition industry survey, but an analysis of the available manuscript census material suggests intriguing patterns.[6]

The business of cinema exhibition differed markedly from region to region in both qualitative and quantitative terms. In Mexico City, operating a movie theater could be lucrative. The *Circuito Olimpia* owned and managed a chain of thirteen cinemas and claimed to be operating with over $1,000,000 MN (approximately US$485,437 in 1923) in working capital. The company employed over 150 men, women, and children who worked regular schedules, seven hours a day and six days a week. At their largest cinema, the *Teatro Olimpia*, male employees earned 30 pesos per week. The young women who worked as *acomadoras* (usherettes) and in the box-office earned an average of 14 pesos a week, both respectable wages relative to salaries in other industries (Cuestionario 550 1923). According to returned surveys for all the chain's theaters, *Circuito Olimpia* employees were uniformly literate. Although management professed ignorance on the issue—"we can't say with precision" they said—the *Circuito*'s skilled employees belonged to the *Sindicato de Empleados de Cinematografó* [Union of Cinema Employees] (De los Reyes 1993, 353).

The well-capitalized *Circuito* was exceptional. Most cinemas in Mexico City had an average of $2,000 MN (US$970) on hand, though this figure does not include the value of real estate or equipment. Outside of the capital, motion picture exhibition was even more likely to be the province of small business owners. Most provincial cinemas operated with $1,000 MN (US$500) and very often much less in working capital. In smaller towns theaters often operated just one or two days a week and their employees held other jobs. For example, the three cinemas which José Jury owned in Morelia, Michoacan (population 68,467 in 1921), employed twenty-five people: twenty-one men and four women. The three projectionists earned 3 pesos for each shift of six hours, their assistants 1 peso. The ticket sellers (the four women) and door staff earned between 1 peso and 1 peso 25 centavos. The musicians who provided accompaniment for the functions earned the most: 2 pesos an hour. Lest the Labor Department's staff become anxious about how people could live on such meager wages when the cinema was only open two days a week, Jury explained that the members of his staff were "artisans and government office employees, having this as an extra job" (Cuestionario 213 1923). In Oaxaca, one of the country's most rural states, one local cinema also served as a *molina* (corn mill), combining the most basic necessity, ground corn for tortillas, with modern entertainment (Cuestionario, Molina San José 1923).

Outside the capital, industrial Monterrey, and the socialist-leaning Yucatán, few cinema workers were members of unions in the early 1920s, a situation that would change in the latter part of the decade. However, cinemas were often associated with local efforts to organize and defend workers' rights or with the rhythm of workers' lives. Francisco Galindo of Túxpam, Veracruz, reported that the cinema he owned, the *Teatro-Cine Variedades*, had closed but that he loaned the space to various groups from time to time for charity shows or dances to raise funds for the town's planned *casa del obrero* [workers' center] (Galindo 1923). Other cinemas listed their business as being for the "recreation of the workers" (Cuestionario 616 1923) or noted that their small business was only open on Saturday, "el día de ralla [*sic*]," [day of the line/limit, e.g. payday] (Maranón 1923) for the workers in the local textile factories.

The census material also shows that the concentration of cinemas followed a definite pattern. Unsurprisingly, given the city's rapid population growth during and after the Revolution, Mexico City had numerous cinemas—fifty-five in 1923—and seats—over 82,000, not including those in temporary or smaller, third-run neighborhood theaters. Rural states had fewer cinemas. Jalisco and Oaxaca are good examples. Jalisco had a population of approximately 1,200,000 in 1921 but only twenty-one cinemas, nine of which were in the capital, Guadalajara. Oaxaca had a population of 975,000 but only eight cinemas in the entire state. In contrast, states with developing industrial or export sectors with strong ties to the United States had both a higher number of cinemas and more seats per capita. The state of Nuevo León had a population of 336,000 and nineteen cinemas that could seat 13,500. Sonora, with an even smaller population of 275,000, had fourteen cinemas that could seat 16,000 patrons. Even more strikingly, Yucatán with a population of approximately 358,000 had *forty-six* cinemas which could seat approximately 35,000 spectators.

These states, whose audiences arguably played a major role in sustaining the national exhibition industry in the 1920s and would welcome the national production of the 1930s, shared certain social characteristics. Nuevo León had strong ties to the United States and powerful steel and beer industries, as well as a developed commercial agriculture sector. Sonora held large mineral deposits that American industrialists had begun to exploit in the late nine-

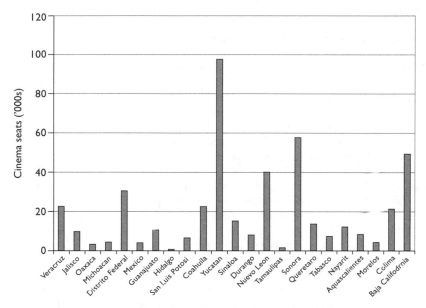

State (in descending order of population, 1921)
States for which there was no data about number of seats do not appear.

Figure 7.3 Number of cinema seats per 1,000 inhabitants.

teenth century. The Yucatán, perhaps the most compelling example, had been part of the United States' early twentieth-century "informal empire" (Joseph 1982, 45). The International Harvester Company controlled the production of henequen, used to produce the twine needed by balers. Although the bottom of the henequen market would fall out in the 1920s, the presence of international capital and wage labor had afforded workers increasing if uneven access to the market, including the market for commodified leisure.

Conclusion

These patterns of cinema development deserve further study. While the revolutionary state promoted Mexico for Mexicans, at least rhetorically, and cinema owners and workers styled themselves as staunch nationalists, in reality both the development of the industry and mass spectatorship audiences relied on the transnational circulation of capital and took place where the local economy and international markets intersected. Those international markets included the market for Hollywood films in Mexico and the market for goods, such as sisal, which created the conditions in which mass spectatorship in Mexico would flourish.

Notes

1. This revisionist approach is well represented by the essays gathered by Stokes and Maltby (2004).
2. In English the standard, textbook history of Mexican cinema is Mora (2005). See also Dever (2003) and the volume edited by Hershfield and Maciel (1999). Blanco (1993) offers a comprehensive account of Mexican filmmaking (in Spanish).
3. Significant exceptions to this trend include Pablo Paranaguá who takes up triangulation between Europe, the United States, and Latin America as the central focus of his account (2003), and Ana M. López who asserts that encounters with foreign cinema shaped not only indigenous production but also "mass spectatorship" (2000, 52).
4. During the first decades of motion picture exhibition in Mexico, cinema owners and distributors commonly paid for complimentary press. Known as *gacetillas* (little cookies), these advertisements-cum-reviews surfaced once in a while in the 1920s (Miquel 1995, 29).
5. For a general discussion of labor and the revolutionary state in the 1920s see Jean Meyer (1991).
6. This research represents the first analysis of the *censo obrero* material relating to the cinema industry. Because of the incompleteness of the material—the surveys from cinemas in states starting with the letters A–L are simply missing—and the inconsistency of responses, it is difficult to offer precise figures. In generating my analysis of the number of seats per 1,000 inhabitants, I combined the survey information with a series of lists, which did include cinemas in all thirty-one Mexican states and then compared the number of reported seats with official population census figures from 1921 to arrive at a suggestive approximation.

Works Cited

Advertisement. 1923. *Excélsior* 10 July: 8.

Advertisements, "La India Bonita." 1921. *Excélsior* 14 September.

Alvarez, José. 1924. "El patriotismo y el cine." *El Hogar* 20 February.

Amador, María Luisa and Jorge Ayala Blanco. 1999. *Cartelera cinematográfica, 1920–1929*. México, DF: Centro Universitario de Estudios Cinematográficos, Universidad Nacional Autónoma de México.

Amor, Hipólito. 1922. *Report to Head of Public Diversions, 29 December, Vol. 812, Exp. 166*. Archivo Histórico del Distrito Federal (hereafter AHDF).

Ayala Blanco, Jorge. 1993. *La aventura del cine mexicano: en la época de oro y después*. Mexico: Editorial Grijalbo.

"El Cine Majestic, vuelve a ponerse de moda," 1924. *Excélsior* 5 April: 5.

Crofts, Stephen. 1993. "Reconceptualising National Cinema/s." *Quarterly Review of Film and Video* 14.3: 49–67.

Cuestionario 213. 1923. Departamento de Trabajo. Vol. 620, Exp. 5, folio 5. AGN.

Cuestionario 550. 1923. Departamento de Trabajo. Vol. 620, Exp. 5, folio 121. AGN.

Cuestionario 616. 1923. Departamento de Trabajo. Vol. 641, Exp. 5, folio 107. AGN.

Cuestionario, Molina San José/Cine Regades. 1923. Departamento de Trabajo. Vol. 641, Exp. 5, folio 57. AGN.

De los Reyes, Aurelio. 1993. *Cine y sociedad en México 1896–1930, Volumen II*

1920–1924: Bajo el cielo de México. Mexico: Instituto de Investigaciones Estéticas; Universidad Nacional Autónoma de México.

"Desde hace tres eses no entra una película americana a la nación." 1931. *Excélsior* 17 October: 10.

Dever, Susan. 2003. *Celluloid Nationalism and other Melodramas: from Post-Revolutionary Mexico to fin de siglo Mexamérica*. Albany: SUNY Press.

Dorfman, Ariel and Armand Mattelart. 2002. *Para leer al pato Donald: Comunicación de masa y colonialismo*. Buenos Aires: Siglo veintiuno editores.

"La empresa Calderón y Salas Porras ensancha a su campo de acción." 1927. *México en Rotograbado*. 11 August.

"Los empresarios de cines piden que se las rebajen las contribuciones." 1919. *Excélsior* 19 June: 3.

"Los espectáculos y el ayuntamiento." 1919. *Matehuala* 15 September: 2.

Espinosa, Candido and Juan Castillo. 1931. Letter to President Pascual Ortiz Rubio, 26 October. Collection Pascual Ortiz Rubio, Caja 66-B, Exp. 306. AGN.

Galindo, Francisco. 1923. Letter to Sección de Estadística, 29 November. Trabajo, Vol. 641, Folder 5, Folio 67. AGN.

García Riera, Emilio. 1992. *Historia documental del cine mexicano, Vol. 1, 1929-1937*. Guadalajara: Universidad de Guadalajara.

Hershfield, Joanne and David Maciel, eds. 1999. *Mexico's Cinema: A Century of Film and Filmmakers*. Wilmington: SR Books.

"El hijo de la loca: película nacional." 1923. *Excélsior* 14 October.

"Hoy es la solemne inauguración." 1924. *El Universal* 19 April: 7.

Jefe de sección, Diversiones Publicas. 1922. Report to Presidente Municipal, 21 June. AHDF, Vol. 812, Exp. 1674.

Joseph, Gilbert M. 1982. *Revolution from Without: Yucatan, Mexico, and the United States, 1880–1924*. Cambridge: Cambridge University Press.

Knight, Alan. 1990. "Revolutionary Project, Recalcitrant People: Mexico, 1910-1940." *The Revolutionary Process in Mexico: Essays on Political and Social Change, 1880–1940*, ed. J.O. Rodríguez. Los Angeles: University of California, Latin American Center Publications, 227–264.

López, Ana M. 2000. "Early Cinema and Modernity in Latin America." *Cinema Journal* 40.1: 48–78.

López, Rick A. 2002. "The India Bonita Contest of 1921 and the Ethnicization of Mexican National Culture." *Hispanic American Historical Review* 82.2: 291–328.

Maltby, Richard. 2004. "Introduction." Stokes and Maltby, *Hollywood Abroad*, 1–20.

Maranón, S. 1923. Letter to C.G. Villalobos, 1 August. Trabajo, Caja 620, Folder 5, folio 54. AGN.

Meyer Jean. 1991. "Revolution and Reconstruction." *Mexico Since Independence*, ed. Leslie Bethell. Cambridge: Cambridge University Press, 227–232.

Mexico. Departamento de la Estadística Nacional. 1928. *Resumen del censo general de habitantes de 30 de noviembre de 1921*. Mexico, DF: Talleres Gráficos de la Nación.

Miller, Toby, et al. 2008. *Global Hollywood: No. 2*. London: BFI Publishing.

Miquel, Ángel. 1995. *Por las pantallas: periodistas del cine mudo*. Guadalajara: Universidad de Guadalajara.

Mora, Carl J. 2005. *Mexican Cinema: Reflections of a Society, 1896–2004*. Jefferson: McFarland & Co.

Paranaguá, Paulo Antonio. 2003. *Tradición y modernidad en el cine de América Latina*. Madrid: Fondo de Cultura Económica de España.

Pezet, Jorge. 1931. "Conflicto Cinematográfico: El negocio del cine en México." *El Universal* 21 October: 9.

"Promedio del salario que ganan los obreros en la Ciuadad de Mexico, D.F." 1922. *Boletín del Departamento de Trabajo* March.

Sección de Estadística. 1923. Letter to Jefe del Departamento de Fomento Industrial, 8 December. Trabajo, Caja 641, Folder 5, folio 217. AGN.

Serna, Laura Isabel. 2006. "'As a Mexican I feel it is my duty,': Citizenship, Censorship, and the Campaign Against Derogatory Films in Mexico, 1922–1930." *The Americas: A Quarterly Review of Inter-American Cultural History* 63.2 (October): 225–244.

Special Municipal Inspector. 1922. Report to the Chief of the Department of Public Diversions. 7 February. Ayuntamiento, Vol. 811, Legajo 1620. AHDF.

Stokes, Melvyn and Richard Maltby, eds. 2004. *Hollywood Abroad: Audiences and Cultural Exchange*. London: British Film Institute.

"Teatro E. Durand." 1918. *Matehuala* 9 September: 2.

Villegas, Alfonso. 1924. Letter to Álvaro Obregón, 4 October. AGN, O-C, 104-P-79.

Chapter 8

The Recording Industry's Role in Media History

Kyle S. Barnett

The Recording Industry and Media History

Despite media history's increasing attention to the cultural aspects of the film, television, and radio industries, such research on the recording industry remains largely absent. In popular music scholar and archivist Pekka Gronow's essay, "The Record Industry: The Growth of a Mass Medium," he writes that while it seems logical to include sound recordings in the study of media, "a glimpse at standard textbooks on mass communication makes us doubt our common sense" (Gronow 1983, 53). Although present-day media studies textbooks often include historical overviews on sound recordings and the recording industry, both topics commonly disappear after introductory classes. While the notion that sound recordings constitute media may seem so obvious as not to be arguable, they have rarely been included in media history, and when we contextualize sound recordings within the industry that produces them, there is less historical research. This is surprising, given the ubiquity of recorded music in media and the long involvement of other industries in ownership and cross-promotion.

In reading existing literature, it sometimes seems that the recording industry emerged in the mid-1950s.[1] The pre-rock'n'roll period saw the industry's institutional culture take shape through a complicated cultural circuit that included musicians, recording engineers, talent scouts, record salespeople, journalists, advertisers, and consumers. An historical approach with the specificity to glean a discursive history of the recording industry's organizing principles *as they emerged* could inform various lines of thought in contemporary research. Going beyond mere historical overviews and technological progress narratives, what is missing is an explanation of how an ever-changing but distinct cultural formation helped to understand, organize, and define popular music.

Perhaps as scholars increasingly recognize the historically close relationship between industries, comparative media histories including the recording industry might be written, but given the complexities of the recording industry, a fuller accounting of its discrete history is just as important. For many years, the two commonly cited industry histories came from outside academe. Roland Gelatt's *The Fabulous Phonograph* was published in 1977 and Oliver Read and Walter Welch's *From Tin Foil to Stereo* had been published first in 1959. These histories focus on technological issues and institutional machinations but do not give a sense of the recording industry as a multifaceted cultural formation. While useful, they also run the risk of reducing recording industry history to a series of technological shifts.

Research from across academic disciplines (mostly by History and American Studies scholars) has been published within the past decade, including William Howland Kenney's *Recorded Music In American Life* (1999), David Morton's *Off The Record* (2000), and Andre Millard's *America on Record* (2005). These histories help fill a tremendous gap in research, though the focus remains on recorded sound technology. In terms of industry history, Sanjek and Sanjek's *Pennies From Heaven* (1996) and Tim Anderson's *Making Easy Listening* (2006) clearly focus on the record business. Sanjek and Sanjek's text remains a key resource in recording industry history, popular music history, and its links to other entertainment and media industries.[2] Anderson's more succinct and discrete social and cultural history brings together commercial practices, consumer listening aesthetics, and technological aspects of the industry as a dynamic cultural institution.[3] The most useful and succinct industry overview is Geoffrey Hull's *The Recording Industry* (1997), though it spends little time on history.

With little recording industry research in media history, perhaps the clearest hope for cultural histories of the recording industry comes from popular music studies.[4] The study of popular music has been interdisciplinary from the start but, through its connection to cultural studies, initially focused on contemporary subcultures research. Simon Frith's "The Industrialization of Popular Music" provided a much-needed historical overview that collapsed the distinction between "music-as-expression" and "music-as-commodity" through suggesting the centrality of the industry in the music-making process (Frith 1987, 53–54). Dave Laing pointed to a lack of historical research in the recording industry by going back to the 1890s (Laing 1991, 1).[5]

Popular music studies is linked to the production of culture/cultures of production research, or cultural industry studies, which has reinvigorated popular music studies in general. If popular music research has yet to create many cultural industry histories now common in other media research, contemporary work on the recording industry is robust. Cultural industry research as practiced by UK scholars Keith Negus, David Hesmondhalgh, and Paul du Gay points to organizing structures and cultural practice within record companies. This research is quite useful in understanding the roles of various cultural intermediaries operating between points on the societal circuit of culture (du Gay and Pryke 1990, du Gay 1997).[6]

A rare example of recording industry research that bridges media history and popular music studies is Richard Peterson's Creating Country Music: Fabricating Authenticity (1997).[7] Peterson brings the specificity of cultural industry research common in contemporary popular music research as he denaturalizes country music in a variety of ways. He places Atlanta, not Nashville, as the center for early country music recording in the United States. He outlines a series of identities that Jimmie Rodgers would employ for different venues and audiences. He also details Henry Ford's significant financial investment in the "old time tunes" of country music through sponsoring fiddle contests (spurred on by Ford's fear of jazz's societal effects) (12–54). Peterson's research points to a whole series of commercial, aesthetic, and sociocultural developments in the early recording industry in need of further study.

What if more scholars were to take Peterson's lead? What might be gained from an approach that would combine media history's attention to industry history with the focus of cultural industry studies on organizing principles and cultural practices? To begin to answer that question and suggest some possibilities for further research, I will use as my case study a little known 1920s record label that played a crucial part in the development of the US recording industry: Gennett Records.[8] Although little remembered, Gennett is perfectly suited to illustrate many facets of the recording industry's production culture in the 1920s during a time after the phonograph's rise and before radio's dominance in the 1930s changed the record industry dramatically.

Case Study: Gennett Records

The story of Gennett Records is of lasting importance because of its role as the first label to challenge successfully Victor and Columbia through adopting the major labels' audio playback technology (lateral-cut recording) and its success in developing viable niche genre markets.[9] Studying the company's cultural practices also gives us a glimpse into how scouts served as intermediaries. In what follows, I will discuss some general institutional qualities of Gennett as a company, followed by some specific company practices.

Gennett Records of Richmond, Indiana, enjoyed surprising importance and reach during its heyday in the 1910s and 1920s. For those familiar with the record label, Gennett's lasting reputation is often associated with jazz, primarily due to the company's involvement in some of that genre's foundational recordings, including early recordings from King Oliver, Louis Armstrong, Bix Beiderbecke, and others. Beyond jazz, Gennett's recorded output was stunningly broad. In its short history, Gennett expanded its involvement to approximately seventy record labels around the world. William Jennings Bryan recorded his "Cross of Gold" speech to musical accompaniment, which was added to the Library of Congress's National Recording Registry in 2003 (National Recording Preservation Board 2003). Gennett recorded "personal records"—one-time pressings for cash—for the Ku Klux Klan. Gennett's mobile truck made recordings across the United States, which included recording Hopi Indian performances at the Grand Canyon with assistance from anthropologist J. Walter Fewkes. The label also had a West Coast operation making sound-effects records for the motion-picture industry (another link in the largely unexamined relationship)—the only part of the Gennett recording operation to survive the Great Depression.

The Gennett label had the infrastructure and distribution network of its parent company, Starr Piano, at its disposal.[10] Starr already had stores in cities around the USA that allowed Gennett Records to be sold in Starr stores as well as in other retail outlets and allowed Starr stores to function as information-gathering centers for the company. The company had recording studios in New York and Richmond, as well as temporary recording facilities when needed. Starr often found out about regional tastes and trends in music, as well as popular performers in a given region, through its employees' interactions with customers. By making recordings meant for various niches, Gennett proceeded in trial-and-error fashion, recording this or that style in the hope that its releases would find an audience. Starr-Gennett employees often learned how to scout talent on the job.

Talent Scouting and Corporate Structure

The Gennett family generally hired their record company employees out of their Starr Piano concern. The figure commonly thought most responsible for Gennett's jazz recordings was longtime Starr employee Fred Wiggins, a de facto talent scout during his time in Chicago in the early 1920s and head of Starr Piano's recording division by mid-decade. Relatively little firsthand information about Wiggins remains (his obituary ignores his recording industry work altogether). We do know that Wiggins had become a key figure in the Chicago store and had likely learned about Chicago's jazz scene there. That Wiggins had little firsthand knowledge of the music nor much experience in scouting talent before his work with Gennett was routine for such labels. Surviving documents suggest that employee roles were not particularly regimented or stratified in its division of labor. To a certain extent, Gennett's relatively flexible, even loose, approach to the recording industry—an industry in which the low barrier to entry has traditionally encouraged experimentation—applied to the industry as a whole. The relatively small expense of making a recording with a given artist encouraged risk-taking among labels like Gennett, looking for their market niche.

If smaller labels like Gennett sought niches because of their marginal status versus the Big Three (Victor, Edison, and Columbia), the recording industry as a whole was marginal when compared to established and respected areas of business. In other words, the labels worked on the edges of the prevailing business culture. Nowhere was this more evident than in terms of race. Tim Brooks writes,

> The white, and mostly young, entrepreneurs who were struggling to build the new recording industry did not set out to change the social order. They simply did not have the luxury of enforcing irrational social conventions like "the color line."
>
> (2004, ?)

African-American recordings were common by the time of Starr-Gennett's entrance into the recording industry in the mid-1910s and would increase dramatically in the 1920s with the popularity of jazz and blues. It may have been enough for Wiggins to see audience responses to performances in Chicago to recognize the music's potential power.

In the early 1920s, Wiggins was named manager of Starr Piano's Chicago store and was soon acting as talent scout for the Gennett label as he learned about that city's music scene (Kennedy 2008). According to jazz researcher George Kay, Wiggins's role as scout expanded over time:

> During the early days of Wiggens' [sic] career, he scouted for artists but the final decision for closing recording deals was left to Fred Gennett. Later, as his ability became more recognized by the Starr officials, young Wiggens' judgment in signing talent and releasing records was accepted as final.
>
> (1953, 4–13)

Starr Piano's Chicago location was at 423 South Wabash, very close to recording studios and nightclubs that dotted the avenue from near north to near south. It was at the Friars Inn (343 North Wabash) where Wiggins first heard a band then known as the Friars Society Orchestra, an all-white jazz group and one of the first jazz groups Gennett recorded.[11] With the jazz craze that followed in the years after the 1917 Original Dixieland Jazz Band recordings, opportunistic club owners searched for their own acts to capitalize on the trend.[12]

Recording and Record Selection

Disagreement exists about who had the specific responsibility for making recording selections. It appears that various Gennett recording engineers and talent scouts made decisions on recordings, but Wiggins—who was brought back to Richmond, Indiana, after a few years in Chicago to become recording director—was one of the central figures who decided what was released. The kind of decision-making Wiggins employed did not always sit well with his staff in the recording division. In an interview with John MacKenzie, Gennett recording engineer Harold Soule "complained bitterly about Fred Wiggins' personal method of selection." Soule reveals that decisions were based as much on technological appropriateness as on quality of performance (MacKenzie n.d.). Soule remembered:

> Wiggins had an old wind-up phonograph in his office that he'd use to listen to the test pressings. It was about as lousy a piece of equipment as you could ask for. I couldn't understand why the test pressings had to be played back on this old style rig. Being a kid in those days, I couldn't see the reason, of course. I can see his viewpoint now.
>
> (MacKenzie 1961)

"Jazz enthusiasts today," Kay wrote in 1953, "would howl with despair at some of his decisions to destroy cherished jazz masters as 'not suitable for release'" (6). But Wiggins believed that their target audiences—not only their jazz listeners—did not have the means to afford better phonographs. Indeed, besides the Starr Piano stores, most Gennett records were sold for less than the record prices of the Big Three. Gennett even had discount labels through which they sold recordings via mail order and chain stores. If Wiggins deemed that a recording did not sound good on cheap equipment, then it would not be released.

Several important differences are evident when comparing Gennett and the 1920s recording industry with the contemporary recording industry. One obvious difference is scale. The level of conglomeration in the contemporary industry greatly exceeds that of the 1920s, though a tendency toward oligopoly was already pronounced then, perhaps made more volatile by the ease with which new players could enter the fledgling recording industry. During their short runs, labels like Gennett played crucial roles in defining new niches, breaking in new artists, and shaping new genres and subgenres.

Another important distinction is in the specialization of roles. In Gennett's era employee roles were much less proscribed. Recording engineers often functioned as talent scouts on recording trips around the country. The job was not only to record the music but also to obtain a sense of the audience to whom this music was to be sold. Narratives of happenstance, and even chaos, played no small role in the fortunes of recording companies, but those working at Gennett were always responding in a variety of ways to what they were learning from musicians, music listeners, and various cultural intermediaries. Then as now, record company employees are constantly involved in an "active response" to this chaotic cultural circuit, predicated on the moving target of "commercial success" (Negus 2001, 151).

But perhaps the most crucial aspect suggested by historiographies is the *provisional* nature of the recording industry during the period between growth in the late 1910s and the bust in the early 1930s due to competition from radio and the effects of the Great Depression. It is during this era that many of the industry's fundamental organizing principles first emerge. These include the recording of music for profit—not the foremost of Thomas Edison's plans for recorded sound but one that created an industry (Edison 1878, 527–536). These would also include aspects common to any media industry: a reliance on genre as an organizing principle, the division of releases into specific subsidiary labels or series, the need for smaller companies to develop niche markets, a marked tendency of the recording industry toward oligopoly, and cyclical battles over technological formats and what we would now call intellectual property.

Conclusion: Everything New is Old Again

There may be good reasons to focus on the contemporary recording industry in what seems like an unprecedented moment of crisis—except that this crisis is not unprecedented. It is true that significant changes are at hand. US consumers' increased preference for mp3s over compact discs continues to reshape the recording industry as it struggles to find equilibrium. iTunes did not exist before 2001 and is now one of the two largest retailers of music in the United States. Wal-Mart, the other big retailer, is putting pressure on recording companies by reducing shelf space for CDs in its stores (Smith 2008, B1). As CD sales fall and audio file sales have yet to make up the difference, companies have turned to video game and cell phone ring tone licensing for new revenue sources. In 2007 year-end shipping statistics, CDs to retailers showed another annual loss, this time by over 17 percent as the market continues to shrink (Recording Industry Association of America 2008). The sky is falling, right?

Yes, except the sky has fallen before. In the early 1930s, the recording industry was on the verge of collapse as consumers chose radio over phonographs in economic hard times. In 1932, *American Mercury* published an article by Dane Yorke in which he recounts "The Rise and Fall of the Phonograph," as if the record industry's fall was a *fait accompli* (it surely must have seemed so) (Yorke 1932, 5–12). Edison, the inventor of the phonograph, left the record business in 1929. In the first years of the Depression, Gennett and other smaller labels were shut down and sold off to a number of different buyers (Gennett's catalog was purchased by Jack Kapp's Decca label). But the same business responsible for the recording industry's supposed irrelevance—the broadcasting industry—would help in its resurgence. The Radio Corporation of America (RCA) bought Victor Records in 1929, in a David-buys-Goliath scenario akin to America Online's purchase of Time Warner in 2000. Columbia fell further, owned by several record and radio concerns, before its eventual purchase by William Paley as part of the Columbia Broadcasting System. Much of this narrative should seem familiar because it is: format battles, corporate mergers, breath-taking changes in fortune. This is not to reduce the two eras down to similarities at the expense of their differences. However, we should not ignore the cyclical nature of media industries and what may be learned with the various formations over time. In this sense, everything new is old again.

And vice versa. The phonograph record that journalist Yorke eulogized in 1932 showed signs of resurgence by the end of that decade ("'Dead' Phonograph" 1940, 1). In the last year, records made yet another unlikely reappearance, having long ago been transformed from shellac to vinyl. 2007 statistics showed that vinyl shipments had increased by 36 percent (Recording Industry Association of America 2008). As compact disc sales continue to drop, some companies are now turning solely to mp3 and vinyl releases. Admittedly a niche format, vinyl's "comeback" nevertheless points out the persistence of sound recording as a medium amidst ongoing changes in delivery technologies and how that technology reflects its changing functionalities for both industry and audience (Jenkins 2006, 13).

At the start of this chapter, I mentioned the unexamined history of connections between the recording industry and other media industries. These issues accumulate, particularly in an age of media conglomeration; but the recording industry's importance is not limited to its relationship with other industries. At the heart of the recording industry is what it records. The bulk of the recording industry's output is the ephemeral pop hit (and a lot more pop misses) through which we recognize so many facets of our own experience. If we think about the industry that produces it, it is usually to castigate it, to hold it accountable for real and imagined wrongs. The reality is rather more complicated than that. In spite of recorded sound's importance in our everyday lives, we have only just begun to account for the industry so crucial in creating it.

Acknowledgments

Thanks to Lisa Barnett, Rob Sloane, Kim Simpson, Janet Staiger, my research group at Bellarmine University, and the panel audience at "Media History: What Are the Issues?" in Austin, Texas, for comments on earlier versions of this chapter.

Notes

1. In fact, academic popular music research too often ignores the 1950s and begins in the 1960s or later, as if the "rock'n'roll" of the previous decade merely set the stage for "rock."
2. This makes sense: *Pennies From Heaven* is based on the last volume of Russell Sanjek's sweeping three-volume history. Its daunting title is *American Popular Music and Its Business: The First Four Hundred Years* (1988).
3. Besides academic studies there is a vast collection of autobiographies and memoirs from industry insiders. These usually cover the post-rock'n'roll era and vary widely in quality and focus. How-to books are also common and understandably tend toward a contemporary focus. The most useful of these is Krasilovsky et al. (2007).
4. Two strong introductions to popular music studies include Bennett et al. (2006) and Frith and Goodwin (1990).
5. As Laing points out, the earliest years of the recording industry "still await adequate and rigorous scrutiny" (1991, 1). Little has changed in this regard since 1991, although an increase in digital reissues suggests this may be changing at last.
6. Negus's work is clearly centered on popular music and Hesmondhalgh's research often focuses on it. For their innovative overview of popular music studies, see Hesmondhalgh and Negus 2002. However, cultural industry research reaches far beyond popular music studies, through research across the arts and media, including foundational work by Richard Peterson, Howard Becker, Paul Hirsch, and others. For useful overviews of cultural production/production of culture research, see du Gay and Pryke 2002; du Gay 1997; and Hesmondhalgh 2002.
7. Compare Peterson's approach (1997) to the more traditional historical, albeit useful, account in Malone 2002.
8. The most useful introduction to Gennett is Kennedy 1994.
9. Gennett's successful court battle against Victor Records over phonograph recording and playback formats was finally decided in the US Supreme Court, which allowed Gennett to continue using lateral cut disc technology. This in turn made their recordings playable on Victor and Columbia phonographs, which allowed for greater potential consumers.
10. Many of the phonograph businesses of the late 1910s and early 1920s grew out of companies involved in domestic furniture production, including pianos. This serves to recontextualize the development of early US record companies around cultural concerns about the phonograph's move from public to domestic space. See Barnett 2006, 301–324.

11. Richard Sudhalter has researched the Friars Society Orchestra/New Orleans Rhythm Kings extensively. See Sudhalter 1999. He makes an important contribution, but the topic would be better served by an integrated history of jazz.
12. For an overview, see Alexander 2008.

Works Cited

Alexander, Scott. 2008. "The First Jazz Records." *Red Hot Jazz* 26 July. www.redhot-jazz.com/jazz1917.html.

Anderson, Tim J. 2006. *Making Easy Listening: Material Culture and Postwar American Recording*. Minneapolis: University of Minnesota Press.

Barnett, Kyle. 2006. "Furniture Music: The Phonograph as Furniture, 1900–1930." *Journal of Popular Music Studies* 18, 3 (December): 301–324.

Bennett, Andy, Barry Shank, and Jason Toynbee. 2006. *The Popular Music Studies Reader*. Abindgon, UK: Routledge.

Brooks, Tim. 2004. *Lost Sounds: Blacks and the Birth of the Recording Industry, 1890–1919*. Urbana, IL: University of Illinois Press.

"'Dead' Phonograph and Record Approaches Peak." 1940. *Advertising Age* 9 December: 1.

du Gay, Paul. 1997. *Production of Culture/Cultures of Production*. London: Sage.

——— and Michael Pryke. 2002. *Cultural Economy*. London: Sage.

Edison, Thomas. 1878. "The Phonograph and Its Future." *North American Review* May–June: 527–536.

Frith, Simon. 1987. "The Industrialization of Popular Music." *Popular Music and Communication*, ed. James Lull. London: Sage, 53–79.

——— and Andrew Goodwin. 1990. *On Record: Rock, Pop, and the Written Word*. London: Routledge.

Gelatt, Roland. 1977. *The Fabulous Phonograph, 1877–1977*. New York: Macmillan.

Gronow, Pekka. 1983. "The Record Industry: Growth of a Mass Medium." *Popular Music* 3 (Producers and Markets): 53–75.

Hesmondhalgh, David. 2002. *The Cultural Industries*. London: Sage.

——— and Keith Negus. 2002. *Popular Music Studies*. London: Arnold.

Hull, Geoffrey P. 1997. *The Recording Industry*. Boston, MA: Allyn & Bacon.

Jenkins, Henry. 2006. *Convergence Culture: Where Old and New Media Collide*. New York: New York University Press.

Kay, George. 1953. "Those Fabulous Gennetts! The Life Story of a Remarkable Label." *The Record Changer* June: 4–13.

Kennedy, Rick. 1994. *Jelly Roll, Bix, and Hoagy: Gennett Studios and the Birth of Recorded Jazz*. Bloomington, IN: Indiana University Press.

———. 2008. "The Man Who Made the Label a Legend." *Starr-Gennett Foundation, Inc. News*, Summer, Starr Gennett Foundation, 7 September. www.starrgennett.org/stories/articles/label_legend.htm.

Kenney, William Howland. 1999. *Recorded Music In American Life: The Phonograph and Popular Memory, 1890–1945*. New York: Oxford University Press.

Krasilovsky, M. William et al. 2007. *This Business of Music* (10th edn). New York: Watson-Guptill.

Laing, Dave. 1991. "A Voice Without a Face: Popular Music and the Phonograph in the 1890s." *Popular Music* 10: 1–9.

MacKenzie, John. 1961. Interview with Harold Soule. 3 August. John MacKenzie Collection, Indiana Historical Society.

——. n.d. "Recording and Record Manufacturing at the Starr Piano Company." Unpublished essay ms. John MacKenzie Collection, Indiana Historical Society.

Malone, Bill C. 2002. *Country Music USA* (2nd edn). Austin: University of Texas Press.

Millard, Andre. 2005. *America on Record: A History of Recorded Sound* (2nd edn). New York: Cambridge University Press.

Morton, David. 2000. *Off The Record: The Technology and Culture of Sound Recording in America*. New Brunswick, NJ: Rutgers University Press.

National Recording Preservation Board. 2003. "National Recording Registry 2003." Library of Congress, 24 July. www.loc.gov/rr/record/nrpb/.

Negus, Keith. 2001. *Producing Pop: Culture and Conflict in the Recording Industry*. New York: Edward Arnold.

Peterson, Richard. 1997. *Creating Country Music: Fabricating Authenticity*. Chicago, IL: University of Chicago Press.

Read, Oliver and Walter Welch. 1959. *From Tin Foil to Stereo: Evolution of the Phonograph*. Indianapolis: Howard W. Sams.

Recording Industry Association of America. 2008. "2007 Year-End Shipment Statistics" 28 June. www.riaa.org.

Sanjek, Russell. 1988. *American Popular Music and Its Business: The First Four Hundred Years*. New York: Oxford University Press.

—— and David Sanjek. 1996. *Pennies From Heaven: The American Popular Music Business In The Twentieth Century*. New York: Da Capo.

Smith, Ethan. 2008. "As CDs Decline, Wal-Mart Spins Its Strategy." *Wall Street Journal* 9 June: B1.

Sudhalter, Richard M. 1999. *Lost Chords: White Musicians and Their Contributions to Jazz, 1915–1945*. New York: Oxford University Press.

Yorke, Dane. 1932. "The Rise and Fall of the Phonograph." *American Mercury* 27 September: 1–12.

Chapter 9

Forging a Citizen Audience

Broadcasting from the 1920s through the 1940s

Richard Butsch

Audience history research was an intermittent enterprise two decades ago. Since then there has been a steady increase in such research. We now have a fairly good picture of audiences through the twentieth century. Most of the work had been social history, documenting who were audiences and how they behaved (e.g. for texts surveying and analyzing this work, see Brooker and Jermyn 2003; Gillespie 2005; Hay et al. 1996; Nightingale 1996; Staiger 2005). This chapter is intended to illustrate a newer approach, to examine audiences as cultural categories (Butsch 2008). I examine not flesh-and-blood audiences but how they have been represented in discourse and constructed by institutions and practices. I will focus on how broadcasting from the 1920s through the 1940s constructed audiences as publics and citizens. By public, I mean an active citizenry that engages in public discussion of issues, the public of Gabriel Tarde (1969), Robert Park (1972), John Dewey (1927), and, more recently, Jürgen Habermas (1989). To varying degrees they define the good citizen as informed, deliberative, rational, and civic-minded, cultural values that were identified with the white, male, middle or upper class (Schudson 1998; Smith et al. 1994). This was not the only discourse on audiences; discourse on propaganda at the time also depicted radio as a tool of demagoguery and manipulation of the masses. But that circulated mostly among elites, whereas the more widespread image depicted radio and its audiences as an invigorated public sphere.

I will examine three aspects of this image-making: the social construction of radio as a deliberative public sphere by federal law and regulation and by radio magazines; the subject position of audience as citizen constructed by public forum programs; and the creation of a representative public sphere by radio programming and corporate sponsors.

Radio Policy and Regulation

From the very beginning, US government policy and regulation defined radio as a public sphere. For six decades it founded policy on a trustee model which presumed that the airwaves are public property held in trust for the benefit of the people and the nation and their uses licensed only to operators under the condition that they serve the public interest. The public's interest took precedent over the private interest of the licensee; the license was a privilege, not a property right, and could be revoked. This model defined radio in terms of the fourth estate tradition of the press as established in the First Amendment of the US Constitution, since the required public service programming was largely journalistic and placed radio and its audiences solidly in the public sphere. Of course, commercial radio and advertisers would frame audiences as consumers, and government ultimately favored commercial enterprises, as several radio scholars have shown (Barnouw 1966; McChesney 1993; Smulyan 1994; Benjamin 2001). However, private media corporations had to justify their actions in terms of the trustee model that defined audiences as citizen publics.

Even before broadcasting, the US government framed radio as a public good. Before the 1920s radio was considered a wireless telephone, a form of two-way communication in which each user could both transmit and receive signals. The Radio Act of 1912 limited amateur radio transmitter operators' use of radio on the grounds that unfettered use of the airwaves interfered with sea and military communication. The law required amateurs to obtain a federal license and reserved part of the radio wave spectrum for shipping and government use. This established the precedent that public interest in the form of governmental uses of the airwaves preceded private use. Using the public safety argument underlying priority for commercial sea communication, amateur radio operators formed the American Radio Relay League to promote themselves as providing a public service by relaying messages for emergencies (Barnouw 1966; Douglas 1987).

During World War I the US government seized the radio patent rights of the Marconi Company as an Italian company. This presented a question about how the government should use or dispose of these patents. The US Navy argued for retention of the patents so it could better control communication at sea. The Navy did not prevail, as the government gave the patents to a consortium of AT&T, General Electric, and Westinghouse, which formed RCA to manufacture radios. But the Navy's argument introduced the idea that commercial development should be secondary (Douglas 1987).

When broadcasting began in the early 1920s, another dilemma again led to framing radio as public rather than private. The Radio Act of 1912, created for wireless telephony, was inadequate to regulate broadcasting. Regulation was in the hands of Commerce Secretary Herbert Hoover who attempted to gain voluntary cooperation from broadcasters to solve problems of interference and other issues. In some ways Hoover was favorable to private station owners, particularly the larger ones. Nevertheless, he expressed the goal of defining the airwaves as public property. In 1924 he wrote:

> We seek to preserve the ownership of the road through the ether as public property that we may maintain initiative by holding it a free field for competition; to keep alive free speech; to avoid censorship; to prevent interference in the traffic.
>
> (*Wireless Age*, October 1924, 24)

After several attempts by Hoover to gain voluntary cooperation among broadcasters had failed and court challenges to his authority limited his ability to control development, and chaos in broadcasting mounted, Congress passed the Radio Act of 1927 and established the Federal Radio Commission to regulate broadcasting (Barnouw 1966; Smith et al. 1994). Representative Luther Johnson expressed the importance of radio in presenting a diversity of political viewpoints to citizens in the debate over the Radio Act of 1927:

> It will only be a few years before these broadcasting stations, if operated by chain stations [networks], will simultaneously reach an audience of over half our entire citizenship. . . . American thought and American politics will be largely at the mercy of those who operate these stations . . . then woe to those who differ with them. It will be impossible to compete with them in reaching the ears of the American public.
>
> (Benjamin 2001,70)

The 1927 Act stated that the Radio Commission should grant a license if it determined that "public convenience, interest or necessity would be served by the granting thereof" (reprinted in Barnouw 1966, 306). The Federal Radio Commission's 1928 Annual Report, interpreting the concept of "public interest," declared that licensees should not use their stations for private interests and that the interests of listeners took precedent over that of the licensee (Smith et al. 1994, 238). In other words, it was not for their use but the public's.

The 1934 Communications Act created the Federal Communication Commission (FCC) with broader scope than the old Radio Commission it replaced and extended the idea of serving the public interest. The FCC and the courts in the 1930s began to construe public interest in a political sense, building upon past association of radio with public service and attaching it to the idea of radio functioning to provide citizens with the information and means of communication that they needed to fulfill their role in a democracy, i.e. as a source of news and public information and a place for public debate, like the press.

This trend began after the passage of the 1934 Act with hearings about non-commercial broadcasting. The networks were successful in defeating efforts to reserve a quarter of the radio spectrum for non-profit stations, a defeat of the actualization of radio as a public sphere. However, in order to defeat the reform, the networks presented themselves as providing public service programming. They thus committed themselves to something that they would thenceforth be expected to deliver. Radio stations began to appoint "public service directors" as liaison with non-profit groups, who sometimes acted as counterweights against commercialism and supporters of the ideal of radio audiences as citizens. When Congress or the FCC began to raise questions or debate issues concerning radio, commercial broadcasters responded by introducing new public affairs programs (Barnouw 1968; McChesney 1993; Smulyan 1994).

Licensing decisions were guided at least since the 1930s by a goal to maintain a diversity of voices on radio on the ground that this enriched public discussion. In 1946 the FCC issued a report intended as a guide to licensees on its interpretation of public service. The report restated that stations were licensed to serve the public not private interest; it described radio as "an unequaled medium for the dissemination of news, information, and opinion, and for the discussing of public issues"; it listed four factors in judging public service: including sustaining non-commercial programs, local live programs, programs discussing public issues, and eliminating "advertising excesses" (FCC 1946, 39, 55). The FCC established the Fairness Doctrine in 1949, based on the trustee model and requiring broadcasters to present public issues in a balanced and fair manner in another effort to sustain diversity of opinion (Smith et al. 1994). Congress reaffirmed the public interest criterion in 1958:

> the spectrum is a natural resource belonging to the entire national public ... may be used for private purposes only insofar as such will benefit the public interest ... the right of the public to service is superior to the right of any licensee to make use of any frequency or channel for his own private purposes.
>
> (US Congress 1958, 54)

In the 1980s, after a half-century, this basic principal of FCC regulation was abandoned for a market model (Smith et al. 1994, 255–259). What is remarkable is the preceding six decades of framing radio in legal discourse as a public sphere, a result of a variety of coincidences and opportunities, an entrenched tradition against which broadcast corporations found they had to work persistently.

While legal and regulatory discourses were framing radio as a public trust, in the early years of broadcasting articles in radio hobbyist and listener magazines echoed this, emphasizing radio's potential as a medium of public information and debate.[1] These magazines expressed what was a widely and long-held view of radio, a public image far more favorable than that of movies, or later of television (Butsch 2008). In these magazines, an oft-repeated idea was the claim that radio brought the world into your home, i.e. the information needed by citizens to engage in discussion on public issues. More than one cartoon or illustration depicted a globe with a radio antenna on it, commenting how radio had shrunk the world. Articles quoted homebound people telling how radio was a blessing for them, one saying he was "better informed than I was six years ago when I could walk" (*Wireless Age*, March 1923, 38). Ads for radios claimed they provided news of the world, high cultural events, and sports in the home (Butsch 2000; Volek 1990). The sum of these messages created a familiar image of radio enhancing and extending the public sphere.

From the beginning of broadcasting in 1922, *Wireless Age* published many articles touting radio's value to the nation, for cultural uplift of the masses and for making the public into better citizens. It declared radio a "non-partisan political medium" in the first national election to involve the use of radio and "an absolutely unbiased and impartial medium through which public expression may be given to subjects that have public interest" (*Wireless Age*, December 1922, 27–29). *Wireless Age* devoted its October 1924 issue to the political significance of radio—exciting greater interest, informing listeners, teaching rational deliberation, and encouraging participation. Editor William Hurd concluded, "It is by radio that he can be aroused to wide apprehensions . . . and through this means come by example to know and by good education to acquire, the scientific habit of mind of wanting to know why" (*Wireless Age*, October 1924, 17).

Public Forum Programs

The FCC requirement to serve the public interest assured that radio stations and networks provided news and information programs. In addition to news and commentary programs, networks broadcast over fifty public affairs programs from 1926 to 1956. Many of these were "public affairs forums" in which experts presented differing points of view on current issues. Some lasted for two decades or more: *University of Chicago Round Table* (1933–1955), *American Town Meeting of the Air* (1935–1956), *Northwestern Reviewing Stand* (1937–1956), and *American Forum* (1938–1956) (Summers 1971). Most were sustaining programs aired by networks without commercial funding as part of the public service obligation of broadcasters. The FCC even recommended that such programs were better kept as sustaining rather than sponsored (Federal Communication Commission 1946).

American Forum was typical. Created by Theodore Granik, a prominent constitutional lawyer, it began broadcasting in January 1928 from station WOL in Washington, DC with two panelists in debate before a live audience that submitted questions to the speakers. It was picked up by MBS radio network and then NBC until 1956. It appeared on NBC TV from 1949 to 1957. To encourage listeners to think about and discuss what they had heard, the producers distributed a weekly pamphlet transcribing the speeches and debate, beginning in 1939 (*American Forum* 1942).

American Town Meeting of the Air, the most famous of these programs, was broadcast for twenty-one years. George Denny of Town Hall Inc., an organization that grew out of the suffrage movement and promoted civic involvement, conceived the program (*Good Evening Neighbors* 1950). George Denny hoped that *American Town Meeting of the Air* would combat one-sided propaganda and bolster democracy (Denny 1937). Public forum programs arose in part as an antidote to propaganda. Radio research pioneer Hadley Cantril, who advised Franklin Roosevelt, expressed a similar hope in his writing in the late 1930s and 1940s. Other organizations as well envisioned radio in this way, including the Council for Democracy, B'Nai Brith Anti-Defamation League, *The Nation*, the *New Republic*, *Harper's*, and the *New Yorker* (Gary 1999).

To support group discussions, *Town Meeting* prepared and mailed out, at nominal costs, a wide range of printed material to assist in organizing groups and leading and participating in discussions. It also provided a service to answer questions from listeners and offer advice in organizing listening groups. This was part of a larger group listening movement in the USA and England that hoped to involve more people in the political process of public discussions of current issues. Civic and educational organizations, including PTAs, universities, religious organizations, high schools, boards of education, and libraries, recruited listeners to groups and provided agendas and other support. Groups gathered in schools, public halls, and homes to listen to broadcasts of programs such as *Town Meeting*, and to engage in discussion after the broadcast ended. Their purpose was to extend participation in the public sphere among lower strata. It seemed to have worked. According to a researcher of the time, "The radio groups reached down into strata unable to afford or to have time for the fairly expensive lunches or dinners which in the 'regular' discussion clubs were usually the preludes to discussion" (Hill and Williams 1941, 53–54).

Participants also apparently enthusiastically accepted their role in these radio publics, as they attested to the liveliness of the discussions (Barfield 1996, 93; Hill and Williams 1941).

Institutional Advertising and Citizen Consumers

Networks and their advertisers promoted another kind of public on radio, the representative public spheres of advertising and programs through which corporations displayed themselves to the public (Habermas 1989). Large national corporations and their advertising agencies began a new approach to advertising: institutional advertising not to sell products but an image of their corporation and industry (Marchand 1998). Radio networks presented their sustaining programs as their generous gift to the nation rather than as a requirement by the FCC. In 1932 to 1933, broadcasting the New York, Boston, Cleveland, and Philadelphia Symphonies, and ten other concert music series made the networks look like cultural philanthropists to the nation. In 1937 to 1938, Toscanini directed NBC's own symphony orchestra, the New York Philharmonic played on CBS, and four networks broadcast eleven concert music programs on a sustaining basis (Summers 1971, 31, 67–68). As media historian Erik Barnouw noted, these highly visible and familiar programs recognized by people across the nation appeared as much greater contributions than those of local educational broadcasters that were often limited to daytime hours and small audiences (1966, 205, 250, 279). The networks promoted these programs as cultivating and educating the nation, and presented themselves as responsible. They used them as a means to display to the public their magnanimity as civic-minded caretakers of the public sphere, just as princes three centuries earlier displayed themselves to their subjects. To use Habermas's term, corporate media "re-feudalized" the public sphere.

In a similar vein, corporate sponsors of cultural and civic programming framed themselves as good citizens and their audiences as consumer-citizens (Bird 1999). In the mid- to late 1930s, Firestone Tires, Ford Motors, General Motors, Armco Steel, Cities Services, Packard Motors, RCA, Sherwin Williams Paints, Carborundum Abrasives, Chesterfield Tobacco, and American Banks each sponsored concert series. Philco Radio, Scott Paper, Sun Oil, Pall Mall, Bromo Quinine, Jergens Lotion, and Campbell Soups sponsored news and commentary (Summers 1971, 51–70).

Under the guidance of emerging modern advertising agencies such as Batten Barton Durstine and Osborne, the nation's largest corporations began to fabricate new public images for themselves and to frame radio and its listeners in the process. They crafted a new vocabulary called "Better Living." The term was short for DuPont's slogan first introduced on its radio program, *Cavalcade of America*, "better things for better living ... through chemistry," a slogan that lasted for decades (Bird 1999, 23). It captured the idea that corporations were the creator and causes of a high standard of American living—ignoring of course the widespread poverty in the depths of the Depression. It placed this idea of domestic comfort at the center of the political agenda by giving it a patriotic quality, as something not only to benefit the individual family but also to make America strong. Similarly, *Westinghouse Salutes* and GM's *Parade of the States* adapted civic pageantry to radio (Bird 1999, 29–30). Each weekly episode was a middle-brow eulogy for a city or state.

Another tactic was for corporations to sponsor highbrow cultural programs. These tended to concentrate their messages in intermission talks by company spokesmen. The *General Motors Symphony Concerts* from 1934 to 1937 included brief talks by the Voice of General Motors (Bird 1999, 41–45). During the sit-down strikes of 1936 to 1937 when auto workers were trying to gain recognition for a union, GM used these more directly for public support. The series was relabeled "The American Way of Doing Things," equating GM's views on public issues such as labor legislation with America and, by implication, the workers' views as un-American. In one ingenious statement, they drew upon the Declaration of Independence's right to happiness to claim that all workers had the "inalienable right to work," i.e. to negotiate individually their own employment and not be bound by a union contract. The talk cleverly wove together citizen rights and domestic bliss. It defined the Declaration's "happiness" in domestic terms, "the security, the independence and the welfare of self and family," and as a political right. By speaking to the audience in terms of their domestic circumstances, it framed them as workers and as consumers who through their work would earn enough for their welfare. By addressing the nation on the subject of political rights and labor law, they framed radio as a public sphere (Bird 1999, 43–44).

The imagined audience for these shows, despite their highbrow fare, were the masses. In a 1935 internal memo, Alfred Sloan of GM remarked, criticizing the musical selections for the concerts, that too many compositions "are very low in melody and appeal to the masses," revealing what audience he sought for his advertising (Bird 1999, 43–44). Sloan, speaking for the GM Board, repeatedly called for more popular music, presumably to reach a less sophisticated audience, not one composed, as Denny described, solely of educated opinion leaders (Bird 1999, 54–59).

These programs with their intermission talks indicate a desire by corporate executives to propagandize the masses. The implicit frame was that of corporate elites using radio as a public sphere for propaganda rather than deliberation; they envisioned audiences of attentive and obedient listeners rather than informed citizens actively participating in debate and politics. Sloan and others clearly did not want debate but rather a docile public who would imbibe and repeat the corporate messages. In contrast to the group listening movement, these programs constituted a kind of Foucauldian governmentality (Foucault 1991) intended to produce an unproblematic public who would listen to the broadcasts, internalize their messages, and follow through in their civic participation.

While some negative discourses existed about radio from the 1920s through the 1940s, the characterization of radio as a public sphere predominated far more than in other twentieth-century media. Movies were rarely conceived as a public sphere, and television received a hostile reception from its start. Similarly, recorded and broadcast music, from tango to jazz to rock 'n' roll, was condemned as exposing middle-class white teenagers to the disorder of lower-class influences. Radio stands out in the history of twentieth-century media for its positive initial reception and continuing characterization as a vital part of American civic life.

Note

1. This research is based on examination of the following magazines: *Popular Radio* 1922–1928, *Radio Age* 1922–1926, *Radio Broadcast* 1922–1927, *Radio News* 1920–1923, *Radio World* 1922–1924, *Wireless Age* 1922–1925.

Works Cited

n.a. 1923. "Work and Play by Radio." *Wireless Age* March: 38.

n.a. 1922. "A Non-Partisan Political Medium." *Wireless Age* December: 27–29.

American Forum of the Air. 1942. January.

Barfield, Ray. 1996. *Listening to Radio: 1920–1950*. Westport: Praeger.

Barnouw, Erik. 1966. *A Tower in Babel: A History of Broadcasting in the United States*. Vol. 1. Oxford: Oxford University Press.

———. 1968. *The Golden Web: A History of Broadcasting in the United States*. Vol. 2. Oxford: Oxford University Press.

Benjamin, Louise. 2001. *Freedom of the Air and the Public Interest: First Amendment Rights in Broadcasting to 1935*. Carbondale: Southern Illinois University Press.

Bird, William. 1999. *Better Living: Advertising, Media and the New Vocabulary of Business Leadership, 1935–1955*. Chicago, IL: Northwestern University Press.

Brooker, Will and Deborah Jermyn, eds. 2003. *The Audience Studies Reader*. London: Routledge.

Butsch, Richard. 2000. *The Making of American Audiences from Stage to Television, 1750–1990*. Cambridge: Cambridge University Press.

———. 2008. *The Citizen Audience: Crowds, Publics and Individuals*. New York: Routledge.

Denny, George. 1937. "Bring Back the Town Meeting." Address at Harvard University. 26 July.

Dewey, John. 1927. *The Public and its Problems*. New York: Henry Holt.

Douglas, Douglas. 1987. *Inventing American Broadcasting 1899–1922*. Baltimore, MD: The Johns Hopkins University Press.

Federal Communication Commission (FCC). 1946. *Public Service Responsibility of Broadcast Licensees*. 7 March.

Foucault, Michel. 1991. "Governmentality." In G. Burchell, C. Gordon, and P. Miller, eds. *The Foucault Effect: Studies in Governmentality*. Chicago, IL: University of Chicago Press.

Gary, Brett. 1999. *The Nervous Liberals: Propaganda Anxieties from World War I to the Cold War*. New York: Columbia University Press.

Gillespie, Marie, ed. 2005. *Media Audiences*. Maidenhead, UK: Open University Press.

Good Evening Neighbors: The Story of an American Institution, 15 Years of American Town Meeting of the Air. 1950. New York: Town Hall Inc.

Habermas, Jürgen. 1989. *The Structural Transformation of the Public Sphere*, trans. Thomas Burger. Cambridge, MA: MIT Press.

Hay, James, Lawrence Grossberg, and Ellen Wartella, eds. 1996. *The Audience and its Landscape*. Boulder, CO: Westview Press.

Hill, Frank and W.E. Williams. 1941. *Radio's Listening Groups*. New York: Columbia University Press.

Hurd, William. 1924. "The Dawn of Politics in Radio." *Wireless Age* 17 October.

Marchand, Roland. 1998. *Creating the Corporate Soul: The Rise of Public Relations and Corporate Imagery in American Big Business*. Berkeley: University of California Press.

McChesney, Robert. 1993. *Telecommunication, Mass Media and Democracy: The Battle for Control of US Broadcasting, 1928–1935*. Oxford: Oxford University Press.

Nightingale, Virginia. 1996. *Studying Audiences: The Shock of the Real*. London: Routledge.

Park, Robert. 1972. *The Crowd and the Public and Other Essays*. Chicago, IL: University of Chicago Press.

Schudson, Michael. 1998. *The Good Citizen: A History of American Civic Life*. Cambridge, MA: Harvard University Press.

Smith, F. Leslie, Milan Meeske, and John Wright. 1994. *Electronic Media and Government: The Regulation of Wireless and Wired Mass Communication in the United States*. New York: Longman.

Smith, Rogers. 1997. *Civic Ideals: Conflicting Visions of Citizenship in US History*. New Haven, CT: Yale University Press.

Smulyan, Susan. 1994. *Selling Radio: The Commercialization of American Broadcasting, 1920–1934*. Washington, DC: Smithsonian Institution Press.

Staiger, Janet. 2005. *Media Reception Studies*. New York: New York University Press.

Summers, Harrison. 1971. *A Thirty Year History*. New York: Arno.

Tarde, Gabriel. 1969. "The Public and the Crowd" and "Opinion and Conversation." *On Communication and Social Influence*. Chicago: University of Chicago Press.

US Congress. 1958. Report of the Committee on Interstate and Foreign Commerce: Network Broadcasting. Washington, DC: Eighty Fifth Congress, Second Session.

Volek, Thomas. 1990. "Examining Radio Receiver Technology through Magazine Ads in the 1920s and 1930s." Vol. 2. Illustrations. Ph.D. dissertation, University of Minnesota.

Chapter 10

Bobby Jones, Warner Bros., and the Short Instructional Film

Harper Cossar

Robert Tyre (Bobby) Jones, Jr., is the most accomplished amateur golfer in history. From 1923 through 1930, Jones won thirteen national golf championships and in 1930 completed the elusive "Grand Slam," winning the British Amateur, the British Open, the United States Open, and the United States Amateur golf tournaments in succession. This feat has only been duplicated by Tiger Woods (as a professional), and even he has not won them all in the same calendar year. Jones was an international hero, a "gentleman" (as an amateur he famously never accepted prize money), a writer, and a scholar holding degrees in mechanical engineering, literature, and law from elite universities such as Georgia Tech, Harvard University, and Emory University, respectively. His exploits have been chronicled in several feature films in recent years such as *The Legend of Bagger Vance* (Robert Redford, 2000) and *Bobby Jones: Stroke of Genius* (Rowdy Herrington, 2004). In 1930 Warner Bros. presented Jones with an exclusive multi-picture deal for a reported $250,000, forcing him to retire from competitive golf or relinquish his status as an amateur. Jones was twenty-eight years old and at the height of his golfing ability, popularity, and fame when the Warner Bros. compensation package effectively ended his amateur golf career.

The Jones/Warner Bros. films are a valuable case study for cinematic history that is underreported in the literature: the importance of short films to the overall production structure of major studios. In addition to newsreels, cartoons, and serials, short films rounded out the "balanced program" (sometimes pejoratively called the exhibition "grind") for what Richard Koszarski (1990) calls "an evening's entertainment." So important are these films to the studios' profits and industrial structure that trade journals such as *Motion Picture Herald* and *Reel Journal* review them as separate entities listed as "Short Features" and even subcategorize them as "Educational," "Comedies," or "Serial." These reviews may occasionally indicate how the audience reacted to certain shorts, the extent of their distribution, and their overall running time. Such indicators were provided to exhibitors to announce short films that may fulfill a billing or exhibition booking engagement.

This chapter examines the case study of the Jones/Warner Bros. golf instruction films in an effort to reveal the importance of short films to the overall studio output. Such short films, whether cartoons, serials, or instructional films, served as a site where studios could experiment with emerging technologies and also as a kind of testing ground where studios could showcase new talent with minimal financial investment or risk. In short, it is important to examine all of a studio's output with regard to filmic texts, not only Class A features or star vehicles. I address an underreported area of film's history: the importance of these short films—financially, technologically, and as a site to debut untested talent—to the overall production structure of the classical studio system.

The Jones/Warner Bros. films are noteworthy for a variety of reasons, but one line of inquiry stands out. What was the impetus for the "studio of the people" (Warner Bros.), a studio closely associated at that time with the introduction of sound to motion pictures, gangster and social problem films, and its Fordist-efficient production strategies, to produce eighteen golf instructional films at the beginning of the Depression? This question requires a discursive analysis of the industrial production of the exhibition "grind" designed to ensure a "balanced program" for theaters. For example, Donald Crafton calls such short films "the sound of custard" on a bill that "acted as a buffer, a curtain-raiser to prepare the audience for the feature that followed" (1997, 381). Not all of the majors produced their own short films, but all of the studios that owned theaters needed such "filler" fare to offer a broad range of filmed entertainment options in an effort to address the broad (and nebulous) desires of their patrons. Warner Bros. was among the few studios that did produce their own short films.

Jones suggested that one of his main attractions to the "talking pictures" was the combination of sound and image for instructional purposes. Douglas Gomery details that Warner Bros. had many reasons to adopt the early sound technology, not least of which was to capitalize on the technology and thus change Warner's standing as a minor studio. More importantly, Warner Bros. "never set out to make talkies as features but rather to provide one- or two-reel length recordings of musical and vaudeville acts that theater owners could provide as 'stage shows'" (Gomery 1992, 218). Thus, for Warner Bros., the short subject offered an additive quality for its audiences; the short subject with sound was a novelty item for filling out "the balanced program." Interestingly, while Warner Bros./Vitaphone made their own short subjects in an attempt to assess new talent and test new technological innovations, larger studios such as Paramount and MGM distributed shorts produced by independents (notably Hal Roach for MGM). Richard Ward suggests that Warner Bros. produced shorts because they "took up slack time in support units (such as the sound department) between major productions, keeping the studio workforce busy and permitting overhead charges to be spread over more product" (2003, 222). Ward further reports that Warner Bros. produced and distributed shorts as a way "to brighten up the program a bit" (222); that is, to balance the studio's output of gangster films or social problem films such as *The Public Enemy, Three on a Match*, or *I Am a Fugitive from a Chain Gang*.

Anecdotal evidence is that, at times, the short films may have eclipsed the features in popularity within a given theater or city. Dana Benelli reports:

> In the trade press, there is ample evidence that theaters promoted the content of their newsreels by giving it marquee status above the feature film listing on those occasions when the newsreels covered events of particularly intense current public interest. . . . Among series of shorts on sport topics, Knute Rockne's demonstrations of football strategy and Bobby Jones's golf tips achieved a degree of popularity which eventually also earned them frequent above-the-feature marquee preeminence in some theaters' promotions of their film programs.
>
> (2002, 5)

Second, the short subject was often the locus of technological and stylistic experimentation by a studio. Crafton notes that studios would often use the short films as "a laboratory in which [a] new technology could be tested and fine tuned" (1997, 381). Certainly this was the case with synchronized sound, color, and widescreen, to name just a few. Walt Disney Animation and Pixar Animation studios still use the production of short films in a similar way. Disney producer Don Hahn says that "shorts have always been a wellspring of techniques, ideas and young talent" (Solomon 2006). In a *New York Times* story on Disney's recent renewal of animated short films, the author states that Walt Disney's "reputation was originally built on shorts" and that Disney used his "Silly Symphonies series to train his artists" for larger, more intensive projects. Veteran Disney story artist Chuck Williams claims that shorts "allow you to develop new talent. Shorts are your farm team, where the new directors and art directors are going to come from" (quoted in Solomon 2006). By "farm team," Williams is describing the hierarchal nature of the studio system as being analogous to that of a baseball team. In baseball, the "minor league" team serves as a "farm team" where promising talent, ideas, and techniques can grow with minimal financial or public exposure and thus minimal risk on the part of the parent organization. As Williams suggests, shorts have a long history of providing a developmental network for studios and/or filmmakers with regard to talent, technology, and techniques.

In terms of the classical studio system production strategy, David Bordwell,

Janet Staiger, and Kristin Thompson would most likely classify the Jones's golf shorts as related to the earlier, silent shorts categorized as "topicals" or possibly even "trick" films. The former relied upon an "exploitation of current events" and "a direct appeal to the freshness of the product," which were certainly applicable to Jones's worldwide golf championships and fame. Further, the authors suggest that "sport was one of the earliest subjects for filming" because "sports films held their value in repeated showings, particularly if controversial calls benefited from replays" (Bordwell et al. 1985, 114–115). While no "controversial calls" occur during the Jones's shorts, the fetishizing of Jones's skills and athletic ability does give way to an early version of "instant replay" via slow-motion photography, an experimental process at the time. As for "trick" films, Bordwell, Staiger, and Thompson report that " 'trick' films provided an extension of the initial marketing appeal of the technology. Once moving pictures as such faded as a novelty, other aspects of the technology were exploited" (1985, 114–115). Again, the aspect of technology as novelty with Jones's films cannot be overstated, and its importance is twofold: Jones's mastery of the various golf clubs and shots and the camera techniques and unique *mise-en-scène* to capture such skills. A textual analysis of several of the films reveals novel uses of slow-motion camerawork, innovative *mise-en-scène*, and costuming that may have ultimately led to the emergence of the modern-day instructional sport films.

Bobby Jones and Teaching Golf in the 1930s

From 1931 to 1933, Jones made eighteen one-reel, instructional films for Warner Bros. studios. These short films are entertaining, informative, and sophisticated in their uses of both technology and style, capturing the essences of both the golf swing and how the sport is played. Jones stated that the "talkies" were the perfect medium for golf instruction. "The talking picture," Jones commented in 1930, "with its combination of visual presentation and demonstration, with the possibility of detailed explanation [via sound], appeals to me as the ideal vehicle for an undertaking of this nature" (Matthew 2005, 183). Mark Frost suggests that perhaps Jones had an additional impetus for wanting to exploit the new "talkies." Frost writes, "An Atlanta friend who owned a string of movie houses interested [Jones] in exploring the idea of a series of instructional films about the game. He could teach what he knew to the masses in a way that had never been done before" (2004, 447). This revelation suggests that the "Atlanta friend" understood the fiscal possibilities associated with golf, Jones's celebrity, and short subjects, and this association may have driven Jones's profits from both series as high as $600,000.[1]

Jones's accomplishments and celebrity helped to increase golf's popularity at a time when the United States was on the precipice of the Depression. The

New York Times ("Golf boomed" 1931) reports that "football, basketball, intercollegiate sport generally ... were in the doldrums during 1930, but not the grand old game the canny Scots popularized. Generally speaking, 1930 was a boom year for golf" (29). The newspaper goes on to detail not only the staggering rise in golfing around the country, but to suggest that golf, like much of Hollywood, was somewhat immune to the effects of the coming Depression:

> At Seattle, 280,000 golfers used the municipal course in 1930, as compared to 190,000 in 1929.... Atlanta, 73,663 more persons played golf last year than two years ago, 20,000 of that number playing on the new John White municipal course of nine holes. "Golf was never more popular and the business depression has had little effect," observers reported. From eleven of the leading courses in the Hudson Valley area around Albany came reports that more persons played over their courses last year than ever before. Wilmington, Del., reported golf booming as did Philadelphia. The stimulation in the Quaker City was traced to the national amateur tournament at Merion, Pa., where Bobby Jones won his fourth major title of the year.
>
> (1931, 29)

Studio veteran (and avid golfer) George E. Marshall (*Destry Rides Again* [1939], *The Perils of Pauline* [1947], *How the West Was Won* [1962]) directed all of the Jones's short films, and they featured appearances by members of the Hollywood elite such as W.C. Fields, Douglas Fairbanks, Jr., James Cagney, Loretta Young, Walter Huston, and Edward G. Robinson. None of the studio actors received any monetary compensation for their efforts, and several welcomed the opportunity to be "exchanged" from their contractual studios to be close to Jones and possibly soak up a few golf tips. Frost reports: "interest in Jones was so great that ... every studio in town signed releases for their own stars so they could appear in the series" (2004, 449–450).

Jones and Marshall admittedly had different opinions about what they wanted to accomplish with the films. Jones stated that he envisioned the films "exhibiting and explaining the methods which I employ in playing the shots ordinarily required in playing a round of golf" (Matthew 2004, 2). Marshall thought the films should appear "as natural and spontaneous as though it was something which might have occurred during an afternoon's golf game or during a conversation at the clubhouse" (4). The plots (virtually ad-libbed on set with dialogue and narration supplied by Jones's biographer O.B. Keeler) generally involve the Hollywood glitterati bumping into Jones on the course (Lakeside Golf Club, Flintridge Golf Club, or Bel Air Country Club, all of which are in or around Hollywood) and asking for an impromptu lesson. Frost characterizes the Jones's golf narratives thus:

Watched in succession, the series suggests that Bob [Jones] is an almost mystical being who materializes from out of the woods to offer soothing words of advice and a laying-on of hands to his anguished supplicants. They bump into him—he's forever strolling by in the middle of his own never-ending round of golf—he applies his gentle ministrations to their troubles, and the stars depart as if magically healed by their friendly neighborhood holy man.

(Frost 2004, 450)

The Jones short *The Driver* (1931) is exemplary of the series in its use of innovative technology. J. Farrell MacDonald (as himself) is struggling with his driver. He falls asleep reading a Bobby Jones instructional manual, and Jones's still picture from the magazine "comes to life" in MacDonald's dream. Here, director Marshall uses an optical printer technique to show Jones in MacDonald's subconscious and entering his dream world. When MacDonald awakes, he has internalized Jones's technique and thrashes his playing partners in short order.

Marshall and Jones also experiment with slow-motion cinematography and creative *mise-en-scène* and costuming for the Jones short *The Downswing* (1933). Jones and Marshall want to show the proper use of a golfer's body and in

Figure 10.1 Jones and director Marshall use optical printer techniques in the short *The Driver*.

Figures 10.2 and 10.3 Jones and Marshall use slow-motion cinematography and creative *mise-en-scène* to fetishize Jones's
body movement by isolating the moving parts of
his golf swing.

particular the proper rotation of the shoulders in relation to the hips during
the golf swing. Jones wears an all-black suit with one white sleeve to isolate
and reveal the shoulder rotation, and later wears a symmetrically divided
half-white, half-black suit to show proper trunk and hip rotation. By using
such techniques, Marshall and Jones presage the instructional sports videos of
the modern era and a key narrative factor in modern sports coverage: the fet-
ishization of the body's performance during athletic endeavors and "instant
replay." The use of slow-motion photography combined with the creative
costuming shows great strides in narrativizing the corporeal, athletic movement involved in the golf swing. Such constructs may be found in most
current sports coverage on television and in instructional, "how-to" sport
videos.[2]

Selling Jones's Celebrity in the 1930s

The initial twelve films (*How I Play Golf* [3]) were shown beginning in April 1931 and ran throughout the summer. Frost reports that the Jones films were "rolled out in April of 1931 and [played] through the summer at a rate of one a week. Screened in over six thousand theaters, they were an immediate smash, well reviewed and financially successful" (2004, 450). Due to their enormous success, Warner Bros. picked up the option for another six films (*How to Break 90*) to bring the total for both series to eighteen. Michael Schoenecke (2005) reports upon the tradition of sports stars such as Jack Dempsey and Babe Ruth, not to mention Red Grange or Bill Tilden, capitalizing on their athletic achievements in Hollywood, and aligns Jones with similar interests. In addition, Lee Grieveson (1998) writes of boxer Jack Johnson's fight films from 1912 to 1915 with regard to the scandalous nature of *watching* (via film) a black man beat a white man and the social/legal consequences for both Johnson and fight films. As indicated by these examples, filming sports and sports figures thus had precedence to drive or enhance a star's popularity in the public mind by the time of Jones's arrival on the international sporting stage.

Warner Bros. sought to capitalize upon Jones's international celebrity and acclaim by selling his genteel, Southern persona (and syrupy Georgian drawl) in addition to his golfing prowess. A Warner Bros./Vitaphone advertisement in *Motion Picture Herald* calls "the one and only Bobby Jones" the "most famous sports personality in the world." The ad goes on to suggest that Jones's alignment with Warner Bros./Vitaphone is "the most successful screen merger of entertainment and education" complete with "filmdom's biggest stars" (Vitaphone pamphlet 1931, 17). Also advertised on this one-sheet pamphlet designed to help exhibitors "complete the perfect program" is another sport-related topical entitled *Sport Slants* with radio broadcaster Ted Husling, a series of Warner Bros.'s *Looney Toons* cartoons featuring the controversial character Bosko, and the *Ripley's Believe It or Not* spectacle series. This line-up of short subjects reflects Warner Bros.'s commitment to the short subject as "filler" to provide a balanced program. To further promote this concept, the shorts are advertised as "every kind of entertainment for every kind of audiences [*sic*]."

In sum, Warner Bros. was using the short subjects to present a balanced bill to the independent theater owner. Crafton suggests that this strategy was part of a larger effort on behalf of Warner Bros. to distribute the risk associated with the sound conversion across many genres and programs. The use of shorts was to highlight the novelty associated with sound and new uses of innovative technology (as with animation and later with color and widescreen) and as a training ground for auditioning new talent (i.e. Jones). Crafton writes:

Instead of packaging shorts with WB features, the company was building a library of varied subjects which exhibitors could rent individually to play with any program, much as they had done with live acts. . . . [T]he shorts on the program were almost the last bastion of the independent owner's effort to individualize his program.

(1997, 383)

To take advantage of the celebrity of Jones and increase the role of sporting short subject films to their own bottom line, Paramount Pictures counter-programmed a series of their own short golf subjects for the Paramount Pictorial series. These twelve short subjects featured professional Walter Hagen (Jones's main golf competitor of the era) along with three other (lesser known) golf professionals. The copy for the Paramount ad suggests that the series will "draw the sport loving millions" and that the shorts feature "personalities every newspaper reader, whether golfer or not, knows and wants to see" (4 great golf stars 1931, 3). The notion of counter-programming production trends for features is widely reported in the scholarly literature, but little has been written with regard to counter-programming short subjects on the playbill.[4]

Unlike the aforementioned athletics stars of his age, including Hagen, one of Jones's chief attractions was his amateur status. Jones did not accept prize money for any of his many victories and, in doing so, presented himself as a "gentleman" who played for sport and competition, not money. So great was Jones's reach and impact upon the world sporting stage that the Prince of Wales (Edward VIII) acknowledged Jones's accomplishment (and, to a lesser extent, that of Charles Lindbergh) at a London dinner engagement shortly after Jones's retirement. The British heir to the throne said: "Not only does the great golfing community of Britain but the whole sporting community admire to the utmost [Jones's] unique achievement . . . we admire particularly the most graceful way in which he retired" (Selden 1930, 3).

Ironically, when Jones accepted the Warner Bros. deal, he was effectively forced to retire owing to the monetary compensation. The reported deal, which paid Jones some $250,000 for the first twelve films, is a striking sum considering what other "stars" of short subjects were paid for their sound films. In a study of Columbia Pictures's short comedies, Ted Okuda reports:

most contract comedians appearing in their own starring series were paid the flat sum of $500 per short. However, there were exceptions. When Buster Keaton was signed to a series, it was considered quite a boon to the department, and his salary per short was $1,000.

(1986, 49)

Keaton was past his prime in terms of compensation (during his years at Columbia from 1939 to 1941), but the disparity in fees illustrates the fiscal attitude of Warner Bros. toward Jones; moreover, the studio must have believed that the short subject could make money.

The Jones/Warner Bros. golf shorts are an intriguing case study of one major studio's production strategy with regard to providing a variety of entertainment programming options for exhibitors and patrons. By utilizing the short film format, Warner Bros. was able to introduce a new "talent" (Jones) and experiment with innovative technological/stylistic strategies such as slow-motion and creative *mise-en-scène* and costuming. This case study unpacks a section of media history that may have been neglected in the past. Currently there is much work that might have to be done in this area, particularly given the importance of shorts to studios and exhibitors. Shorts were all but abandoned by filmmakers and studios with the coming of the television era of the 1950s. Therefore this case study of the Bobby Jones's golf series, *How I Play Golf* and *How to Break 90*, serves to fill a small but important gap in the history of film studios' overall production strategies.

Notes

1. A recent *Golf Digest* article (2008, 64) suggests that Jones's compensation was $600,000 or the modern equivalent of "the $29.2 million that Arnold Schwarzenegger got for *Terminator 3*." Jones's compensation may have reached as high as the *Golf Digest* reported figure after *both* series (1931 and 1933) had completed their run, and he may have also benefited from exhibition proceeds. In either case, his carefully constructed and perpetuated amateur status had to be relinquished because he accepted monetary compensation for his golfing efforts.
2. The fascination with technology in sports coverage persists as CBS recently won a special technical Emmy for their use of an ultra high-speed camera (1,000 fps, Swing Vision) used to dissect various golfers' swings during televised rounds (George Wensel Technical Achievement Award, Swing Vision, *Golf on CBS*, 2007–2008).
3. Jones specified this title to denote that this series is not a monolithic "how-to" but rather a personal perspective which thus reinscribes Jones as author and celebrity.
4. For a more complete picture of counter-programming of shorts by studio (MGM, Warner Bros., and Universal) from 1929 to 1939, see Ward 2003, Appendix A, 235–242.

Bobby Jones Warner Bros./Vitaphone Short Films

How I Play Golf series (1931):
The Putter
Chip Shots
The Niblick
The Mashie Niblick
The Medium Irons
The Big Irons
The Spoon
The Brassie
The Driver
Trouble Shots
Practice Shots
A Round of Golf

How to Break 90 series (1933):
The Grip
Position and Back Swing
Hip Action
Down Swing
Impact
Fine Points

Works Cited

Benelli, Dana. 2002. "Hollywood and the travelogue." *Visual Anthropology* 15: 3–16.

Bordwell, David, Janet Staiger, and Kristin Thompson. 1985. *The Classical Hollywood Cinema: Film Style and Mode of Production to 1960*. New York: Columbia University Press.

Crafton, Donald. 1997. *The Talkies: American Cinema's Conversion to Sound 1926–1931*. Berkeley: University of California Press.

"4 great golf stars." 1931. Paramount shorts advertisement. *Motion Picture Herald* 103. 8: 3.

Frost, Mark. 2004. *The Grand Slam: Bobby Jones, American and the Story of Golf*. New York: Hyperion.

"Golf boomed throughout country in 1930; marked increase in players and courses." 1931. *New York Times* 27 January: 29.

Gomery, Douglas. 1992. *Shared Pleasures: A History of Movie Presentation in the United States*. Madison: University of Wisconsin Press, 218.

Grieveson, Lee. 1998. "Fighting films: race, morality, and the governing of cinema, 1912–1915." *Cinema Journal* 38.1: 40–72.

Grillroom. March 2008. *Golf Digest* 64.

Koszarski, Richard. 1990. *An Evening's Entertainment: The Age of the Silent Feature Picture 1915–1928*. New York: Charles Scribner's Sons.

Matthew, Sidney L. 2004. "Along came Jones." In "Bobby Jones and Hollywood." *Bobby Jones: How I Play Golf* DVD liner notes. Turner Home Entertainment.

———. 2005. *Bobby: The Life and Times of Bobby Jones*. Ann Arbor: Sports Media Group.

"Nominees for the 29th annual sports Emmy Awards." 2008. Press release. Available at: www.emmyonline.org/mediacenter/sports_29th_nominees_data.html.

Okuda, Ted. 1986. *The Columbia Comedy Shorts: Two-Reel Hollywood Film Comedies, 1933–1958*. Jefferson: McFarland.

Schoenecke, Michael K. 2005. "Bobby Jones, golf and his instructional reels." *Film and History: An Interdisciplinary Journal of Film and Television Studies* 35.2: 67–70.

Selden, Charles A. 1930. "British heir lauds two noted Americans." *New York Times* 28 November: 3.

Solomon, Charles. 2006. "For Disney, something old (and short) is new again." *New York Times* 3 December: B 22.

Vitaphone shorts advertisement. 1931. *Motion Picture Herald* 103. 8: 17.

Ward, Richard. 2003. "Extra added attractions: the short subjects of MGM, Warner Bros. and Universal." *Media History* 9.3: 221–244.

Part III

New Approaches

Chapter 11

Bonding with the Crowd

Silent Film Stars, Liveness, and the Public Sphere

Sue Collins

When Mary Pickford appeared in Chicago in 1918 on behalf of the war bond drive, "bankers and babes" turned out in droves to see her even though it was "raining pitchforks." Movie columnist Mae Tinee insisted that there was "nobudda" for whom this many people would go to such lengths. Gossip columnist Louella Parsons, keen to deflate the exclusivity of the café society crowd, reported on a similar scene:

> I suspect some of the mothers and wives of these dignified gentlemen would scarcely have recognized them if they had seen them—pushing each other and pawing the air in their eagerness to get a look at Mary Pickford. One man said it was worth $1,000 just to get a look at "Little Mary." Another clutching his photograph of her said the picture was worth more to him than the paltry $5,000 he had just paid for a Pickford-signed Liberty bond.
>
> (1918)

The *San Francisco News Letter* likewise reported that socialite women traded in their privilege for an excuse to deign themselves in the presence of a "movie queen" and to reveal themselves as fans ("High Class" 1918).

This chapter explores the political import of live film star appearances during the Liberty Loan Bond Drives of 1917 to 1919. Adhering to a policy of neutrality during the start of World War I in Europe, upon US intervention the Wilson administration faced the task of reshaping public opinion in support of the war. Part of the government's propaganda campaign involved the recruitment of the film industry and its biggest stars—Charles Chaplin, Douglas Fairbanks, and Mary Pickford, also known as the "Big Three"—to lend their celebrity capital for the purposes of war mobilization. In short, stars toured the country appearing live before massive crowds to whom they preached the virtues of Liberty Bond investments, thrift, and Americanization.

In discussing this case study, I am interested in problematizing liveness in early film stardom as a discursive mechanism of political authority. By live-ness, I mean film stars appearing before the public as themselves. A distinction exists between liveness in stage performance and the film star appearing live as the "real" person, or more accurately within the confines of a persona, which appears as real to the spectator. I focus on the live film star persona as a phe-nomenon in the 1910s that operated within the interstices of filmic texts, the beginnings of celebrity journalism, and, for the first time, the public sphere. Of course, live star appearances were mediated for the much larger non-present public, while publicity efforts by exhibitors and studios also antici-pated them. Experiential understandings of live appearances inhabited most people's imaginations of what it would be like to see the star through their screen memories.

I consider live appearances with respect to two methodological issues. The first concerns thinking about how live appearances by silent film stars figure into calculations of the star image in a way that might respond to Janet Staiger's call to treat a history of cinema less in terms of film history and more in terms of media history (2004, 127). The corporeality of live star bodies in the public sphere during the Liberty Loan tours signified more than film's arrival into the pantheon of communications. I argue that political authority of entertainment celebrity was written into the construction of stars at the moment they began to appear live on behalf of the nation for war mobiliza-tion. Put another way, live appearances by stars articulated model citizenship in the public sphere for the first time during the war. Given film's entrance into a media environment characterized primarily by the rhetorical practices of political elites—which is to say long-standing traditions of print and oratory and renegotiations with the rhetorical salience of images—I treat the new-found political authority conferred on popular culture's emissaries as a cultural technology expedient for the propaganda campaign of the moment. At the same time, celebrity political authority comes on to the scene in everyday life as a regulatory guide to behavior.

In thinking about stardom in a historically specific case but also the broader category of celebrity as a cultural technology, I highlight, first, the reproduci-bility of celebrity as image constituting a culturally valorized form of visibility that communicates meanings distinct to the celebrity in question. Second, and consequently, I call attention to the celebrity testimonial deployed as a form of power in the naturalization of particular meanings. When this happens as policy in conjunction with the state, celebrity as a central part of popular culture, to borrow from Tony Bennett, is "brought within the province of government" in the management of populations (1995, 18). This represents a move away from the dominant propaganda model of centralized top-down power toward a reconceptualization of the relationship of the state to popular culture in terms of governmentality. In other words, the government's success with its domestic propaganda campaign may be understood vis-à-vis its ability to diffuse culturally its policy objectives by inviting apparatuses of popular culture (managed independently) to aid in the formation of patriotic subjects who "voluntarily" financed the war.

If, as media theorists might argue, existing relations of social power are disrupted when new uses of technology arrive on the scene, then we might expect to find resistance to the idea of film stars as sources of political authority, given persistent attitudes respecting distinctions between high- and lowbrow cultural tastes and steadfast policy initiatives to censor and reform cinema in the first few decades of the twentieth century. Unsurprisingly, we do not find signs of disapproval in the trades or the dailies for the most part, which brings me to my second methodological issue: apprehending liveness as a construction by film industry press and print dailies during wartime. Here I simply wish to reiterate Donald Crafton's warning to scrutinize our faith in the early presses to speak for audiences. More to my point, Crafton notes that film industry professionals and publicity personnel "have been instrumental in trying to shape films' critical evaluation" (1996, 462). Anthony Slide puts it this way: "Page after page of early trade periodicals is filled with the most unbelievable nonsense" (1978, 122)!

The film industry, from the start of World War I and throughout US intervention, worked relentlessly through the trades to declare its value to the government as on a par with the written word, then ultimately superior to it. This was, in part, a strategy to win essential industry status (DeBauche 1997), but it was also an industry-wide ethos responding to an unprecedented opportunity made by wartime conditions: at stake was the industry's utility to political elites and the reimagining of cinema as a cultural form equivalent to or better than other venerable modes of persuasion, expressions of national identity, and tools for political and cultural policy. To be sure, the dailies and industry trades detailing the stars' involvement in the bond drive tours are rife with celebratory hyperbole during a period, first of anti-interventionist sentiment, and later of increasing bond fatigue, trends that are evident through discursive fissures found in other contemporary historical documents. Thus the press, and particularly the trades, must be read with these competing realities in mind.

The public's initial fascination with film actors coincides with an important history of industry strategy designed to create star value, which began years before the stars were called upon to do their "bit." The ontological underpinning of the star image is the idea that fans, in varying degrees, want to know who the person behind the screen image "really is"; thus they turn to extratextual discourses such as fan magazines to gain the dope on the star. Before studios identified their players, curious fans sought out information about their favorite players by pestering exhibitors, writing to studios, and turning to the industry's trade publications (Bowser 1994). The public's exuberance with the stars' private lives was largely circumscribed by fan magazine discourses starting in late 1910, which became a strategy to control knowledge about the star (deCordova 1990), except for the advent of live star appearances in theaters to promote their films. But these appearances were restricted geographically to big cities so that very few fans could actually glimpse their screen idols in public. Prior to 1910 people living in or visiting New York City could manage fairly easily to watch a film being made or even to meet movie actors, "most of whom," Kathryn Fuller writes, "had the same meager celebrity as traveling stock-company performers" (1996, 129).

Richard Abel's work (2006) affirms that the first live appearances by film stars date back to the IMP stunt in 1910 during which Carl Laemmle publicized Florence Lawrence, formerly "the Biograph Girl," by faking her death in a news story, only to resurrect the "film star" in a series of articles published in the *St. Louis Times*. Stories published in advance alerted fans to her two-day live appearance upon which she was greeted at the train station, allegedly, Abel points out, with a reception comparable to that given to President Taft or Commander Peary (232).[1] The stunt spawned others and by 1913, stars were touring theaters to promote their films, attending balls sponsored by the various segments of the industry, and making appearances on behalf of their studios at the exhibitors' trade conventions.

The exhibitors' national conventions started in 1910. Star appearances privately wooed the exhibitors who, like the public, held their favorite stars in high esteem. Essanay was the first to capitalize on this strategy at the second annual convention held in Chicago. Having set up an "office" at the La Salle hotel in Chicago, the studio provided refreshments, handed out souvenirs, and made sure popular stars from its eastern stock company were there to "welcome and meet the exhibitors and their friends personally" ("Essanay's" 1912). "Room 1811," as it was called, was such a success that it initiated an industry standard. The following year, studios assigned themselves days (e.g., Biograph Day, Vitagraph Day) during which they publicized that exhibitors and the public would have a chance to meet "the players who have been their favorites for so long but who until recently existed as unnamed personages" ("To Entertain" 1913). Within two years, the crowds grew so big that the convention was augmented with an exposition to accommodate the public but also to provide exhibitors' privileged spaces to conduct their business dealings, including chances to meet the stars privately. In 1916, the *Exhibitors Herald* claimed that a quarter of a million people attended the Chicago Exposition ("Film History" 191b, 17).

By the time of the bond drives, live appearances became controversial within the industry. Initially they publicized the studio as a brand of film production through the star vehicle, which afforded select exhibitors profit from packed houses generated by the publicity of a star appearance. The business ploy seemed to work so well that Equitable announced that it planned to stipulate personal appearances at theaters two nights a week in its stars' contracts ("Equitable" 1916). But there were problems too. For one, promised appearances did not always materialize and the public's disappointment with no-shows was a point of admonishment in the trade editorials. In addition, having their stars present at the national conventions and various regional ones put considerable demand on the studios, prompting them to push for one annual convention, which was agreed upon in 1916. The stars themselves were heavily taxed by having to appear, particularly when the crowds required police control. The more well known the stars, the more likely they had to contend with the nervous tension of large crowds.

Soon personal appearances were called into question for their risk of overexposure and the breakdown of the stars' auratic function as critical in the reproduction of stardom, the linchpin to the industry's economic success. In 1914, the *Dramatic Mirror* had warned that "the 'illusion [so] valuable [for telling a story] on the screen' could be undermined by 'too great a familiarity' with the players" (quoted in Abel 2006, 247). In August 1917, *Motography* published an editorial denouncing star appearances as "bad business." Stars, it was argued, should not be known to their public in person, for once they appear in the flesh, the picture loses its special hold over audiences: "The most magnetic of personalities, the most beautiful of forms and faces, the most delicious of voices, cannot compare with the unreal beauty and the unheard voices of the screen" ("When Players Appear" 1917).

In a similar way that talking pictures would be thought to break the spell of glamour and romance on the silent screen, live appearances threatened to demystify film stardom's discursive construction of aura. This measure of authenticity is different from Walter Benjamin's conception, which is critically tied to "the presence of the original," and at the same time to a sensation of distance provoked by the artifact's uniqueness (1969, 386). For Benjamin, film precludes aura because film actors act not for live audiences but for the camera in a disjunctive and fragmented process out of which the whole is identically reproduced along with the viewing experience. Catherine Kerr, however, has argued that once actors adjusted to the technology by learning to be "gazed upon without gazing back," viewers' engagement with the medium moved away from its technical apparatus and toward the production of an "aura of realism," which worked to produce audience desire and which made film "the special forum for the actor's authentic self-expression" (1990, 397–403). The industry made its own claims to cultural legitimacy and located aura in the star image, dependent upon the apparatuses of cinematic expression (including extra-textual ones). The star closeup on the screen signified an intimacy and certain immediacy; yet it was effectively allusive and distant and should remain that way. Fan magazines provided privileged and controlled access to the "real" of the stars' private lives. Live appearances, then, risked the very enigmatic mechanism upon which the system existed.

Three weeks after the editorial, *Motography* reported that screen stars had started a movement to curb their appearances in theaters. The stars argued that while appearances might add to their popularity and increase theater attendance, in the long run and "on the whole it detracts from the glamour and mystery that motion pictures must have, and because of that is not good publicity" (" 'Split Reel' " 1917). Likewise, *Moving Picture World* affirmed for manufacturers that filmic aura is more properly protected and reproduced in the fantasies of audiences:

> How in the world it increases the popularity of a star to drag him or her before the footlights away from the atmosphere of the picture is beyond us. "I thought he was tall. Shucks! He's short! I thought he had a deep voice. Fudge! He's squeaky" . . . But you say, "The people want it." That's just it. Make them want it. Continue to shroud the pictures and the stars in a certain mystery. . . . Let them think of the star only as they see him or her in the pictures. Give them the pictures they want, if you are lucky enough to know what the public like, but don't bust up that perfectly good little illusion.
>
> (Fisher 1918)

Two months later, notwithstanding this argument to manage stardom's aura on screen and through controlled avenues to knowledge about the stars' private lives, film stars began to step up and associate their names, film titles, studios, and live bodies with war work.

Despite claims that the Big Three were not arousing publicity in advance of their arrival to open the third loan drive, the cross-country trip to Washington was punctuated with stories in the dailies depicting hordes of fans awaiting the arrival of the stars at each rural station whether the train stopped or not. In Salt Lake City, 30,000 people blocked the Pullman from its station such that the police and a company of soldiers were needed to clear space for the train to pull in ("A Valuable Load" 1918). *Moving Picture World* reported opening day to be one of the largest meetings ever held in Washington, as the three stars and Marie Dressler appeared together on the steps of the Navy Building. Swarms of people managed to "wedge their way" to the booths to subscribe to the bonds, but "the vast majority had to content themselves with looking at the screen idols from a distance and shouting greetings." Later, at the ellipse, as the stars tried to make their way to their respective booths, they "found themselves hemmed in on all sides, the space around them constantly growing smaller," while "tens of thousands in the back were surging forward" ("Film Industry" 1918). Chaplin and Fairbanks pushed their way through to get to their booths, and though police mounted on horseback struggled to clear a path for Pickford, it took her forty-five minutes to reach hers which she ended up having to share with Dressler ("First Day's Sales" 1918). Yet the pandemonium of the scene was representatively diffused when "Chaplin and Fairbanks then mounted the tops of trucks and made addresses and kept the crowd shouting with merriment" ("Film Industry" 1918).

The *New York Sun* estimated the noon turnout to see Fairbanks and Chaplin on Wall Street to be an incredible 50,000–100,000 people with only 150 police officers stationed for crowd control ("Fairbanks and Chaplin" 1918).[2] During Chaplin's appeal, fifteen people suffered injuries from being trampled. Still, the fans were held in captive "delight" at the antics of the two, particularly when Fairbanks carried Chaplin on his shoulders and Fairbanks's "golden smile" caused the crowd to "roar" with approving pleasure ("Film Industry" 1918). When Pickford appeared on the same platform three days later, *Moving Picture World* informed its readers that a record-breaking crowd had been expected, so the police department took "extra precautions for the protection of the public" ("Film Industry" 1918). Nevertheless, an "army" of fans wanting to hear her "broke the lines several times and were half way up the steps of the Sub-Treasury before they could be turned back by the police"

Figure 11.1 Chaplin and Fairbanks on Wall Street, 1918.

("Mary Pickford Appeals" 1918). Yet Pickford's smile and the kisses she blew to the crowd seemed to be enough to convince one reporter of her command in convincing the crowd to buy bonds. As she spoke futilely, through a megaphone, the multitude surged to come closer, which frightened Pickford, who began regularly to fear her fans in aggregate numbers. Pickford shouted for them to remain orderly, throwing down her glove "to stem the onrush." As she resumed speaking, *The Tribune* reported, "out of respect" for her, the crowd complied and "became more orderly." In between pronouncements, "the crowd cheered and applauded merrily," and though most could not hear a word she spoke, "who cared about that? Every one could see her smile and sigh and throw kisses" (Mary Pickford Convinces" 1918).

These scenes among others are testimony to David Marshall's supposition on celebrity's discursive emergence at the turn of the century as a site working to house the perceived irrationality of the modern mass (1997). Indeed, the bond drive tours bear out this framework. Recurring narrative journalism describing scenes requiring police forces for crowd control are repeatedly diffused by journalists' accounts of how the stars managed to contain the unruly mass, interpolating them into fun-loving and well-intentioned fans, while channeling their energies into bond sales and patriotic sentiments. At the same time, Marshall argues, celebrity represents conceptions of individuality, for which it is celebrated as a part of democratic capitalism. As a signifier of upward mobility, celebrity indicates dominant modes of subjectivity that audiences, from "bankers to babes," are encouraged to emulate. Awarded unprecedented access to the public sphere, the stars modeled ideal citizenship and normalized modes of patriotism as they contributed to the suppression of anti-interventionist dissent.

Embodied access to the site of elite spectacle imbued film stardom with new-found political authority as it also signified that movie-going was an essential American experience. If moving pictures had been perceived as lowbrow entertainment, live star appearances for the state bridged the gap between popular and elite tastes. Although the stars beckoned large crowds on to the streets, they more effectively functioned to separate out the social elite who could afford to buy bonds in large denominations and who were interested in hosting them. From surging crowds to private settings, the stars' efforts were reflected in subscriptions in the tens of thousands from extremely wealthy patrons and heads of institutions. When Pickford auctioned her "priceless curls" to the highest bidder at the Board of Trade in Chicago, she showed that the so-called crowd spanned the social strata ("Mary Pickford Adds"). The stars' celebrity capital invoked more bond sales and worked to offset bond fatigue through enterprising exploits.

During war mobilization, the stars functioned to incite the crowd's energy through their live presence, reconfiguring their charismatic aura as a function of live spectacle. Within the domain of the state's spectacle, the live film star underwent a privileged form of public subjectivity, serving as a point of class convergence and cultural commonality. Endowed with political opinion leadership status, film stars evoked obligations to nation, polity, and civil society, positioning the collectivity into citizen subjects, eager to do their bit and to share in the reconfiguration of national identity. However, as this study's approach to understanding film stardom in the public sphere has argued, a certain scrutiny is warranted to correct for the early industry trades' unrelenting superlative accounting of the stars' power. More to the point, government officials *thought* the stars were powerful motivators, which signaled a new star discourse and a broader signification for Hollywood celebrity.

Notes

1. Lewis Jacobs also makes this claim (1968, 87).
2. Other accounts estimate the crowd in the tens of thousands.

Works Cited

Abel, Richard. 2006. *Americanizing the Movies and "Movie-Mad" Audiences, 1910–1914*. Berkeley: University of California Press.

"A Valuable Load." 1918. *New York Star*, 17 April, Mary Pickford Scrapbook 30, Margaret Herrick Library, Los Angeles.

Benjamin, Walter. 1969. "Art in the Age of Mechanical Reproduction," trans. Harry Zohn. *Illuminations*, ed. Hannah Arendt. New York: Schocken Books, 348–408.

Bennett, Tony. 1995. *The Birth of the Museum: History, Theory, Politics*. London: Routledge.

Bowser, Eileen. 1994. *The Transformation of Cinema, 1907–1915*. Berkeley: University of California Press.

Crafton, Donald. 1996. "The Jazz Singer's Reception in the Media and at the Box Office." *Post-Theory: Reconstructing Film Studies*, ed. David Bordwell and Noël Carroll. Madison: University of Wisconsin Press, 460–480.

DeBauche, Leslie Midkiff. 1997. *Reel Patriotism: The Movies and World War I*. Madison: University of Wisconsin Press.

deCordova, Richard. 1990. *Picture Personalities: The Emergence of the Star System in America*. Urbana: University of Illinois Press.

"Equitable Stars to Appear in Person." 1916. *Motography* 8 January: 77.

"Essanay's Convention Activities." 1912. *Motography* 31 August: 165.

"Fairbanks and Chaplin Thrill Wall Street Hosts." 1918. *The Sun* 9 April: 16.

"Film History Made at Chicago Convention." 1916. *Exhibitors Herald* 29 July: 11–18.

"Film Industry Working for Liberty Loan." 1918. *Moving Picture World* 27 April: 519.

"First Day's Sales Lead to Belief Doug and Charlie Will Double Thirteen Million." 1918. Mary Pickford Scrapbook 30, Special Collections, Margaret Herrick Library, Los Angeles.

Fisher, Thorton. 1918. "Grinding the Crank: Disillusionment Thy Name is 'Personal Appearance.'" *Moving Picture World* 16 February: 956.

Fuller, Kathryn. 1996. *At the Picture Show: Small-Town Audiences and the Creation of Movie Fan Culture*. Washington, DC: Smithsonian Institution Press.

"High Class Vaudeville at Orpheum This Week." 1918. *San Francisco News Letter* 12 October. Mary Pickford Scrapbook 31, Special Collections, Margaret Herrick Library, Los Angeles.

Jacobs, Lewis. 1968. *The Rise of the American Film*. New York: Teacher College, Columbia University.

Kerr, Catherine. 1990. "Incorporating the Star: The Intersection of Business and Aesthetic Strategies in Early American Film." *The Business History Review* 64. 3: 383–410.

Marshall, P. David. 1997. *Celebrity and Power: Fame in Contemporary Culture*. Minneapolis: University of Minnesota Press.

"Mary Pickford Adds Million to Bond Sale Here." 1918. Mary Pickford Scrapbook 30, Special Collections, Margaret Herrick Library, Los Angeles.

"Mary Pickford Appeals for Loan." 1918. *The Sun* 4 April: 5.

"Mary Pickford Convinces 20,000 in Wall Street Loan Should Succeed." 1918. *New York Tribune* 12 April: 5.

Parsons, Louella. 1918. *Chicago Herald*. Mary Pickford Scrapbook 30, Special Collections, Margaret Herrick Library, Los Angeles.

Slide, Anthony. 1978. *Aspects of American Film History Prior to 1920*. Metuchen, NJ: The Scarecrow Press.

"'Split Reel' Notes for Theater Men." 1917. *Motography* 11 September: 573.

Staiger, Janet. 2004. "The Future of the Past." *Cinema Journal* 44. 1: 126–129.

Tinee, Mae. 1918. "Mary Sells Her Little Bond for a Million." *Chicago Tribune* 21. Mary Pickford Scrapbook 30, Special Collections, Margaret Herrick Library, Los Angeles.

"To Entertain Lavishly." 1913. *Motography* 12 July 3: 11.

"When Players Appear in Person." 1917. *Motography* 25 August: 394.

Chapter 12

The Comfort of Carnage

Neorealism and America's World Understanding

Karl Schoonover

In 1952, *Life* magazine predicted that Italian cinema would pose an increasing commercial threat to Hollywood's domination of the US market if Italy continued to produce both "provocative films" and "provocative beauties" ("Italian Film Invasion" 1952). Indeed, *Life* traces the recent American success of these European imports to the seemingly contradictory lures of the realist image: the "raw honesty" of films like Roberto Rossellini's *Open City (Roma, città aperta,* 1946) derives, *Life* argues, from both their "moral conscience" and their "frank treatment of sex and violence."[1] Here, Neorealism provokes American spectators in two ways: it forces them to confront the urgent relevancy of foreign matters, while at the same time overwhelming them with prurient views of imperiled bodies. Above the headline "Italian Film Invasion," for example, the magazine supplies a promotional still from a recent import to illustrate the characteristic allure of this new and raw aesthetic. The caption reads: "Heroine of new Italian film *Voice of Silence*, a decent girl led into delinquency, sells off her clothes to get money to buy a car" (107).[2] For *Life,* the still "sums up the mixture of sex and naturalism which is the trademark of the postwar Italian film." The right-hand side of the image shows the back of a young woman's bare legs and arms. The body of this "half naked girl" looks awkwardly exposed and vulnerable—her flesh indecently white against the gloss of her high heels and the sheen of her black satin undergarments. Her legs hang as limp as her arms and are suspended in front of a crowd of smartly dressed young men and boys. This image raises the question: how was the American spectator for Neorealism envisioned during this period?

Any attempt to theorize the arrival of Italian post-World War II cinema on movie screens across the USA must contend with two divergent accounts of the mid-century American filmgoer that emerge during this period. On the one hand, critics suggested that the unprecedented success of Neorealist films such as *Bicycle Thief (Ladri di biciclette,* 1949, Vittorio De Sica), *Shoeshine (Sciuscià,* 1947, De Sica), *Paisian (Paisà,* 1948, Rossellini), *Germany Year Zero (Germania anno zero,* 1949, Rossellini), and *Open City* indicated the new commercial

HEROINE OF NEW ITALIAN FILM "VOICE OF SILENCE," A DECENT GIRL LED INTO DELINQUENCY, AUCTIONS OFF HER CLOTHES TO GET MONEY TO BUY A CAR

ITALIAN FILM INVASION

Figure 12.1 Illustration and title for an article appearing in *Life* (20 October 1952).

viability of "human interest" stories (Verdone). For perhaps the first time, moreover, distributors and theater owners believed that by appealing to humanitarian concerns and global communalism a film could increase its box-office receipts (Thompson and Bordwell 2003). Here, Neorealism's success would echo André Bazin's original aspirations for these films, which he thought would "open the hearts of everyone" and, at the same time, confirm the existence of "a wide moral audience among the Western nations" (1971, 71, 20). On the other hand, Neorealism's US promotion often emphasized the salacious character of these imported films, suggesting that their commercial viability depended upon the films' unique exposure of a sexualized and/or violated body. These contrasting accounts of humanitarianism and prurience combine in *Life* magazine's imagining of Neorealism's audience. At first glance, we see the magazine aligning us—and, implicitly, the US audience for Neorealism—with the young male viewers in the photograph. As readers and as members of a potential audience for foreign films, we are asked to join the voyeuristic crowd. We provide another set of leering wide eyes—our mouths agape—focused on a body. Our spectatorship is correlated to the boys' reactions: their eager eyes stand in for the American audience for imported films. However, the boys themselves are not only a corollary of our gaze. They are also its object. The limpness, nakedness, and blankness of the woman's body forces us to ask serious questions about why and how these boys ended up partaking in this scenario in the first place. In this context, the woman's body starts to look both sexualized and imperiled. In fact, upon closer inspection, some of the boys appear more troubled and disoriented than stimulated. This image ultimately illustrates how the realist film's "raw honesty" invites two gazes at once: one of titillation, but also one of concern.

If Neorealism invites both the socially concerned contemplative gaze of art cinema and the sensationalized voyeuristic gaze of exploitation cinema, then should we simply describe its audience as an incoherent bundle of contradictions? The simple answer is no. It is widely accepted that film audiences are internally diverse composite entities that often fail to confirm the coherence of industrial reception categories. Nor do they line up neatly with any particular social grouping that exists outside of the movie theater. Yet this fact should not dissuade us from analyzing how a period's dominant discourses imagine reception, anticipate engagement, and in so doing condition the sociopolitical remunerations of filmgoing. Over the course of this chapter, I plan to do just that by returning to the archive of Neorealism's US promotion and criticism to see how it articulates a vision of a mid-twentieth-century American spectator who is both less contradictory and more politically coherent than recent historicism would suggest. The orthodoxy of current film reception history understands the audience as a multifarious shape-shifter who makes a mockery of spectatorship theory. When applied to mid-century America, I argue, this intense focus on the pluralism of the spectator obscures an emergent ideal spectator envisaged by these films and their US advocates. What this imaginary viewer tells us about actual audiences is empirically inconclusive. However, I believe that apprehending this spectator—whom elsewhere I dub "the bystander"—is crucial for understanding the political aspirations of these films and for reassessing their supposed progressive impact (Schoonover).

Many histories of mid-century filmgoing anecdotally mention that Neorealism was often marketed as a quasi-pornographic spectacle, but rarely does the nature of this promotion significantly color historical accounts of the transitioning postwar film industry and its consumers. In his meta-critical essay, "Art, Exploitation, Underground" (2003), however, Mark Betz usefully identifies a "yes, but" gesture in the conventional historiography on this period: *yes*

Neorealism drew audiences by promising lurid content, *but* the popularity of these imports also points to the moral and cultural ascendancy of US audiences. This rhetorical evasion attempts to protect the idea of the newly reformed American viewer. In other words, this strategy sidelines any details that do not confirm conventional narratives of the American viewer's moral and cultural improvement after World War II. The "yes, but" gesture is only one way that historians retrofitted the duality of the realist image. A second strategy, also noted by Betz, revels in Neorealism's bi-vocal hailing of audiences, recognizing its heretical contradiction as historically significant. This inconsistent address is seen as either a harbinger of the fluid spectatorial affinities of the mid-century filmgoer or a symptom of a quasi-poststructuralist implosion of high and low genres. Coded taste distinctions that were once assumed to segregate social groups are, upon closer inspection, turned topsy-turvy by this period's texts, resulting in a leveling of cultural hierarchies. More recent studies approach the duality of Neorealism's address to US audiences by adopting a third strategy: a partial embrace of contradiction. Barbara Wilinsky, for example, draws on discourse theory to argue that Neorealism's promotion marks an "inconsistent public rhetoric" (2001, 67). For this historian, contradictions in this promotion's doublespeak symptomatically expose the nature of an emerging arthouse ideology, where commercial interests commingle with a sociocultural mission of goodwill and art snobbery. In their efforts to ignore, account for, or repurpose the duality of the realist image, each of these critical strategies clings to certain ethical ambitions for the mid-century audience. Since this duality of the realist image troubles recent scholars more than it did criticism from the period, however, these more recent approaches seem committed to distinguishing ethos from pathos in a way that this period's film culture did not. In the third strategy, for example, lurks an implicit moralism. Does the fact that viewers came to these films for cheap thrills necessarily contaminate the idea that Neorealism helped establish an audience aware of their global citizenry? Must ethical humanism begin with a bracketing of affect?

Positing hybridity, inconsistency, or multiplicity as an endpoint of our analysis of these audiences evades the possibility that this apparently contradictory address actually cues a single spectatorial protocol. Furthermore, the critical strategies described above distract us from how adroitly the period navigates the realist image and its draw on the viewer. Refusing to preserve a traditional division between pathos and ethos, the realist image that emerges from the US promotion of Neorealism is, I want to argue, principled and illicit at once. It is simultaneously artful and trashy, sensitively observant and brazenly beguiling, morally attuned and salaciously corporeal, intellectually rigorous and dissolutely excessive. Even if we account for the various industrial shifts in censorship, theater ownership, and product shortages, it remains clear that many Americans came to Neorealism for precisely this duality. I also want to emphasize that early advocates of these films did not see the duality of the realist image as a contradiction. Critics, distributors, promoters, and exhibitors depended upon the term "realism," I claim, not only as a code word for carnally explicit content (as Thomas Guback and others suggest), but also to reference a new practice that allows otherwise incommensurate extant modes of filmgoing to merge into a single viewing practice. As Betz states, art and exploitation cinemas "proceeded not simply as parallel alternate modes of film practice, but as shared discourses and means of address" (2003, 204). The postwar realist image made previously distinct, inflexible, and opposing categories of spectatorship suddenly appear analogous, coterminous, or commingled. In other words, the promotional materials and criticism from this period are uniquely sensitive to the competing lures of the realist film image and uncommonly aware of postwar filmgoing as an experience that invokes, enlists, and manages the viewer's multiple and conflicted identifications with the world onscreen. What we might today mistake for contradiction or inconsistency was in fact the invention of a new politics of engagement. Take, for example, Harold Barnes's review of *Germany Year Zero*, which proclaims that the film is "relentless," "savage and shattering" (1949, 18). In spite of this "inexorable impact" on the viewer (or perhaps because of it), the film is able to make a "coldly dispassionate appraisal" of the situation it depicts. As does Barnes, Neorealism's early advocates repeatedly posit sensate spectating as an experience integral to the new American postwar humanism. In their view, the experiential structure of the realist image works by assaulting the viewer with both an ethical plea and affective onslaught. In this account of realism's impact, an acutely postwar version of humanism appears in which somatic arousal grounds geopolitical sympathy and spectatorial sensation underwrites political judgment. In its concomitant address to both charitable humanism and puerile curiosity, I want to suggest, the realist image thus mirrored the structures of sympathy and disengagement underwriting large-scale international aid.

Returning to *Life*'s use of the still from *Voice* in this context, the unusual point of view that the realist image grants us comes into focus. In that image, our gaze originates from an extremely low and slightly canted angle that lends our perspective an exteriority. Alongside the image's contextualization by the article, this exteriority suggests that our relationship to corporeal spectacle does not exactly overlap with that of the audience of boys pictured. We are detached onlookers who both take in the spectacle of the female body *and* watch that body's viewing audience.[3] If *Life*'s text uses the photograph to allegorize the US spectator's encounter with recent Italian cinema, then we discover that realism not only expands the parameters of what the movie screen contains but also revises the terms of our engagement with that screen. The realist image provokes curiosity, generates enthrallment, and offers a venue for increased awareness through its lurid and unseemly implications. However, according to *Life* magazine's visualization of Neorealist spectatorship, the viewer often encounters the most startling of Neorealism's spectacles through an exterior viewpoint. In this sense, if the realist image supplies the immediacy of affect, it also offers the viewer the comforts of subjective alterity.

The writings of Manny Farber channel this movement between affect and alterity. In his review of *Open City*, Farber never quite resolves how depictions of war-torn Italy impact him (1946). He begins his assessment as if beleaguered by the film, suggesting that the onscreen world of worrisome destitution imposes wears and tears on the spectator. "There is a spirit of such depression, leadenness, consuming exhaustion and poverty in every note of . . . *Open City* that you wonder whether its extreme morbidity was intended" (1946, 46). Then suddenly Farber switches tone, delightedly spying on Italy's sordid physical and moral disrepair: "a dope addict, a 15-year-old prostitute, plus a lot of people on the fringes of scenes who look wonderfully shady and as if they would murder you for car fare" (46). For this critic, realism allows the viewer to confront and dismiss his/her reactions to the wretchedness of war. For example, Farber is conscious of how the film depends upon displays of corporeality to secure the realism of the image and to build audiences: the actors' bodies are all too convincingly worn-down and shrunken as a "wet string," as if from "years-long strain, bread-crumb existence, tension, and rebellion." "*Open City* shocks you because of its excessively realistic look," but this realism is not without its pleasures—pleasures that Farber both critiques and indulges. He admonishes the film for attempting to exploit moments of "unseemliness" and sex to generate box-office revenue, only to then change his moral course mid-sentence by adding snidely that *Open City*'s treatment of sex should teach Hollywood how better to depict women undressing.

We can trace a patterned repetition of alternating responses to the realist image in Farber's essay. Despite the "burdensome, graveyard quality" of watching this "grayest of all war movies," there are "flashes" when the film seems particularly fresh, and "these moments have the effect of a draft in the theatre." These graphic sequences not only distinguish the film aesthetically but also provide the viewer with intermittent flares of voyeuristic glee that pop out of an otherwise worrisome mix of poverty and oppression. Each seems to offer Farber a kind of consumptive pleasure akin to rubber-necking or common somatic responses to fireworks: "[T]he most graphic scenes [of violence and suffering] develop with the burst and intensity of an oil-dump fire." For Farber, cinema itself may supply an effective device for juggling contradictory political affects: Neorealism invites viewers to experience the realist image as both overwhelming engagement and a means of divesture.

Farber's account demonstrates the contiguity of two otherwise opposite ethics of viewing. His constant alternation between immediate empathic response and distanced mediated viewing reflects neither the incidental doublespeak of crass commercialism nor any simple reshuffling of taste, class, and political allegiance. Rather, it evinces a historically productive rearranging of the political work of spectatorship. The new spectator that emerges in the imagination of this period is, like Farber, a moviegoer comfortable with his/ her schizophrenic oscillation between overwhelmed engagement and conscious detachment and ultimately reconciled to his/her paradoxically intimate distancing from the onscreen world. The *Christian Science Monitor* outlines a similar journeying for *Germany Year Zero*'s spectators.

> [A]s the violent shock ... subsides, a perspective begins to emerge.... [The film's achievement] lies in the fact that each member of the world audience with what Mr. Rossellini calls "a heart capable of loving and a brain capable of thinking" will feel himself compelled to grasp for the deeper answers to the hard questions.
>
> (Beaufort 1949, 8)

The film initially devastates the viewer with shocking images and then offers that same viewer a means of transcending his/her own shock. In the process, the film has granted the viewer a special entry and status in the world community.

One critic—James Agee—was vocally suspicious of realism's graphic quality and expressed concern over how cinematic corporeality might actually detach the American psyche from the urgent social frailties brought on by the war. Like Farber and others, he appears aware of the strangely proximate distance afforded by realism. But more than these other critics, Agee remains deeply unsure of its political potential. He chastises Hollywood for the "safe fearlessness" of the social problem film and remains unimpressed with the caricatured realism of *The Best Years of Our Lives* (William Wyler, 1946), which "makes every punch [seem like] a kind of self-caress" (Agee 2005, 268). Agee accepts that a Hollywood pro-military film, like Paramount's *Wake Island* (John Farrow, 1942), strives to "convince, startle, and involve an audience" (475). In other words, the film reaches for complete spectatorial enthrallment in

> an effort to fill civilians with the image and meaning of a terrible and magnificent human event.... Toward that end, faces, bodies, machines,

rhythms, darkness, light, silence & [*sic*] sound must build up a tension which is a plausible parallel to human fact.

(475–476)

Yet, for Agee, "*Wake Island* is a cinematic defeat because it builds up this tension for brief moments, then relaxes" (476). At stake in this review is Agee's fear that films can cheapen the witnessing of violence, eroding the culpability of all Americans in the violence of war. We see this in his critique of *Wake Island*'s technique: "The silky panchromatic light which properly drenches a grade-A romance softens the strongest images of courage or death into a comfortable fiction" (475).

Agee finds this dangerous sequestering of affect at play in documentary as well as fictional realism. Ending his review of an American combat documentary in 1945, Agee suddenly questions why he has, just sentences earlier, advised readers to see the film, suggesting that its violent imagery may have unhinged his own critical equanimity. "I am beginning to believe that, for all that may be said in favor of our seeing these terrible records of war, we have no business seeing this sort of experience except through our presence and participation" (Agee 1945). For Agee, the shattering sensations of documentary realism so warp our perception that we gradually lose touch with political reality. The realist image of violence compares to the effects of pornography, and thus leads to the almost certain degradation of the viewer. While Agee's comments may sound retrograde and iconophobic at first, his analysis proceeds to make a startling link between realism's dependence upon the corporeal and the self-righteous geopolitical orientation of the postwar American subject. What pornography threatens to degrade in the viewer is not what we would immediately assume. The consumption of pornographic images leads neither to psychological deviance nor to socially destructive behaviors, but rather it encourages a self-satisfied smugness in the American viewer about his/her own place in the world. Pornography, it seems, is the guardian of a complacent status quo.[4]

As Agee describes this danger, his writing participates in a larger discourse seeking to imagine the postwar US moviegoer as a bystander, but he also harshly condemns that position:

> If at an incurable distance from participation, hopelessly incapable of reactions adequate to the event, we watch men killing each other, we may be quite as profoundly degrading ourselves and, in the process, betraying and separating ourselves the farther from those we are trying to identify ourselves with; none the less because we tell ourselves sincerely that we sit in comfort and watch carnage in order to nurture our patriotism, our conscience, our understanding, and our sympathies.

(Agee)

Compared to other cautionary tales of subjective numbness and affective lethargy that result in subsequent misbehavior, Agee's warning arises from his fear that graphic images disorient American viewers spatially, allowing them to disengage from a true political situatedness by projecting themselves into the sphere of false sympathy where conscience and understanding are mere affectations. Here, Agee is most troubled by the American viewer's acceptance of a position *incurably distant from participation*. The comfortable consumption of carnage precipitates a renewed political complicity.

This passage anticipates the ways in which American critical discourses would exploit the realist image. Inasmuch as the explicitness of that image triggers automatic ethical outreach, it also provides a transnational space in which spectators can ascertain their own political sovereignty in the new geopolitics of postwar recovery. This spectator is able to bear witness even when viewing from afar. Moreover, the spectator embraces the separation offered by the corporeal image because it strengthens the rightness of his/her inaction. In other words, the image perpetuates complacency by bolstering the idea that political action is best carried out by proxy.

Perhaps for these reasons, Agee's praise for Neorealism appears more fraught than the accolades of other US critics. Agee admires how Neorealist films transform affect into information and vice versa. In this respect, his assessment of these Italian imports seems similar to his colleagues. For example, the effectiveness of *Shoeshine*'s realism, a film "bursting at the seams with humane sympathy," is that it makes "information eloquent to the eye" (2005, 516). Agee also agrees that Neorealist films uniquely enable "understanding." However, his version of understanding does not originate from witnessing bodily violence. In fact, he applauds the American censors when they cut details of *Open City*'s torture scenes, arguing that the original print would only further indulge the "backstairs sadism" of American audiences. What makes Agee especially unique is how he uses his reviews of Italian films to insist upon the incongruence of US foreign policy and an ethics of humanism. For him, patriotism can never be humane. In his review of Luigi Zampa's *To Live in Peace* (*Vivere in pace*, 1947), he daringly identifies himself as, first and foremost, "a human being, [one] who would rather be a citizen of the world than of the United States" (2005, 328). Agee points out that the film's "deeply humane" outlook results from the way it dismantles the very same all-knowing and morally superior spectatorship so often fostered by lesser realisms. The film condemns any aspirations to impartial judgment as delusional by making all such positions untenable. The strength of this film's extreme perspectivalism is that no one escapes its soaring gaze: not even the filmgoer's point of view avoids its ruthless pitying or mocking scrutiny (2005, 328). In other words, Agee applauds the film for its interrogation of a spectatorial mode that we have seen elaborated in other texts and that I have called "bystanding." What makes this review so complex is how Agee claims Zampa's film provokes distanciation as a means of achieving a true humanism, while the film simultaneously exposes the hypocritical moralism of a false humanism based on the observer's detachment, removal, and self-appointed distinction from the object of his/her gaze.

In 1949, an American magazine for art movie fans, *The Foreign Film News*, announced the launch of its own national movie club: "Thousands of moviegoers from coast to coast are joining this new type of film society because they enjoy a different kind of screen entertainment and are interested in seeing foreign films gain popularity throughout the nation" ("Foreign Films" 1949). A benefit of becoming one of the club's "discriminating moviegoers" was the opportunity to view "complete versions of those films of adult entertainment that have not passed the censorship boards for release to the general public." Alongside this promise of uncensored content, the *News* reveals the club's lofty mission: "The Foreign Film Movie Club hopes it will be instrumental in fostering international good will and world wide understanding through the medium of the motion picture." Arguments for the worldwide circulation of films after the war reinvigorated the idea of moviegoing as a mind-"broadening" process. This revamping of spectatorship adopted the language of a liberalism that emerges with the formation of non-governmental organizations (NGOs), suggesting that an affective engagement with the realist image be considered equivalent to actual involvement in the global community. Through the experience of cinema, viewers could *feel* themselves participating in world politics without leaving their home town.

Considering the weight that American film history accords Neorealist films in the postwar transformation of film style and exhibition, it is tempting to read their initial box-office success as a sign of an emergent global humanist ethic in America. Even today, critics continue to cite postwar realism when they advocate for a cinematic "fostering [of] international good will and world wide understanding" ("Foreign Films" 1949). Jonathan Rosenbaum, for example, points to Bazin's religious faith in photographic registration as an effective premise for arguing that cinema is "a way for the world to keep in touch with itself—and that's clearly an issue today, even an urgent one when faced with the consequences of, say, American isolationism" (vii). However, if we are to accept the idea that Neorealism both fostered the American audience's intimacy with the postwar European condition and provided an aesthetic venue for the international ethics of sympathy, then, like Agee, we must also understand the exact aesthetic terms that Neorealism and its promotion negotiated for this transnational engagement. A postwar geopolitical attitude emerged from the interplay of distanced knowing and immersive affect that the realist image enabled.

For all its rawness and shattering effects, the realist image left the American viewer with a version of "world understanding" entirely commensurate with the political and social priorities of postwar US policy. These texts conceived of a spectator who was happy to have reaffirmed just how *incurable* was the distance between human rubble and the movie theater. The discourses surrounding Neorealism in the USA extended to the viewer the position of bystander. As an alternative to truly humane responses to suffering, this compromised mode of engaging in the world proposed an active involvement that came at little cost. In the end, we find the popularity of "human interest" and imported films in this period entangled with a paradoxical internationalism in which the gestures of sympathy, outreach, and aid strengthen only one nation's global sovereignty.

Notes

1. Conventional practice dictates that film titles are listed in the language of their country of origin. Because of this chapter's focus on the American context, I will be referring primarily to the US release titles and dates.
2. *La Voce del silenzio*, 1953, G.W. Pabst.
3. Neorealism's corporeal spectacles involve male and female bodies, as well as male and female viewers. *Open City*'s extended scenes of torture, for example, focus on exposed male bodies that were often subjected to the look of female characters.
4. For a different reading of Agee's use of "pornography" as a means of describing how violent images produce subjective exhaustion in the context of postwar culture, see Chapter 1 of Carolyn Dean's *The Fragility of Empathy after the Holocaust* (Ithaca, NY: Cornell University Press, 2004).

Works Cited

Agee, James. 1945. "Films." *The Nation* 24 March: 342.
———. 2005. *Film Writing and Selected Journalism*. New York: Library of America. Distributed in the US by Penguin Putnam.
Barnes, Harold. 1949. "The Truth Exactly [*Germany Year Zero* Review]." *New York Herald Tribune* 20 September.
Bazin, André. 1971. *What Is Cinema?*, trans. Hugh Gray. Vol. 2. Berkeley: University of California Press.
Beaufort, John. 1949. "Rossellini Film Shown in New York." *Christian Science Monitor* 24 September: 8.
Betz, Mark. 2003. "Art, Exploitation, Underground." *Defining Cult Movies: The Cultural Politics of Oppositional Taste*, ed. Mark Jancovich. Manchester: Manchester University Press, 202–211.
Farber, Manny. 1946. "*Open City* [Review]." *The New Republic* 15 July: 46.
"Foreign Films Movie Club Launched." 1949. *The Foreign Film News*. February, n.p.
Guback, Thomas. 1969. *The International Film Industry: Western Europe and America since 1945*. Bloomington: Indiana University Press.
"Italian Film Invasion." 1952. *Life* 20 October: 107–113.

Rosenbaum, Jonathan and Adrian Martin. 2003. *Movie Mutations: The Changing Face of World Cinephilia*. London: BFI Publishing.

Schoonover, Karl. 2008. "Neorealism at a Distance." *European Film Theory*, ed. Temenuga Trifonova. New York: Routledge, 302–318.

Thompson, Kristin and David Bordwell. 2003. *Film History: An Introduction* (2nd edn). Boston, MA: McGraw-Hill.

Verdone, Mario. 1951. "The Italian Cinema from Its Beginnings to Today." *Hollywood Quarterly* Spring: 270–281.

Wilinsky, Barbara. 2001. "Discourses on Art Houses in the 1950s." *Exhibition, the Film Reader*, ed. Ina Rae Hark. London/New York: Routledge, 67–75.

Chapter 13

"Talk About Bad Taste"

Camp, Cult, and the Reception of *What's New Pussycat?*

Ken Feil

During the "Springtime For Hitler" production number in *The Producers* (Brooks, 1968), an audience of Broadway first-nighters sits stunned and gaping-mouthed amid chorus lines in SS-dress piping praise for the Führer in swastika formations. Disgusted spectators stomp out, one blurting, "Well! Talk about *bad* taste." Moments later, the remaining crowd realize that "Springtime" deliberately aspires to what Susan Sontag calls the "good taste of bad taste": the blending or inversion of high and low taste categories, as well as a perverse delight in cultural works historically defined as "low" (Sontag 1966, 291; Taylor 1999, 51–52; Betz 2003, 202–203). *The Producers* remains one of the most memorable tributes to the good taste of bad taste (or good-bad taste) in 1960s cinema, but it is not the first.

Three years earlier, the sex comedy *What's New Pussycat?* (Donner, 1965) offers one of the first instances of when the "official" voices of film interpretation perceive a *mainstream* film *intentionally* to aspire to good-bad taste: as "camp" and "cult," among other trendy terms circulating. These labels also signify particular avatars of good-bad taste, namely urban bohemians, gays, and rebellious youth. My argument is that *What's New Pussycat?* poses a dual menace to culture critics in 1965: the threat of jettisoning traditional, bourgeois conceptions of high and low culture and the related hazards of intermingling "low" taste publics with the mainstream.

The larger argument of this chapter pertains to how scholarly histories approach this "talk about bad taste." Histories of bad taste, cult, and camp in the USA from the 1960s onward usually undertake the "marginal" method. Marginal histories tend to delimit the scope of study to one disenfranchised subculture, its oppositional activities, and, in some cases, its relationship to mainstream culture. Andrew Ross unpacks camp sensibility, for instance, as the separate expression of gay culture and the youth counterculture (1989, 135–144, 148–165). William Paul privileges youth culture when discussing politicized challenges to cultural hierarchies, from the "Dirty Words" movement to Hollywood movies (1994). Sasha Torres's and Barbara Klinger's

Figure 13.1 Poster of *What's New Pussycat?*

studies of mass camp treat gay, subcultural camp as the authentic original by contrast to its mainstream absorption and "de-gaying" (Cleto 1999, 16–22; Feil 2005, 166–169; Klinger 1994, 139–140; Tinkcom 2002, 187–194; Torres 1999, 339). These and other studies de-emphasize the "dialogues" among minority taste publics and foreshorten investigation into the margins *within* the mainstream. The talk about bad taste that pervades *mainstream* culture of the mid-1960s forces a reconsideration of this framework.

The popularizing of good-bad taste occurs through the interplay of a number of marginalized taste publics, namely African-Americans, gays, and young people, but crucially involves recalcitrant members of the mainstream who take "part-time" interest in these marginalized groups and sensibilities (Gans 1999, 110, 123; Taylor 1999, 87–88). Investigating these events requires inquiries into the intersections of marginalized groups and tastemak-ers, a dialogic conception of the margins and the mainstream, and a reconsideration of majority culture as more than just oppressive or cooptive toward minority culture and sensibilities.[1]

This chapter explores the interplay among various subcultures of good-bad taste in the mid-1960s—urban bohemains, gays, and young people—the mainstream negotiation of their sensibilities, and concern by critics about the toxic impact of "minority" tastes on "majority" taste and value systems. The reception of *What's New Pussycat?* provides the centerpiece for this historical investigation. Released six months into the popular "camp" craze, reviewers establish *Pussycat*'s good-bad taste through such labels as "camp," "cult," "hip," and "far out." They describe these sensibilities in terms that evoke subcultures of rebellious gays and young people: "homosexual," "childish," "juvenile," and "decadent," among others. In the spirit of good-bad taste, *Pussycat* also plunders the style and racy subjects of art films but, commentators claim, without any more meaningful content than celebrating vulgarity and immorality. Good-bad taste remains relatively harmless as the private plaything of urban artists, gays, and other disaffected hipsters. Once it reaches the mainstream, critics fear, "Art for art's sake" will devolve into "vulgarity for vulgarity's sake."[2]

Critics worry that if *Pussycat* achieves popular success, mainstream audiences will confuse this "vulgar," counterfeit art film with true art. Worse still, innocent spectators could adopt the perverse, "unwholesome" sensibilities that inform the film's aesthetic and message. In the eyes of bourgeois traditionalists, *Pussycat* muddies the distinctions between high and low, undermines "authentic" art, and blurs the lines between safe, mainstream taste publics and dangerous, deviant subcultures.

Camp, Cult, Gay, and Youth Culture: The Loss of Tradition and the Rise of Good-Bad Taste

For bourgeois purists of the 1960s, the popularizing of good-bad taste threatens what Pierre Bourdieu describes as "the sacrilegious reuniting of tastes which taste dictates shall be separated," an unacceptable offense to critics "who regard themselves as the possessors of legitimate culture" (1986, 192–193). Paraphrasing Lawrence W. Levine, good-bad taste's inversion of cultural hierarchies is "translated almost inevitably into an attack on the idea of culture itself" (7). *Film Quarterly*'s Diana Gould voices these concerns about "Establishment Camp" which enables audiences to "enjoy form without content" and films that defy critical evaluation, explaining: "a film cannot possibly be taken seriously by anyone" (1966, 57).

The "transgressions" of good-bad taste derive, in part, from the lifestyles of its dissident practitioners. As Bourdieu explains, "At stake in every struggle over art there is also the imposition of an art of living, i.e. the transmutation of an arbitrary way of living into the legitimate way of life which casts every other way of living into arbitrariness" (1986, 193). Earlier in the 1960s, such stakes fueled critics' homophobic jabs at the "camp" underground film movement, but this remained a safely insulated battle between high culture and various urban demi-mondes (Staiger 2000, 134–144; Suárez 1996, 91–94). Once good-bad taste reaches youth culture, traditionalist critics begin to worry about its impact on the "civilized" status quo.

Throughout 1965, the word "camp" circulates as a "catch-all term" for good-bad taste, prompted by the publication of Sontag's "Notes on 'Camp'" in 1964. Thomas Meehan's *New York Times* story from March 1965 defines this new sensibility through its headline: "Not Good Taste, Not Bad Taste—It's 'Camp'" (1965, 30). Culture pieces in *Time* (December 1964), *Life* (August 1965), and numerous others commonly identify camp as an inversion of taste categories, seizing on Sontag's "it's good *because* it's awful" (1966, 292). Pundits also notice inversion in camp's preference for style over content.

Mainstream newspapers and magazines pitch camp as a maverick sensibility cultivated by urban, underground, and queer constituencies. Even before Sontag's "Notes," reports about the New York underground cinema movement crystallize these associations (Staiger 2000, 142–148). Janet Staiger illustrates the "radical agenda" of the underground through a range of anti-bourgeois behaviors: midnight screenings of "camp" tributes to cinematic "trash"; spectators who talk back to films; and full frontal challenges to sexual, racial, and artistic norms (130, 136; Suárez 1996, 127–140). Meehan perpetuates a similar chain: "homosexual," "anti-Establishment," "perverse"; thriving throughout Manhattan, especially the "East Village" within "the so-called Underground" (1965, 30, 113). *Time* traces camp to "Manhattan's" Sontag, observes that "In matters sexual . . . Camp goes against the grain," and quotes Sontag about "Homosexuals" as camp's "vanguard" ("Camp" 1964, 24). In *Life*, Gloria Steinem flatly attributes a dissident, underground attitude to camp: "Homosexuals, who have always had a vested interest in knocking down bourgeois standards, are in the vanguard of Camp, though no longer its sole custodians" (1965, 84).

The attribution of good-bad taste to middle-class youth culture swiftly shifts camp's historical meanings.[3] Two 1965 articles about "cult" movie phenomena connect youth culture with "camp." Prompted by a Humphrey Bogart film festival at the New Yorker Theater (according to Meehan, "the most Camp movie theatre in Manhattan"), a *New York Times* article quotes theater owner Daniel Talbot about the youthful Bogart "cult." Bogart is "so hip," appealing to "college generation" admirers "disillusioned by idealism" and "suspicious of content"; "as content becomes less important, style becomes more important."

The article concludes by placing Bogart in "the cultural netherworld of 'camp,'" as "the modern anti-hero ... attempting to live outside the established code" ("Old Bogart" 1965, 19).[4]

Time magazine's description of the *Batman* youth cult closely resembles the underground in its affection for camp, Pop art, sexual perversity, comic books, B films, unruly behavior, and progressive attitudes. Once demonized by Dr. Frederic Wertham as "a wish dream of two homosexuals," Batman and Robin now reign as "high-camp folk heroes." Observations about college-town cultists watching the "badly produced" 1943 *Batman* movie serials approximate the "'camp' atmosphere'" and anti-racist politics of the underground: laughter at the overacting, yelling, and "boo[ing of] the opening episode's racist slurs" ("Return" 1965).

Articles abound declaring traditionalist alarm about the inversion of taste codes and moral codes. In a 1965 *New Yorker* short story, Calvin Trillin satirizes youth culture's adoption of "camp" and "androgyny" as the pretentious pursuit of status in a culture devoid of authentic values (1965, 40–41). A young man in drag (and member of the "all-male" Batman Club) explains, "'I myself am so heterosexual it's fantastic ... but if the ticket of admission to the avant-garde is an occasional pair of high heels, I say pay it" (41). The same character observes glibly that camp "'could spread until nothing in the culture has any value anymore'" (43).

Time magazine's "On Tradition, Or What is Left of It" (April 1966) offers an engaged censure of good-bad taste.[5] A theme of inversion and blurring runs among the litany of concerns, tying good-bad taste to the loss of values. The new "sexual morality" trumpets "nothing is inherently right or wrong." Theatrical productions parade "incest," "homosexuality," and "nudity," and "nearly every drugstore or bookshop is loaded with hard-core pornography ... solemnly reviewed by serious critics." In architecture, music, fashion, and décor, "'vulgar' is no longer a nasty word," but "good taste" is. Highbrow critic John J. Enck labels this condition "campopornography," a "monstrous triumvirate" (1966, 176–177).

Pundits agonize over a youth culture that inverts or blurs every value hierarchy, celebrating vulgarity as the "in" taste (Enck 1966, 170; "On Tradition" 1966). Within such anxious reasoning, once good-bad taste contaminates youth culture, it inevitably infects the mainstream. Steinem playfully confirms these fears, arguing that "camp" provides a "warning system" for future fashions while "teen subculture" and "college fads" signal "in" trends (1965, 73, 80).[6] Good-bad taste emerges through the 1960s art and underground cinemas, movie cults, and Pop art, generated by subcultures of hipsters, gays, and other habitués of urban bohemia. Youth culture discovers it, and eventually, so do mainstream audiences of *What's New Pussycat? Pussycat* presents the exact threats described by Bourdieu. As commercialized good-bad taste that shamelessly mimics art films, it pushes "the sacrilegious reuniting of tastes."

Notes on 'Cat, Knocks on Camp

When it opens June 22, 1965, *What's New Pussycat?* appears to traditionalists as a violation of art, mockery of monogamy and marriage, and a tribute to

Figure 13.2 Italian poster: *Ciao Pussycat*.

aesthetic vulgarity and moral degradation.[7] Detractors discredit *Pussycat* as an ersatz art film, its "far-out" and "campy" aesthetic of good-bad taste all superficial style without content. Authentic art movies unify form and content into a *whole work* of "art," making meaningful and motivated such stylistic innovations as fragmented form, references to films, and explicit sexuality (Bürger 1989, 55–56, 65–82). The perception of "art" enables critics to rationalize controversial content through the ethic of *ars gratia artis*, but *Pussycat*'s fragmentation, film quotations, and sexuality appear irrelevant, "decadent": vulgarity, style, and pleasure seem ends in themselves. Critics allude to the sources of *Pussycat*'s "decadence"—queer camp and youth cults—and signal its threatening impact.

Harriet R. Polt systematically illustrates how *What's New Pussycat?* trashes the traditional discourse of art by exalting style over content. Polt distinguishes "meaningful" stylization in 1960s films, such as *À Bout de Souffle* (*Breathless*, Godard, 1960), from the "cheaply come by and irrelevant" stylization of *Pussycat* (Polt 1966, 26–27). *Pussycat* apes the art film techniques that *Breathless* originates and others perfect, turning stylization into "a fashionable fillip to be given to every new, 'mod,' or 'camp' picture" (29) and offers the sorest symptom of stylization "used as an end in itself" (27).

Mainstream reviewers likewise identify *Pussycat* as style devoid of content or formal unity and, according to *Newsweek*, an art film forgery: "the whole nasty business is tricked up to look like an exotic flowering of the avant-garde cinema—frenetic, disjointed (above all disjointed)—and it batters the senses with the mindless insistence of a discothèque loudspeaker" ("Out" 1965, 91). Richard Schickel's review declares, "*Pussycat* has no internal rationale or logic" and "just more situations, each less logical and connected" (1965, 12). Among Bosley Crowther's many pans, he calls *Pussycat* "the loosest-jointed film" and kvetches later, "so aimlessly is it written and so wildly is it played" (1965a, X5; 1965b, 49).

Pussycat steals more than "disjointed" form from art movies; as Polt explains, it also pilfers "allusions to past films" (1966, 26). No one else in the sample connects this with art movies, but several view it as "hip," "in," "far out," or "camp."[8] *Commonweal*'s Philip Hartung wonders why "a comedy that means to be so far out ... is amazingly clogged with clichés ... O'Toole bumps into Richard Burton in a bar and says, 'Haven't we met before some place?' the obvious take-off on the whip scene in '8½'" (1965, 473). For Schickel, Woody Allen's screenplay "faithfully follows one of the cult's favorite sub-notions ... to resurrect the almost-forgotten, just too-much popular styles of other eras" (1965, 12). As Polt admonishes, "Style per se, like camp aesthetics, is momentarily amusing, but finally a dead end. Perhaps this is true decadence" (1966, 27).

The morbid "decadence" of *Pussycat*'s stylization materializes in the concept of good-bad taste and the word "camp." Schickel aims to expose the "star-filled, expensive, vulgar" *Pussycat* as "a witless attempt to cash in on the spirit of Camp which now blights our land . . . the esthetic view that something is good precisely because it is awful." The film's exploitation of "Camp" defines its "self-indulgent" goal, to assert "cultural superiority to those who . . . persist in the square notion that style is merely a tool, not an end in itself" (1965, 12). Crowther disparages *Pussycat* as "outrageously cluttered and campy, noisy and neurotic" (Schickel 1965b, 49) and defines *Pussycat*'s "deliberate absurdity" using the vocabulary of psychological and social disorder: "more expressive of madness than wit"; "the wildest kind of slapstick farce"; "anarchistic burlesques." Alongside *Cat Ballou* (Silverstein, 1965) and other current releases, *Pussycat* proves the most unstable patient in this new cinematic Bedlam. Its "neurotic decadence" strikes Crowther as "disturbing in its positive unwholesomeness" (1965a, xi).

"Absurd," "camp," and "decadence" converge as emblems of artistic and social decline and, by being associated with mental illness, immaturity, and sexual perversion, signify two increasingly disruptive social groups: gays and young people. Schickel's evaluation invokes current psychobabble and collapses the two groups, condemning camp as "regressive in its self-assertiveness. It is juvenilia. Which is why, of course, those pathetically arrested people, the homosexuals, are leading Camp followers." Such deviant immaturity in *Pussycat* resembles "an awful home movie in which . . . smug and bratty children grow sillier and sillier, naughtier and naughtier" (Schickel 1965, 12). For Crowther, *Pussycat*'s "neurotic decadence" also conjures up scenes of sexual perversity and immaturity, "as though the characters were all disturbed children engaged in violent, sex-tinged water-play" (1965b, 49). *Newsweek* likewise envisions a kinky kindergarten for maladapted adults: "**What's New Pussycat?** recommends itself 'For Adults Only' . . . It is only for adults who are willing to accept childish prattle about sex blocks, nymphomania, aphrodisiacs, virgins, sin and orgies as a substitute for adult entertainment" ("Out" 1965, 90–91). As Crowther sermonizes, *Pussycat* finally "goes into a wallow in slapstick sexuality and vandalistic antagonism toward the disciplines of society" (1965a, X5).

Crowther inspires two *Times* readers to endorse *What's New Pussycat?* by inverting traditional moral-aesthetic discourses. Robert A. Friedman supports *Pussycat* for the "young people of 1965" and dismisses the *Times* critic's comments as dated, bourgeois artistic criteria: "there is no standard by which to judge what is good and real. The picture is written aimlessly and wildly because it is realistic . . . an articulation of the contemporary scene that the reviewer has no knowledge of." Friedman challenges moral denunciations of the film as "'unwholesome' and 'antagonistic toward the disciplines of society'" with a political critique of US class exploitation and militarism

("Readers" 1965, xii). Friedman defends *Pussycat*'s aesthetic for the "young people of 1965," but the nearest example of a queer response arises in Saul Kent's correspondence. Reminiscent of Joe Orton's "Edna Welthorpe" letters,[9] Kent enlists the "put-on" and dons the drag of a concerned citizen objecting to *Pussycat*'s "corrupting influences." Appearing either woefully obtuse or covertly flirtatious, Kent venerates "Mr. Crowther" as "messianic" and glorifies "the tensile strength of his moral fiber." In light of Kent's "affection for pussycats," Crowther has rescued him from the film's "pernicious and hypocritical lure." Without righteous saviors such as Crowther, "society would soon crumble and disintegrate into dust" ("Readers" 1965, xii).

Schickel ends his review of *What's New Pussycat?* by inciting a "revolt against this latest form of cultural tyranny. Nothing could be a better corrective for Camp than a big expensive flop" (1966, 12). His wishes remain unfulfilled. The fifth highest-grossing film of 1965 and the top-grossing comedy, *Pussycat* helps solidify a mainstream market for good-bad taste and standardize a style (Bart 1965, xii; Cray 1965, 50; "Gross" 1966; "United Artists" 1965, 65; Vogel 1965, X7). Sexual frivolity, movie send-ups, and Pop color palettes spread among mainstream films and television such as *Casino Royale* (1967, produced by *Pussycat*'s Charles K. Feldman); *The Producers*; *Watermelon Man* (Van Peebles, 1970); *Myra Breckinridge* (Sarne, 1970); and TV's *Batman* (1966–1968), *The Monkees* (1966–1968), *Rowan and Martin's Laugh-In* (1968–1973), and *The Flip Wilson Show* (1970–1974). Mel Brooks's movies bring Jewishness into the mix of identities associated with good-bad taste, *Watermelon Man*, *Flip Wilson*, *Laugh-In*, and *Car Wash* (Schultz, 1976) incorporate African-American expressions of good-bad taste. Simultaneously, the "Midnight Movie" scene emerges as a kind of post-underground, cult-camp venue for queers, youth counterculture, and mainstream "part-timers." The peak of such convergence occurs when audiences rediscover two mainstream cult-camp failures, *Harold and Maude* (Ashby, 1971) and *Rocky Horror Picture Show* (Sharman, 1975). Fans form cults that renew mainstream interest and incite box-office success (Taylor 1999; Hoberman and Rosenbaum 1991, 1–14, 174–213, 298).

What emerges so vividly from this brief, *partial* history of good-bad taste in the 1960s is the continual location of the margins within the mainstream. *What's New Pussycat?* marks a breakthrough in the commercialization of good-bad taste, a sensibility with direct ties to purportedly subversive subcultures. To my knowledge, "marginal" histories of gay taste and youth fashions overlook *What's New Pussycat?* altogether, probably due to lack of much compelling evidence about either subculture's interest in the film. "Marginal" histories would probably characterize *Pussycat* as, to paraphrase J. Hoberman, "repackaged 'camp' for the American Heartland" (1991, 79) and, worse, "de-gayed" camp (Torres 1999, 339).

The mainstream reception of *What's New Pussycat?* engages impassioned talk about bad taste that invokes, not erases, the sensibilities and lifestyles of subcultural gays and young people. When critics merge these two groups, the film materializes radical potential. Here, the elasticity of sensibilities like "camp," "cult," and others actually works to the subversive advantage of "perverse spectators," neither reducing good-bad taste to a single subculture nor erasing ties to the margins. Good-bad taste's perceived threat to cultural stability and normativity consists in its resistance to compartmentalization, in terms of inverting or blending the categories of high and low taste, as well as the social constituencies of mainstream and subculture. This is precisely the menace discerned by reviewers of *What's New Pussycat?*.

Acknowledgments

Many thanks to Michael S. Keane, Carl Perry, Eric Schaefer, Michael Selig, Janet Staiger, and Jessica Wilton for their invaluable input; and Stoughton and Stucka, our "far-out" pussycats.

Notes

1. See Cleto (1999), Diawara (1992), Hall (1992), and Tinkcom (2002) for informative critiques of the "cooptation" argument.
2. Schickel (1965) makes this distinction between "private" camp taste and "deliberate" mainstream camp.
3. See Torres (1999, 333–340) and Robertson (1996, 120–129) on "Pop Camp" and the erasure of gay identity. See also Ross, who makes the application to 1960s youth culture (1989, 136, 151–152).
4. Meehan disputes "the opinion held by some" that Bogart is camp but concedes "there are camp performances in Bogart movies" by Peter Lorre, Sydney Greenstreet, and Elisha Cook, Jr. (1965, 113).
5. The article hints at camp through an opening quotation of Oscar Wilde. Following Sontag's lead (1966, 277–291), *Time* places special emphasis on Wilde ("Camp" 1964), and Meehan mentions him (1965, 30, 114).
6. Without making the connection to youth culture, Gans defines camp as a high cultural sensibility (1999, 105).
7. Objections to *Pussycat* compare closely to the impassioned denunciations of *Kiss Me, Stupid* (1964). The art film trend toward nudity and sexual explicitness drives reviewers to distinguish *Stupid* as a *vulgar, adult, commercial* film, *not* an art film or anything approaching art (such as satire). These concerns multiply with *Pussycat*. See Feil forthcoming.
8. *Time*'s review, "Tired Tabby," identifies *Pussycat*'s "rummaging eclectically through a whole range of comedy styles," and Crowther (1965b, 49) comments that the "many imitative tricks" warrant the title, "'What's New, Copycat?'"
9. Playwright Joe Orton wrote "trickster" letters, often under the pseudonym "Edna

Welthorpe," to various conservative establishments in 1950s/1960s London (Lahr 1987, 136–139).

Works Cited

Bart, Peter. 1965. "When the Cookie Crumbled." *New York Times* 7 November 7: xii.

Betz, Mark. 2003. "Art, Exploitation, Underground." *Defining Cult Movies*, ed. Mark Jancovich, Antonio Lázaro Reboll, Julian Stringer, and Andy Willis. Manchester: Manchester University Press, 202–222.

Bourdieu, Pierre. 1986. "The Aristocracy of Culture." *Media, Culture and Society*, ed. Richard Collins, James Curran, Nicholas Garnham, Paddy Scannell, Philip Schlesinger, and Colin Sparks. London: Sage, 164–193.

Bürger, Peter. 1989. *A Theory of the Avant-Garde*. Minneapolis: University of Minnesota Press.

"Camp." 1964. *Time* 11 December: 24.

Cleto, Fabio, ed. 1999. *Camp: Queer Aesthetics and the Performing Subject*. Ann Arbor: University of Michigan Press.

Cray, Douglas W. 1965. "Sidelights." *New York Times* 24 June: 50.

Crowther, Bosley. 1965a. "Is This Cinema of the Absurd?" *New York Times* 27 June: X5.

———. 1965b. "The Screen." *New York Times* 23 June: 49.

Diawara, Manthia. 1992. "Afro-Kitsch." *Black Popular Culture*, ed. Gina Dent. Seattle: Bay Press, 285–291.

Enck, John. 1966. "Campop." *Wisconsin Studies in Contemporary Literature* Summer: 168–182.

Feil, Ken. 2005. *Dying for a Laugh: Disaster Movies and the Camp Imagination*. Middletown: Wesleyan University Press.

———. forthcoming. "'Esthetically As Well As Morally Repulsive': *Kiss Me, Stupid*, 'Bilious' Billy, and Middlebrow Taste." Untitled Billy Wilder Collection, ed. Karen McNally. Jefferson: McFarland Publishers.

Gans, Herbert. 1999. *Popular Culture and High Culture*. New York: Basic Books.

Gould, Diana. 1966. "*Arabesque*." *Film Quarterly* 20 (Autumn): 57.

"The Gross Is Greener." 1966. *Time* 14 January. Time.Com. 2 February 2007 www.time.com/time/magazine/article/0,9171,835003,00.html.

Hall, Stuart. 1992. "What is this 'Black' in Black Popular Culture?" *Black Popular Culture*, ed. Gina Dent. Seattle: Bay Press, 21–33.

Hartung, Philip T. 1965. "The Screen." *Commonweal* 2 July: 473–474.

Hoberman, J. and Jonathan Rosenbaum. 1991. *Midnight Movies*. New York: Da Cappo Press.

Klinger, Barbara. 1994. *Melodrama and Meaning: History, Culture and the Films of Douglas Sirk*. Bloomington: Indiana University Press.

Lahr, John. 1987. *Prick Up Your Ears*. New York: Vintage Books.

Meehan, Thomas. 1965. "Not Good Taste, Not Bad Taste—It's 'Camp.'" *New York Times* 21 March: 30–31, 113–115.

"Old Bogart Films Packing Them In." 1965. *New York Times* 28 January: 19.

"On Tradition, Or What is Left of It." 1966. *Time* 22 April. Time.Com. 3 February 2007. www.time.com/time/magazine/article/0,9171,899152,00.html.

"Out of Joint." 1965. *Newsweek*, 12 July: 90–91.

Paul, William. 1994. *Laughing/Screaming*. New York: Columbia University Press.

"Pitching Camp." 1964. *Time* 25 December: 2.

Polt, Harriet R. 1966. "Notes on the New Stylization." *Film Quarterly* (Spring): 25–29.

"Readers Appraise Two New Films." 1965. *New York Times* 18 July: xii.

"The Return of Batman." 1965. *Time* 26 November. Time.Com. 3 February 2007. www.time.com/time/magazine/article/0,9171,834730,00.html.

Robertson, Pamela. 1996. *Guilty Pleasures: Feminist Camp From Mae West To Madonna*. Durham, NC: Duke University Press.

Ross, Andrew. 1989. *No Respect: Intellectuals and Popular Culture*. New York: Routledge.

Schickel, Richard. 1965. "A Witless Junkette to Too-Muchville." *Life* 9 July: 12.

Sontag, Susan. 1966. *Against Interpretation and Other Essays*. New York: Farrar, Straus & Giroux.

Staiger, Janet. 2000. *Perverse Spectators: The Practices of Film Reception*. New York: New York University Press.

Steinem, Gloria. 1965. "The Ins and Outs of Pop Culture." *Life* 20 August: 73–84.

Suárez, Juan A. 1996. *Bike Boys, Drag Queens, and Superstars: Avant-Garde, Mass Culture, and Gay Identities in the 1960s Underground Cinema*. Bloomington: Indiana University Press.

Taylor, Greg. 1999. *Artists in the Audience: Cults, Camp, and American Film Criticism*. Princeton: Princeton University Press.

Tinkcom, Matthew. 2002. *Working Like A Homosexual: Camp, Capital, Cinema*. Durham, NC: Duke University Press.

"Tired Tabby." 1965. *Time* 2 July. Time.Com. 2 February 2007. www.time.com/time/magazine/article/0,9171,833887,00.html.

Torres, Sasha. 1999. "'The Caped Crusader of Camp': Camp, Pop, and the *Batman* Television Series." Cleto, 330–343.

Trillin, Calvin. 1965. "Barnett Frummer and Rosalie Mondle Meet Superman." *New Yorker* 17 April: 40–43.

"United Artists Sets Profit Mark." 1965. *New York Times* 2 December: 65.

Vogel, Amos. 1965. "Films: Fashion of the Fashionable." *New York Times* 5 September: X7.

Chapter 14

Selling Out, Buying In

Brakhage, Warhol, and BAVC

Dan Leopard

In many historical studies of media-based art, Stan Brakhage and Andy Warhol stand as exemplars of a binary relationship situated as a struggle between oppositional and conformist versions of the avant-garde. Often, this relationship is understood as the degree to which media artists retain "autonomy" over the production of their work. In the historiographical sketch that follows, Brakhage and Warhol set the terms for understanding the discourse which grounds the avant-garde goal of an autonomous art practice while providing an opening for a look at the ways in which this goal has moved from individuals to institutions, notably the Bay Area Video Coalition in San Francisco. While admittedly brief, this chapter seeks to attend to the particular effects of a metaphor of agency—autonomy—on specific forms of media practice and production.

Selling Out

> The category "autonomy" does not permit the understanding of its referent as one that developed historically. The relative dissociation of the work of art from the praxis of life in bourgeois society thus becomes transformed into the (erroneous) idea that the work of art is totally independent of society. In the strict meaning of the term, "autonomy" is thus an ideological category that joins an element of truth (the apartness of art from the praxis of life) and an element of untruth (the hypostatization of this fact, which is the result of historical development as the "essence" of art).
>
> (Bürger 1984, 46)

It is not hard to find artists—painters, writers, filmmakers—who proclaim that their work remains "autonomous" from the commercial demands of consumer society (look to film festivals and gallery openings for specific examples). And it is hard to refute that some forms of art, such as painting and sculpture, retain a more or less "semi-autonomous" relationship to the social spheres in which they circulate (museums, galleries, and academia for the most part). It follows by drawing upon certain ideas in Hegel's aesthetic, in particular his linking of a world historical moment to a given style of art, that some art practices are more in sync with the larger political and social discourses within a society during a specific historical period (Hegel 1997). These assumptions may appear self-evident, but they represent the habitual acceptance of ideas previously considered radical or controversial. In becoming accepted as common sense, these radical notions over time have been incorporated into the intellectual fabric of daily life.

"Selling out," "giving in" to corporate culture, or even "dropping out," for that matter, are all the linguistic residue generated by the once radical idea of an autonomous social sphere encompassing art practice. What theorist Peter Bürger recalls, in the quotation cited above, is that the concept of artistic autonomy is itself a historical entity and that it represents an idea developed by artists confronting the industrial production of art under capitalism. Thus each new industrial form of art takes a turn at center stage in Hegel's world-historical moment: in the early twentieth century, cinema; at mid-century, television; now, in the early twenty-first century, the Internet. Each of these technological art forms sets the standard for influence and significance within contemporary visual culture. Not that the new forms have extinguished prior forms of art, but they have shunted them to the side, to a position observably distinct from the "praxis of life."

Given the shift in popular influence from the easel to the cinema in the early twentieth century, it makes sense that some visual artists chose to experiment with film as a new material for art. By adhering to the romantic notion of the individual artist as singular creative genius, these early film artists—such as Hans Richter and Marcel Duchamp—deployed filmmaking as an extension of the plastic arts and refused the larger production models developed at the time by Hollywood and the various emerging world cinemas. Thus they supplied the film-as-art movement with its founding assumption that an artist can take industrial tools and fashion a non-industrial product. The fragmented nature of film editing, the plasticity of the film negative, and the dissolution of the image into multiple frames matched well with the shock tactics and the disruption of the essential unity of the work of art that defined the project of what Bürger calls the historical avant-gardes. This term "avant-garde," associated in particular with Dada and Surrealism, took on greater significance in postwar America as a way to indicate clusters of radical artists working in advance of the general populace in matters aesthetic and, at times, political. More importantly, exploiting the term's origins in military jargon, the avant-garde in art stood against the encroaching visual culture of commercial advertising and Hollywood movies (what Theodor Adorno famously called the "culture industry") (Wood 2002).

The notion of the avant-garde within painting and sculpture found a parallel development in the, at times, overlapping world of alternative film practice and culminated in a form of bourgeois individualism most fully realized by the film work of Stan Brakhage. Brakhage's scratched painterly films of the late 1950s and early 1960s expressed the need for an autonomous outside, a transcendental space of possibility, beyond the stifling conformity that dominated art and cultural discourse of the period. Brakhage, by taking POV (point of view in film lingo) as the basis for the shot and by scoring and manipulating the physical material of the film, developed a practice that broke with the assumed photographic correspondence between representation and its subject, and thereby allowed what he saw as a purified expressivity to enter filmmaking. Although earlier filmmakers had used abstraction, Brakhage, following on from Jackson Pollock and the Abstract Expressionists, linked abstraction to the larger psycho-temporal features of human consciousness. He produced films as a form of myth-making by sticking tenaciously to his elemental fascination with film as the poetic expressive practice of an individual artist.

Of course, at the most basic level, Brakhage relied on the tools and materials of industrialized production to create his art films. Cameras and film stock, lenses and filters, all became necessary objects of consumption during the process of making his films. As 16 mm equipment and film stock grew in price (and following the theft of his camera in New York City), he eventually moved to working in Super 8. This smaller gauge consumer format allowed Brakhage to produce films at a lower cost and with more immediate results. He could shoot his film, have it developed, and then screen the actual reversal camera film positive without the need to use a lab to cut the negative or make a print. With this process, Brakhage assumed as autonomous a position one can have while still relying upon the industrial tools of filmmaking, but the results of this autonomy may also be seen as subjecting Brakhage and his work to a withering of influence.

Over time Brakhage's films have been canonized within the narrowly institutional discourse of avant-garde film scholarship while having been for the most part forgotten by the mainstream academic and popular discourse of film culture. Bürger identifies the social position of avant-garde artists (not to be confused with the status of their artworks) by suggesting that the "aesthetic experience is the positive side of that process by which the social subsystem 'art' defines itself as a distinct sphere. Its negative side is the artist's loss of any social function" (1984, 33). Beyond accruing cultural capital for academics and fellow avant-garde filmmakers, it is unclear what function Brakhage had within society (to say this is to make a sociological as opposed to an aesthetic judgment). His handwritten signature—"By Brakhage"—on films such as *Dog Star Man* (1962–1964) seeks to signify the hand of the artist in fashioning an art object out of an inherently technological medium. But this mark of the romantic genius isolates the work and the artist from the sociality necessary for the production of art and culture using the industrial model. It is a refusal that comes with a price. It is harsh to say that Brakhage the artist is functionless (though *not* autonomous), but it follows from the value system generated by capital.

Buying In or Selling Out as Artistic Gesture

> Even if the problem of where exactly to site the crucial rupture is set aside, to think of [Andy Warhol's] early films as categorically different from the late ones is thus possible only by disregarding the master thematics that continue through them: the mass mediation of all subjectivity, and the permeation of all artistic activity by the culture industries, a fact that has deterred neither the proponents of autonomous art from dismissing the late works nor the mass culture apologists the early ones.
>
> (James 1996, 154)

The "crucial rupture" that film historian David E. James refers to in Andy Warhol's film work is the one separating Warhol's early films such as *Empire* (1963–1964) and *Sleep* (1963–1964), composed of static shots held for long durations, and the later films such as *The Chelsea Girls* (1966) and *Lonesome Cowboys* (1967), essentially homages to Hollywood genre films revolving around the cult of the micro-celebrity. Many Warhol scholars find one set of films to their taste and need to exclude the others in the terms laid out by James.

Contrary to Brakhage's practice as sole expressive force behind his work, Warhol assumed a duplicitous relationship with the very culture from which earlier artists had tried to remain autonomous. If the historical avant-gardes hoped to find the essence of art in its autonomy from the compromised social world of institutions, then Warhol seemed to counter with a non-essentialized position that situated his art practice in dialogue with mass culture, as critique and homage, thereby frustrating both autonomous and mass cultural readings of his work. He actively cultivated celebrity status for himself and for the performers associated with his art. He appropriated imagery from commercial advertising and Hollywood cinema as subjects for his paintings and silkscreens. Going further, in his later art and films he sought to mimic the production model of capitalism by instituting an art world production line in his studio which he christened "The Factory."

His early films had been grounded in formal approaches that confounded the conventions of avant-garde film practice as exemplified by Brakhage. Many of these formal tropes were later incorporated into the body of theory and practice surrounding structural film: long takes, static shots, and few signature effects that could be attributed to the artist (of course, Warhol's formal anti-style became identified as his signature style by critics referencing his early films). These early films were not necessarily more challenging for audiences than other avant-garde films at the time, but they provided an aesthetic position in opposition to the majority of these other films. By upsetting the conventions that had developed within the avant-garde itself, Warhol altered the discourse that was viable within the framework of an increasingly historically situated, and less politically potent, avant-garde. His explicit incorporation of the structures of commercial art production, including the publicity machine that envelopes Hollywood celebrities and his use of the burgeoning media culture as subject matter, implicated art as complicit with the power of capital: whether intentional on his part or not, this point is often debated within art critical circles.

As his early films gained success within the limited domain of art film production, he once again initiated a change in his art practice. He began to "produce" films that were conspicuously co-directed, at first, and then wholly directed by others in his Factory entourage, most often Paul Morrissey. However, by distancing himself from the actual hands-on work of art-making, by reducing his role to signing art after its completion by others, either directly as in paintings and silkscreens or indirectly as in credits for films and performances such as those by the rock group Velvet Underground, Warhol invoked earlier traditions within art production while assuming the role of producer as conceived by the Hollywood studio system. Thus, the Factory may be viewed as a 1960s version of the Renaissance guild system with those who frequented the Factory standing in for apprentices (the celebrities and groupies) and journeymen craftspeople (more accomplished artists such as Morrissey and Lou Reed).

Of course, Warhol's signing of works not directly produced by him may also be seen as a critique of artisanal forms of artistic technique and creative authorship: the basis for Brakhage's work. Whereas Brakhage's signature reaffirms the hand of the artist in producing a given film, Warhol's signature through productive absence is at once a thumbing of his nose at the institutionalization of art (in line with Bürger's reading of the historical avant-gardes) but also a marking of an object with the force of artistic signature. Warhol's work produced by the Factory does not hide the author so much as it confers a singular authority on his signature as artistic gesture. The technique of art is effaced—that signature style or brush stroke by which artistic careers are made—to be replaced by the signature itself: sole repository of the role of the artist in a society of exchange value.

All of Warhol's later work may be seen as some version of this gesture of signature. Warhol seemed to be fully aware of the celebrity nature of his gestural act: his stated desire to be a "business artist," and his ads for Seagram's and Absolute Vodka function as riffs on celebrity not dissimilar to his silkscreens of the rich and famous (or his white shock wig for that matter). Thus *Andy Warhol's Dracula* (1974, Paul Morrissey) is a Warhol film by virtue of the signature embedded in the commercial nature of the work itself as much as it is a film by Morrissey. *Andy Warhol's Dracula* stands as an extension of the production models that Warhol had already initiated in the work of the Factory.

A Model for Selling Out

> The institutional and nonprofit worlds have converged in unique ways in the field of independent video. The very reproducibility of videotape as well as its time-based properties placed it squarely outside of the commercial art world market ... The notion of an art form intrinsically set outside of the traditional art market dovetailed easily with the anti-art-market movements of the 1960s. Here, many thought was a medium that simply could not be co-opted by the commercial art world.
>
> (Sturken 1990, 111)

The introduction of the Sony Portapak in the late 1960s at once opened up the possibilities that eventually led to video art while simultaneously closing down other possibilities, in particular those that had come to define avant-garde film production. The conversion to one-half-inch video as the format for consumer and industrial use was not in response to the needs of artists, filmmakers, or even home movie enthusiasts but arose from an effort by corporations, such as Sony and RCA, to expand the market for event recording through easier-to-use (and more expensive to acquire) technology. The relatively rapid adoption of video ended any misplaced conviction that avant-garde film artists could retain a vestige of an autonomous art practice as the film stocks on which they depended were discontinued and the corresponding cameras became relics maintained by collectors.

Given this background, it is notable that the comments by communication scholar Marita Sturken come from a book co-published by the Bay Area Video Coalition (BAVC) (Hall and Fifer 1990). BAVC was one of a group of alternative media organizations that opened in San Francisco in the late 1970s. BAVC presents a particular case in that it was initiated by a coalition of video artists and community-based media producers and was funded by a series of grants from the Rockefeller Foundation (Sturken 1987). By providing video production and post-production rentals at low cost to artists and community activists, BAVC created a space for production situated between the workaday world of industrial video and the increasingly cliquish world of public television (which had provided key support for early video art under the aegis of other Rockefeller initiatives such as The New Television Workshop at WGBH in Boston and the National Center for Experiments in Television at KQED in San Francisco).

At the outset, BAVC embodied the aesthetic radicalism and the equally radical politics that characterized the San Francisco media arts scene of the 1970s. Given this, BAVC seems to represent the goal of Bürger's historical avant-gardes in that the interpenetration of art and the praxis of life guided the process by which projects were selected to receive production support. Projects that seemed too commercial were simply turned away or charged fees that matched commercial facilities. Projects that reflected the underlying left politics or modernist aesthetics of the BAVC selection committee, regardless of the experience or technical abilities of the project's producer, would find increased access to equipment and funding. At least initially, under this selection process a considerable amount of video art came to fruition due to the clearly defined mandate to support alternative forms of media: a mandate that leads back to, in many instances, the critique of institutions favored by the historical avant-gardes.

As Brakhage and Warhol depended on relatively low-cost tools in order to produce their films, many video artists in the early 1970s also embraced a low-tech, do-it-yourself aesthetic. Shooting on tape, then leaving the tape unedited or minimally edited, these artists produced work that refused the conventions of network television. But just as Warhol had initiated a more complex and more ambivalent relationship with the glitzy lowbrow culture of Hollywood, many video artists moved in the early 1980s toward producing increasingly visually sophisticated work that came to depend on expensive high-end technology. Consequently production values were ratcheted up as using the latest in video post-production techniques, and special effects became the norm. Even a modest grant of $10,000 from the American Film Institute (modest by Hollywood standards) could no longer cover the budgets needed by established video artists.

Video art became a practice dependent on institutional support of one kind or another. Universities and colleges, media arts organizations, and galleries and museums all functioned as intermediaries in the process of making work "that simply could not be co-opted by the commercial art world" as Sturken suggests was the thinking at the time (1990, 111). As the 1980s progressed, video art outside of these institutions became difficult to produce. With the advent of MTV, there was a brief moment when artists with viable technical skills could support their more personal and political artworks by producing music videos on the side. Other artists simply stopped producing video and returned to painting or photography as conservative politicians attacked government grants for media art and systematically defunded them, resulting in the majority of public financial support for media-based art being discontinued altogether.

Within this transformed cultural and economic terrain, BAVC found it necessary to transform itself from an arts institution emphasizing the production of video art and community-based media into a regional training center for video production and new media technologies. Silicon Valley companies such as Apple Computer, Macromedia, and Sun Microsystems heavily funded and supported this transformation (Hochleutner 2001). BAVC continues to provide support for alternative media, but the actual daily activities engaged in at its facilities—training for jobs in industry—suggest that any form of social or cultural critique, by necessity, will be extremely compromised. As the move to video had shut down the possibilities available to film artists, the advent of new media and money flowing up the peninsula from Silicon Valley has shut down historically important media-dependent forms of radical politics and aesthetics.

Looking at Brakhage, Warhol, and BAVC, one sees several responses to the desire of the avant-garde for an autonomous art practice. As I have suggested throughout this chapter, each response actually represents a "semi-autonomous" practice in negotiation with the historically and politically contingent forces of industrial production. Brakhage sought to find autonomy by refusing the aesthetic demands of the culture industry. Warhol sought to endgame the culture industry by producing a critique through an aesthetic of excess consumption. And BAVC sought to create an institution that fostered autonomy (bringing with it the residual notions of the artist as individual expressive agent—Brakhage's signature—and as collective entity—Warhol's signature), but market forces and a withering of the dynamics of post-1968 politics eventually undermined the goals of its original charter (Blau 2004). As of now, BAVC's signature is its brand as applied to the various areas of its website and to its training brochures.

Of course, what I outline here is the history of one phase of a metaphor that has sustained artists during modernity (and, for the most part equally, during the period that has been delimited as postmodernity). But how does autonomous art practice as a metaphor of agency—metaphor in the sense used by George Lakoff and Mark Johnson as a conceptual frame that structures action (2003)—transfer from individuals to institutions? One possible answer is that the people who organize these institutions are themselves drawn to autonomy as a political and artistic goal. A second possibility is that the intertwining of artists and institutions within the historical avant-gardes has blurred the boundaries between agency as individual action and agency as collective action. As Warhol famously stated he wished to become a "business artist," then perhaps as Warhol retained the whiff of the *au courant* artist while shilling for Seagram's and Braniff, BAVC should be considered as advancing its original mandate by exploiting the culture and commerce of Silicon Valley corporations for the benefit of independent media producers.

While the gap between the history of the media-based avant-gardes and those of more mainstream media needs bridging (which involves crossing disciplinary boundaries), it is also important to look at the intellectual trajectories of ideas that bleed across "discourse networks." As media theorist Friedrich Kittler suggests, one must look at "the *source* of these discourses, of the *channels* or the *receivers* of discourse in the form ... of readers or consumers" (Armitage 2006, 19). In this instance, the channels for the discourse networks of the idea of an autonomous art practice are Brakhage, Warhol, and BAVC. After all these years (and following the decline of the historical avant-gardes), the notion of an autonomous form of art practice still plays as large at Sundance with its auteurs of independent cinema as it does on the Internet with its activist's vision of "information wants to be free" (as a common slogan bandied about the web during its formative period proclaimed). This is not to say that the compromised position of art and media in relation to institutions is necessarily one that needs to be condemned as an a priori "bad" discourse. But it is important to state that simply to discount the possibility of at least a negotiated form of "semi-autonomous" art practice, whether applied to film, video, or new media, is to deny the possibility of a future praxis grounded in a politics that can imagine alternatives.

Works Cited

Armitage, John. 2006. "From Discourse Networks to Cultural Mathematics: An Interview with Friedrich A. Kittler." *Theory Culture Society* 23.7–8: 17–38.

Blau, Andrew. 2004. *Deep Focus: A Report on the Future of Independent Media*. San Francisco: National Alliance for Media Arts and Culture.

Bürger, Peter. 1984. *Theory of the Avant-Garde*, trans. Michael Shaw. Minneapolis: University of Minnesota Press.

Hall, Doug and Sally Jo Fifer, eds. 1990. *Illuminating Video: An Essential Guide to Video Art*. New York: Aperture.

Hegel, G. W. F. 1997. *Reason in History: A General Introduction to the Philosophy of History*, trans. Robert S. Hartman. Upper Saddle River, NJ: Prentice Hall.

Hochleutner, Mike. 2001. *Bay Area Video Coalition (BAVC)*. Stanford, CA: Graduate School of Business, Stanford University.

James, David E. 1996. "The Unsecret Life: A Warhol Advertisement." *Power Misses: Essays across (Un)Popular Culture*. London: Verso, 153–171.

Lakoff, George and Mark Johnson. 2003. *Metaphors We Live By*. Chicago, IL: University of Chicago Press.

Sturken, Marita. 1987. "Private Money and Personal Influence: Howard Klein and the Rockefeller Foundation's Funding of the Media Arts." *Afterimage* 14.6: 8–15.

———. 1990. "Paradox in the Evolution of an Art Form: Great Expectations and the Making of a History." *Illuminating Video: An Essential Guide to Video Art*. Eds. Doug Hall and Sally Jo Fifer. New York: Aperture, 101–121.

Wood, Paul. 2002. "Modernism and the Idea of the Avant-Garde." *A Companion to Art Theory*, ed. Paul Smith and Carolyn Wilde. Oxford: Blackwell, 215–228.

Chapter 15

Whatever Happened to the Movie-of-the-Week?

[The Shocking True Story of How Made-For-TV Movies Disappeared from the Broadcast Networks]

Alisa Perren

In 1991, Gary Edgerton published an essay in which he called for a reconsideration of the made-for-television (MFT) movie and its importance to network television (2003, 209–230). By the early 1990s, made-for-television movies were widely perceived to be a disreputable form, full of clichés, overly dramatic moments, and overwrought performances. Edgerton's essay provided a corrective to such conceptions. He illustrated how, during the classic network era, the genre was not only among the most prestigious of televisual forms but also a "fundamental programming staple of network television" (211). To understand MFTs, Edgerton argued, one had to understand the economic and industrial conditions in which they were made (221).

More than fifteen years have passed since Edgerton wrote his essay. Today, MFTs have all but disappeared from network television. Whereas in the mid-1970s more than 100 such films aired annually on the broadcast networks, by 2006 the number had fallen below a dozen (Reynolds 2005, 14). This is not to suggest that MFTs have disappeared from television. In fact, they remain a prominent form on several cable networks. Throughout the mid-2000s, more than a hundred total original films aired annually across such varied program services as Lifetime, HBO, the Sci-Fi Channel, and Hallmark (Moss 2005, 8).

Although MFTs continue to have a presence on television, they are usually targeted to and viewed by much more narrowly defined audience niches than they were during the classic network era in the 1970s. Indeed, MFTs' industrial and economic roles—as well as the ways they are valued culturally—have shifted dramatically in recent years. This chapter explores how the made-for-television movie has changed from the mid-1970s to the present day. The first section returns to Edgerton's work, re-examining claims he makes about the industrial and textual characteristics of the MFT. The second reframes his assertions in light of the significant developments that have taken place both in television as well as in the larger media landscape. This section also traces the gradual ways in which the movies themselves underwent notable shifts during the 1990s and early 2000s. The third section explores key factors contributing to the nearly complete disappearance of MFTs from broadcast schedules during the mid-2000s.

The following study of the transformation of the MFT provides a focused means by which to assess how television's cultural and institutional roles have shifted from the classic network era into the present digital age.[1] This study also suggests the extent to which MFTs as a genre have become associated with specific taste cultures. In particular, the vast majority of MFTs now produced are targeted to (and thus associated with) viewers who, by virtue of their gender (female), location (rural/suburban), and age (over 50), broadcast networks devalue. The popular press and industry often see those who watch MFTs as being less desirable as viewer-consumers.

Toward the end of the classic network era, critics and the press began to view MFTs as low-culture products. This was partly a function of the genre growing tired due to excessive recycling of storylines and overdependence on the form throughout the program schedule. In the contemporary post-network era, MFTs have not only fallen out of favor with the press but with the broadcast networks as well. As broadcasters have become more focused on pursuing upscale "quality" audiences and younger viewers with edgier fictional series and reality programming, MFTs—and their assumed audience—have been marginalized. MFT viewers, in turn, have been relegated to a limited number of niche channels such as Hallmark and Lifetime.

In order for an MFT to avoid being perceived as undesirable, it needs to be explicitly framed as an "event" or positioned as a "motion picture" rather than a "made-for-television movie." The very label of "made-for-TV movie" has come to evoke powerful negative connotations. Notwithstanding Edgerton's call for greater respect, MFTs remain absent not only from the broadcast networks but from recent scholarship on television (but see Gomery 1984; Levine 2007).

To some extent, the limited discussion of MFTs in scholarly literature is not surprising. MFTs are far more difficult than series television programs to track in reference books, trade publications, and newspapers. They are rarely covered or reviewed unless they are high-profile event programs such as *Broken Trail* (AMC, 2006) or they come under scrutiny for their historical accuracy, as was the case with ABC's *The Path to 9/11* (2006). Typically, only those movies that have won numerous awards or attracted media attention are released on video.

These factors all pose problems for scholars wanting to understand their presence—or lack thereof—on television.[2] Yet as I will indicate, by thinking more about why and where MFTs have and have *not* shown up on contemporary television, we can come to a fuller understanding of the medium's shifting economic, institutional, and cultural roles. Prior to this, it is important to highlight the key components of Edgerton's essay.

A Scheduling Staple: The Made-For-TV Movie in the Classic Network Era

Edgerton provides a useful foundation to begin the comparison of classic MFTs with contemporary MFTs.[3] He notes a number of prominent traits typifying MFTs—traits which, in retrospect, may be seen as fundamental characteristics of the network era itself. First, by the early 1970s, MFTs aired regularly on all three broadcast networks. At different points, each network had at least one regular time slot devoted to the movie of the week (Edgerton 2003, 221).

The second trait was their consistency in content from one network to the next. Edgerton observes that the same small group of suppliers produced programming for all three networks. Further, the networks viewed women aged between 18 and 49 as the primary demographic (though often the audience would be much broader than this). In order to appeal to the most viewers, networks favored "soft" content. "Softness" here meant the films lacked sex, violence, action, and special effects (218).

A third trait involves the cultural status of MFTs during their heyday. Namely, they were "prestige" products that in the best of cases, as with *Brian's Song* (1971), *Eleanor and Franklin* (1976), and *Something for Joey* (1977), garnered awards and accolades. Praise accompanied many of the MFTs, regardless of whether they were contemporary docudramas or historical dramas, stand-alone programs or mini-series. Only when they entered what Edgerton calls their "mature" phase in the late 1970s did MFTs come to be seen in an unfavorable light (224). He perceives this to be when innovation and variation in MFTs diminished. In the wake of a seemingly never-ending deluge of "disease of the week" and "women in jeopardy" stories, the genre appeared to be exhausted. Nevertheless, the networks did not cease production of such films but rather continued apace into the 1990s. At the same time, the emerging Fox network along with cable program services including Showtime, TNT, and HBO regularly featured MFTs on their schedules.

Cumulatively, the industrial, textual, and cultural traits of MFTs were consistent with television programming during the classic network era. They were suited to the three-network system, a system that relied on regularity and standardization. In sum, MFTs were often among the most widely viewed programs in television history. Their popularity reinforced television's status as America's mass medium. As Edgerton observes, with 130 million people watching one of the most successful MFTs, "a case can be made that *Roots* was the programming peak of the network era" (223). Such numbers were only possible at a time of limited channel choices and few technological alternatives.

Into the Neo-Network Era: The "Mature" Phase of the Made-For-TV Movie

Roots (1977) was more than the peak of classic network era television. It also marks the beginning of the end of television as a mass medium and the decline of the decades-long hegemony of the three-network system. During the neo-network era of the mid-1980s to the mid-2000s, the long-standing authority of the networks gradually diminished. Although the networks continued to target mass audiences with some programs, they focused their efforts on pursuing certain niche audiences (e.g. teen girls, young professionals) viewed as especially desirable to advertisers.[4]

Following the lead of cable and the newer broadcast networks, the Big Three increasingly cultivated and promoted their own brand identities. New types of programming were acquired that sometimes clashed with the long-established images of these networks. The older skewing CBS thus began its partnership with super-producer Jerry Bruckheimer—a lucrative relationship which ultimately led to such graphic crime dramas as *CSI* (2000) and *Cold Case* (2003). By the early 2000s, CBS's forensic mysteries so heavily dominated its schedule that it was jokingly referred to as the "Crime Broadcasting System" (Schneider and Adalian 2006, 1).

As CBS's move into crime dramas suggests, the emphasis on more demographically targeted material came in tandem with the broadcast networks' growing focus on "edgier" content (Curtin 1996). Such programming continued to test the boundaries of acceptability in terms of sex, violence, language, and the FCC's indecency regulations. The networks began pushing the decency envelope in an effort to stem the tide of viewer erosion and to stand out amidst an ever-more crowded media-sphere.

By the early 2000s, the networks had become something very different. Not only were there twice as many of them, but they had also altered their programming and marketing strategies and redefined what demographic groups were considered most "ideal." In addition, they were now vertically and horizontally integrated. The programming they developed needed to serve the interests of their reconstituted structures. As I will show, made-for-TV movies held a smaller and smaller place within these structures.

Looking at the shifting status of the MFT from the 1990s to the mid-2000s indicates the extent to which the transition into the neo-network era was a gradual and uncertain one for the established networks. Off and on, the broadcast networks retained a weekly slot on their schedules for MFTs. Such films as *Leona Helmsley: Queen of Mean* (CBS, 1990), *A Place for Annie* (ABC, 1994), and *Serving in Silence: The Margarethe Cammermeyer Story* (NBC, 1995) continued to dot the air. However, the movies themselves started to veer away from the docudramas, biopics, and historical dramas that previously predominated.

Along with these types of movies came a growing number of literary adaptations, costume dramas, musicals, and epic mega-productions.[5] For example, ABC and Oprah Winfrey co-presented a handful of MFTs including *Tuesdays with Morrie* (1999) and *Their Eyes Were Watching God* (2005). These films suited Oprah's brand image and featured prominent actors such as Jack Lemmon and Halle Berry. Concurrently, ABC initiated a series of musicals and musical-based productions including *Cinderella* (1997), *Annie* (1999), and *Life with Judy Garland: Me and My Shadows* (2001).

While ABC focused on sentimental literary adaptations and colorful musicals, NBC teamed with producer Robert Halmi, Sr. for grandiose action-packed, star-laden spectacles including *Gulliver's Travels* (1996), *Merlin* (1998), and *Jason and the Argonauts* (2000).[6] Here the focus was on fairy-tales, classic literature, biblical stories, and fantasy. These were "event" broadcasts which simultaneously echoed 1950s programming executive Pat Weaver's "spectaculars" and the 1960s-era Hollywood studios' theatrical super-productions. They were designed to bring big ratings boosts to the networks and were usually aired during sweeps weeks. Although initially they performed well, their ratings declined as the 2000s wore on. The last Halmi production to air on NBC was *The Poseidon Adventure* (2005). Subsequently, ABC broadcast the two-part mini-series *The Ten Commandments* (2006). For its time slot the biblical epic earned the highest ratings in terms of total viewers with an audience of 13.8 million. However, the *Los Angeles Times* perceived its performance as just "so-so" because it lost in the crucial 18 to 49 demographic (Collins 2006, E3). Notably, the rating of 4.4 for part one of *The Ten Commandments* brought it into second place behind Fox's serialized drama *24*, which earned a 5.0 rating in the 18 to 49 demographic.

Much as 1960s-era theatrical releases *Cleopatra* (1963) and *Dr. Doolittle* (1967) represented an out-of-touch Hollywood begging to be restructured, many of these overblown MFTs signaled a network system once again on the brink of a substantial reorganization. By 2005, made-for-television movies no longer served as a "fundamental programming staple of network television" (Edgerton 2003, 211). They had morphed into event-level productions that, more often than not, failed to yield event-level ratings. In short, MFTs were out of step with emerging institutional and business imperatives in the digital age.

Into the Digital Era, Out of the Made-For-TV Movie Business

MFTs became incompatible with the broadcast networks' economic models and programming strategies in the new millennium for several reasons. Due to a range of factors—including their status as "one-off" programs, the mounting marketing costs, the growing disconnect between the content of the films and the networks' emerging target audiences, and the fall-out from several high-profile failures—MFTs all but disappeared from the networks by 2005.

To begin to understand their disappearance from network television, it is important to note that since the 1980s, independent companies have produced most MFTs. The networks decided that direct investment in them was not worthwhile due to the slim profit margins. To make them profitable, a producer often had to cobble together income from a variety of sources around the world.

Independent producers had crafted a business model that limited networks to receiving revenues from advertising dollars in the initial run of the program. During the classic network era, this model would have been acceptable because MFTs often commanded large advertising rates due to their high ratings. By the 2000s, however, this was no longer as tenable. A key component of the now vertically integrated broadcast networks' financial models involved having ownership over many of their programs' rights. This enabled the conglomerates to recycle a given program (e.g. *Law & Order: SVU*; *That '70s Show*) over a range of properties including cable and DVD.

A scenario that worked well with series programming worked much less easily with MFTs. Not only did the programs not rerun well on the network on which they were initially broadcast, but networks also could not recycle them on their other platforms because they usually did not have the rights. During much of the 1990s and early 2000s, the broadcast networks justified the low profit margins of MFTs because the films were perceived as "loss leaders." In other words, they brought in a large enough number of viewers and a high enough ratings boost for networks to view them as useful tools by which to promote other programs and facilitate future ad rate increases. However, the networks were meeting with growing success turning their regular programming into event-level programming. For instance, a "supersized" segment of *The Office* could bring in the same kinds of ratings numbers as an original MFT. What is more, they did so without interrupting their regular schedules.

In the age of DVRs, YouTube, and social networking, regularity and predictability became more important scheduling strategies for the broadcast networks. With so much competition for people's limited time—and an ever-more fragmented media universe—little upside resulted to adding yet another program to the schedule. Another original program was expensive to produce and took a great deal of time and money to promote. What would be the benefit of introducing new characters and a new storyline to viewers already overwhelmed with media options? And why do it when limited potential advantage could be had in ancillary markets? The networks' marketing challenges further increased because nearly 20 percent of viewers now owned digital video recorders (Levin 2007). These DVRs were often set up to record viewers' favorite series, which worked to the disadvantage of MFTs. In addition, promotions for upcoming MFTs could easily be bypassed by the DVR remote.

Younger, wealthier, and more technologically savvy men most heavily used DVRs at this time. The networks were going to great lengths to develop relationships with these viewer-consumers. To do so, they employed all sorts of interactive digital technologies, including live blogging from the sets of shows and production of mini-episodes of programs for cell phones. As Henry Jenkins discusses (2006), this new culture of convergence has helped unite some producers and consumers and has contributed to a creative interchange between fans and talent. Since these relationships often develop over a period of time, series television proves ideal for this kind of convergence. Certain types of shows (e.g. *Lost*, *Heroes*, *24*) prove more amenable to interactive relationships. While a show like *Lost* might not reach the top ten in the ratings, it attracts a devoted audience willing to consume and re-consume it in a variety of media forms. The same is generally not true for MFTs. To create a website for them would be counterproductive owing to their ephemeral quality, the kinds of subjects they present, and their older, predominantly female audience base.

Within this context, the near-complete disappearance of MFTs from network television begins to make sense. MFTs have become niche products, but they do not appeal to the "right" niches for the broadcast networks. The niches they do attract are those perceived by the industry to have less economic and cultural capital: older, rural, and/or female viewers. In other words, these are the viewers of the cable networks where the majority of made-for-TV movies are most likely to show up today: the Hallmark Channel and Lifetime.

What might be seen as the official death-knell for the MFT on broadcast television came in 2006. CBS followed ABC and NBC in dropping its Sunday Movie of the Week. Perhaps symbolically, *Cold Case* took the time slot. The move came after several recent MFT embarrassments, both for CBS and the other broadcast networks. Among the most notorious humiliations were CBS's *The Reagans* (2003) and ABC's *Fatal Contact: Bird Flu in America* (2006). CBS shifted *The Reagans* to sister company Showtime in the wake of protests from conservative groups about its depiction of the former First Couple.

No such controversy surrounded *Fatal Contact*. This show is worth mentioning merely for reinforcing how much television had changed, and how much the value of the MFT had diminished, since the classic network era. A great deal of media attention surrounded its broadcast. ABC had high hopes for the movie, positioning it in the middle of May sweeps. Yet in spite of the hoopla, *Fatal Contact* proved to be an unmitigated disaster, coming in fourth for the night (Kissell 2006, 5). A mere 5.28 million Americans watched it—approximately the same number who watched the sitcoms that normally aired in its time slot. For comparison, 28.85 million viewers watched Fox's *American Idol* that same evening (5).

Very few MFTs have since appeared on the broadcast networks. According to the *Hollywood Reporter*, the 2006 to 2007 season was the first time in thirty-five years that a made-for-TV movie did not appear on ABC (Richmond 2007, 15). This is particularly startling considering that ABC has often touted its role in "creating" the movie-of-the-week format (Pulley 2005).

By the mid-2000s, the networks had all but ceded the MFT and its viewers to a limited number of cable program services. For different cable networks, MFTs served different purposes. With HBO, in keeping with its "quality television" brand image, MFTs were reframed as "movies on television" as opposed to television movies. Here they were heavily promoted and featured big-screen stars (e.g. Annette Bening and Ben Kingsley in *Mrs. Harris*, 2006). MFTs provided HBO with a means of attracting and retaining the discriminating (affluent) viewers the pay cable network prided itself on having. With the Disney Channel, MFTs were part of the larger "franchise-building" efforts undertaken by the Disney conglomerate. The *High School Musical* (HSM) films (2006, 2007), for instance, were just one part of the larger multi-pronged, multimedia push for HSM-related media products.

Most frequently, however, MFTs were just an ordinary, mundane form appearing on a medium in the midst of dramatic transformation. These MFTs were the ones that appeared with great frequency on services such as Lifetime and Hallmark. In both style and storyline, such MFTs were markedly similar to the ones that appeared on the broadcast networks during the 1970s and 1980s. Typically soft, safe, and reassuring by their conclusion, these movies featured B-level stars in tales suitable for viewing by the whole family (e.g. Sarah Paulson and Dean Cain in Lifetime's *A Christmas Wedding*, 2006; Richard Thomas and Nancy McKeon in Hallmark's *Wild Hearts*, 2006). Nothing was especially remarkable about these MFTs, nothing particularly distinctive. They were "just television." Thus, in spite of the fact that numerically these were the predominant form of the genre appearing on television in the new millennium, they largely evaded discussion by the popular press and scholars.

The Cultural Stakes of the Fall of the MFT

As this discussion illustrates, while MFTs remain a viable format on television in the post-network era, they are mainly accessible now on a few cable channels rather than on the broadcast networks.[7] As noted above, about a hundred MFTs continue to air on television annually. This is approximately the same number broadcast on the Big Three during the classic network era. However, there are important cultural implications to their shift from the broadcast networks to cable. Most significantly, MFTs—and by extension, the audiences that view them—have been marginalized. The movies still retain the cultural stigma they held during the latter part of the classic network era. In fact, that stigma may be even stronger now. Due to their omnipresence on cable outlets such as Lifetime, some critics dismiss all of them as (to paraphrase *Variety*) "melodramatic stories about women as victims who suffer abuse at the hands of a contemptible man for seven-eights of the plot, turning the tables at the end" (Dempsey 2005, 18).[8]

In dismissing MFTs as marginal to contemporary television, their audiences and their interests also seem less valuable than those who view channels such as Comedy Central, HBO, or Fox. It is important that we be attentive not only to what the industry and the press perceive as new and hip but also that which is dismissed as old and uncool. Further, we must question precisely why these conceptions exist in the first place and how they indicate cultural distinctions made on the basis of class, race, gender, and age.

Given the methodological difficulties involved in studying MFTs, the cultural stigma attached to them as a form, and their near absence from contemporary *broadcast* channels, there might be an impulse to dismiss them or minimize their importance to media history. However, as I have illustrated here, their disappearance from the most high-profile and highly publicized program services is a product of changes not only in the television industry but in the media landscape at large. By focusing on how and why they can no longer be found on the broadcast networks' schedules, we can arrive at more complex media histories than we might reach should we focus only on the predominance of reality television and serialized dramas on these networks. Significantly, the same economic and institutional forces that contributed to the rise of shows like *American Idol* and *CSI* have helped push MFTs to the industrial and cultural margins.

Notes

1. The label "neo-network" era comes from Michael Curtin (1996, 181–202). Amanda Lotz (2007) revises Curtin's model to account for changes since his essay.
2. Several different methods were used to assess the number and types of MFTs aired

in the mid-2000s. These included: (1) keyword searches in databases such as Lexis-Nexis; (2) power searches by network on www.imdb.com; (3) tracking programs nominated for awards; (4) surveying the websites of broadcast and cable networks; and (5) scanning trade publications.

3. Edgerton's original piece also provides an excellent discussion of how these programs developed and the ways they spread across the larger network landscape.
4. See Lotz (2007) for more on key industrial developments.
5. Much as had been the case during the classic network era, a relatively small number of independent producers oversaw the lion's share of the MFTs broadcast.
6. Many of these shows also involved Hallmark Entertainment and Jim Henson's Creature Shop.
7. MFTs work well on contemporary cable in part because cable networks can replay them dozens of times. The broadcast networks' programming practices and business strategies prevent this.
8. This phrase was used to describe the kinds of stories Lifetime began to move away from as of the mid-2000s.

Works Cited

Collins, Scott. 2006. "Biblical Tale Can't Help ABC's Ratings." *Los Angeles Times* 12 April: E3.

Curtin, Michael. 1996. "On Edge: Culture Industries in the Neo-Network Era." *Making and Selling Culture*, ed. Richard M. Ohmann. Hanover: University Press of New England, 181–202.

Dempsey, John. 2005. "Lifetime Reels in Telepix." *Variety* 8–14 August: 18.

Edgerton, Gary. 2003. "High Concept, Small Screen: Reperceiving the Industrial and Stylistic Origins of the American Made-For-TV Movie." *Connections: The Broadcast History Reader*, ed. Michele Hilmes. Belmont, CA: Wadsworth Thomson, 209–230.

Gomery, Douglas. 1984. "The Rise of the Telefilm and the Networks' Hegemony over the Motion Picture Industry." *Quarterly Review of Film Studies* 9.3: 204–218.

Jenkins, Henry. 2006. *Convergence Culture: Where Old and New Media Collide.* New York: New York University Press.

Kissell, Rick. 2006. "Fox Flies by 'Bird Flu.'" *Daily Variety* 22 May: 5.

Levin, Gary. 2007. "Viewers' Shifting Habits Redefine TV 'Hit.'" *USA Today* 23 October. Accessed October 26 2007. Available from www.usatoday.com/life/television/news/2007-10-23-tv-hits_N.htm.

Levine, Elana. 2007. *Wallowing in Sex: The New Sexual Culture of 1970s American Television.* Durham, NC: Duke University Press.

Lotz, Amanda. 2007. *The Television will be Revolutionized.* New York: New York University Press.

Moss, Linda. 2005. "Programming Booms as Cable Grows Up." *Multichannel News* 29 August: 8, 10.

Pulley, Brett. 2005. "The Dealmaker." *Forbes* 5 September: 108–109.

Reynolds, Mike. 2005. "Basic Cable's Boffo Brand Builder: Made-For-TV Movies are More Than Just a Ratings Draw." *Multichannel News* 7 November: 14, 16.

Richmond, Ray. 2007. "The Telefilm Continues its Long, Slow Descent." *Hollywood Reporter* 16 January: 15.

Schneider, Michael and Josef Adalian. 2006. "A Wandering Eye." *Variety* 19 October: 1.

Part IV

Research Issues

Chapter 16

Doing Soap Opera History
Challenges and Triumphs

Elana Levine

Genre has long been a key analytic concept in media scholarship, with theoretical, historical, and critical work seeking to understand how genres are defined, how they do and do not change over time and place, and how and why they tell the stories they do. In television studies, the soap opera is one of the most examined genres. It has been a major object of analysis for feminist media scholars, central to conceptions of gender and genre, female spectatorship, and women as socially positioned audience members.[1] Indeed, soap opera has been central not only to explicitly feminist scholarship but also to a host of television research concerned with the medium's storytelling capabilities and its distinctiveness from other media.[2] Pair this with the attention to the genre's variations in multiple national and global contexts, and it becomes clear that a substantial, even foundational, body of soap opera scholarship is at the center of television studies.

Yet significant gaps remain in our understanding of soap opera, particularly historical gaps. For the most part, the existing soap opera scholarship focuses on the genre's heyday in the 1970s and early 1980s, basing its at times universalizing claims on a relatively narrow historical moment. Much of this scholarship conceives of soap opera as a stable and static media institution, treating the genre synchronically rather than diachronically, assuming generic features that remain in place across a changing media industry, changing reception practices, and a changing culture. Take Tania Modleski's work as an example, first published in 1979. While Modleski identifies many prominent features of the genre that continue to pertain, other points of her argument are difficult to reconcile with more recent developments. For instance, her emphasis on the "good mother" character as a stand-in for the spectator's ideal mother positioning is complicated in the US daytime soaps of the past ten to fifteen years, since most of the shows' increasingly youthful casts keep the older mother characters off the story canvas. So, too, do Modleski's assumptions about the soap opera viewer as housewife, and the pleasures the genre brings to a woman in such a social position, seem out of touch with the soaps' more recent institutional and reception contexts. Even Robert Allen's *Speaking of Soap Opera* (1985), one of the few takes on the genre to place historically specific analyses at the center of its inquiry, admittedly offers only a start at conceiving what such a history might be. Otherwise, much of Allen's analysis concerns the structure and narrative form of soaps as a genre, although he recognizes that those features can and do change over time.

The soap opera scholarship so central to both television studies and feminist media studies is more often critical or theoretical than it is historical. This tendency is in keeping with the existing body of genre scholarship. Although scholars have engaged in important, historicizing work on genre in recent years, the concept itself—one that steers our inquiries toward the style, form, and content that define a category—pulls the preponderance of existing genre scholarship away from the historical, speaking to those features that continue rather than change over time.[3] In the case of soap opera, while the existing scholarship on the genre has been foundational in many senses, the tendency in such scholarship to conceive of soap opera in universalist terms shapes the ways in which scholars do—and more often do not—examine the genre in contemporary practice. In this chapter, I challenge that practice by arguing for the value of an historical approach to daytime soap opera and, by implication, to genre scholarship as a whole. By drawing on examples from my own past and present soap opera research, I explore not only the reasons why soap opera scholarship has seemingly fallen out of fashion but also suggest what an historical approach to the genre might offer. I do so primarily by grappling with some of the key historiographic challenges such research is likely to encounter and also by suggesting ways I have found to manage these challenges.

There are two chief reasons why soap opera scholarship—and historical work on US soaps in particular—has been an infrequent, almost non-existent, subject of media scholarship since the early 1990s. First is an assumption many media scholars likely hold that we already know what we need to know about soap opera. This may also be the case with many long-standing film and television genres about which much has already been written. In the case of soaps, this stance is surely rooted in the large body of existing work.[4] But lurking underneath this faith in the existing knowledge may also be a sort of acceptance of soap opera's denigrated cultural status, particularly in the current context, in which the US television industry is increasingly losing confidence in the genre's ability to deliver the audiences and advertiser dollars essential to fiscal solvency.

Placing these concerns about scholarship falling prey to the inclinations of the media industries aside, however, the other chief reason that soap opera historiography is so infrequent is surely the daunting nature of the task. As Allen pointed out, grappling with the text of even one daily soap opera would "require 233 days of nonstop viewing, during which time another 164 hours of text would have been produced" (1985, 13). Add to this the radio years of a soap such as *The Guiding Light* or the twenty-two television years from Allen's writing to the present, and the size of the text alone makes studying it in any comprehensive way an impossibility. In addition, grappling with such a text is daunting not only because of its size but also because of its inaccessibility. Before the mid-1960s, all daytime soap operas were broadcast live, and are thus largely unavailable to us in their originally produced form. Even with the coming of videotape to soaps in the 1960s and 1970s, episodes were not always saved. For example, in the late 1970s, videotaped episodes of the Procter & Gamble-produced *As the World Turns* were kept for just thirty days before being erased (Adams 1980, 140).

For these reasons and more, an historical approach to daytime soap opera presents significant challenges. Yet such an approach is both possible and valuable, not only in terms of our understanding of soaps but of media genres as a whole. Indeed, an historical approach helps us to see that all genres are historical, and thus changeable, constructs (Feuer 1992). As recent theorizations of film and television genre assert, genres are constructed and circulated differently in different historical moments and geographic contexts.[5] As Jason Mittell argues, "Genres are cultural products, constituted by media practices and subject to ongoing change and definition" (2004, 1). Studying one of broadcasting's most enduring genres from this perspective can put such theorizations into practice.

A second value in an historical approach to media genres in general and to soap opera in particular is the opportunity it offers for examining the media's role as a site of hegemonic negotiation over time. Owing to the soap opera's long existence and daily schedule, as well as its tendency for ongoing development of characters and their story arcs, the histories of the soaps' production and reception can illustrate the minute ways in which televisual discourses shift across years and decades. This is especially so for discourses of gender, sexuality, and interpersonal relationships, arguably the main fodder for soap opera stories across their history, and also the aspects of social identity and experience to which US soaps are most often articulated, given their assumed audience of women and their status as a feminized form. An historical analysis of the US daytime soap allows for the tracing of shifts and consistencies in such discourses across the history of the genre, at levels of production, reception, and broader cultural circulation. Such an approach serves the interests of feminist scholarship as well as the concerns of media critics and historians. However, to take on this kind of project requires access to a range of different kinds of evidentiary materials, all of which can be difficult to access and many of which hold an uncertain status as historical evidence.

The historical study of the daytime soap opera faces some significant archival absences. In certain respects, recovering the soaps' past is little different from historiographic efforts centered around other kinds of entertainment media and popular culture, especially denigrated forms such as the tabloid press, exploitation cinema, or even much of primetime television. Yet the problems of archival absence common to multiple cultural forms are amplified in the case of soaps. For example, media industry trade publications have much scantier coverage of daytime television, and daytime drama in particular, than they have of primetime programming. This is the case for the mainstream press as well, which does not devote the same kind of regular business or arts coverage to daytime serials as it might to higher profile television programming or other media.

The fan press is another valuable resource for much popular culture history, soap operas included. However, the soap press first emerged in the 1970s, leaving at least twenty years of television soapdom without fan-targeted publishing. The soap press can be extremely helpful for its storyline summaries and feature stories, as well as for the letters to the editor. But libraries rarely save these publications. Currently, only a few libraries within the USA have collections of *Soap Opera Digest* that begin with the magazine's debut in 1975, and libraries' commitment to preserving these publications is questionable. For example, the South Central Wisconsin public library system's main branch, in Madison, Wisconsin, recently disposed of their full run of the publication, citing space restrictions. For an earlier research project, this collection allowed me unique access to information about the spate of rape stories appearing on the soaps in the late 1970s, from comments by writers and producers to plot summaries and viewer responses (Levine 2007). The magazines' total disappearance from this library's collection is all too familiar to researchers whose pursuit of ephemeral and culturally discounted forms is laden with absences and losses of all kinds.

Soap-related holdings in official archives can also be problematic. While script and correspondence archives exist for several soaps and some key writer/producers, few moving-image archives preserve soap opera episodes. Even when an archive, such as that at UCLA, has such episodes in its collection, they are not always available for viewing. For example, UCLA's film and television archive houses thousands of episodes of the ABC soap *General Hospital*, including a full run of episodes from the program's debut in 1963 into the early 1970s. However, most of these episodes require videotape transfer to be viewed, and because this is a labor- and resource-intensive process, the archive tries to limit transfers to ten hours of programming per researcher.[6] As this would only allow for the viewing of twenty episodes of the 1960s *General Hospital*, it cannot remotely approach the number of episodes one might want to view to obtain a full sense of a soap across its long history, or even the number of episodes necessary to watch a single storyline play out over months. Allen was right about the impossibility of consuming most soap texts in their entirety, but the archival situation makes it extremely difficult to screen even a meaningful portion of a particular text, especially for episodes aired before the home videotape era. Thus, while other archives do have a smattering of soap episodes, this sort of random selection impedes an understanding of a soap text in any systematic way. Because soap stories play out over weeks and months rather than one day, access to a single episode, even if it highlights a significant narrative event, does little to communicate the complications and convolutions of a soap story.

The corporations that own the rights to many daytime soaps may have more materials in their private archives. Both Procter & Gamble and ABC/Disney, two of the primary soap producers, have corporate archives that are not generally open to the public. ABC/Disney's archive is stored in the vast, underground vault in Burbank, California, known as Iron Mountain. The company has released some materials for airing on its specialty cable channel Soapnet, but the extent of its holdings remains something of a mystery. So, too, has Procter & Gamble made some of its holdings available through its online P&G Classic Soaps service. Still, the proprietary interests of these companies keep whatever holdings they may possess largely inaccessible to researchers.

Despite all of the historiographic challenges facing soap research, a rich well of material is still available, and that can help enable partial histories of US daytime soaps. The existing public archives are major resources. Thus, the collected papers of soap pioneer Irna Phillips or other radio serial creators such as Jane Crusinberry have allowed for several scholarly histories of the genre's radio years. I have found multiple treasures in the papers of soap writer Ann Marcus, whose contributions to a number of soaps in the 1970s are well documented through her archived correspondence, script outlines, and handwritten commentaries. Script collections are also valuable sources for tracing storyline specifics. Most recently in my research, the *Another World* scripts in the Irna Phillips collection revealed the ways in which this soap represented a young woman's 1964 abortion, the first such story in daytime and one that would help set the tenor for those to follow.

Scripts are also valuable elements in soap historiography for the changes in dialogue that are at times noted on them. Procter & Gamble's script collection allowed me to reconstruct three different rape stories on *The Guiding Light*, the first in the mid-1960s and the other two in the late 1970s. More than what happened in such stories, accessing these scripts and the handwritten notations on them allowed me to examine the specific choices made in producing them.

For example, I was able to see the ways in which future rapist Roger Thorpe's dialogue was altered so that his threats to Rita Stapleton communicated more physical menace than sexual titillation. This evidence helped me to point to one of the many ways in which this soap's representation of rape participated in the anti-rape movement's efforts to shift discussion about the motivations for rape away from sexual desire and toward hostility and violence (Levine 2007).

In addition to this kind of archival evidence, the soaps' ardent, long-lasting fan base also provides some significant research material. In addition to the fan-targeted soap press and especially the published letters to the editor (a selected group of viewer responses, to be sure, but valuable ones nonetheless), scholarly soap history benefits from a fan-targeted book-publishing industry. Although this industry has since died down, from the mid-1970s to the mid-1990s, trade and mass-market presses published a number of tributes to the soaps' pasts.[7] These volumes summarize storylines and celebrate particular actors, writers, and producers in ways that may not be especially useful to a scholar interested in a cultural history of the genre, but they can be incredibly helpful in grappling with the convoluted plots and character relationships of dozens of programs over decades-long stretches. Brief mentions of rape stories in such volumes tipped me off to storylines I otherwise had no way of finding, and gave me general time frames for when such stories aired that I could then pursue further in archival materials or the more detailed summaries of the soap press. With the necessary partiality of soap opera historiography, the storyline summaries these books provide offer an initial filter through which a researcher can zero in on particular points of interest.

As in many popular cultural realms, online fan activity is another resource increasingly essential to soap opera historiography. Not only do fan websites, blogs, and YouTube posts document soap history and identify individuals with memory stores to query, but they also allow for access to fans' own archival collections. Fans' tape-trading networks are more transparent and reachable in this online environment, and fans' eagerness to share their rare collections is encouraging. For example, as I research abortion stories across soap history, I have been able to find full runs of *The Young and the Restless* in 1986 or the key weeks in an *As the World Turns* story from 1992. Since soap fans have had VCRs, this kind of recording and archiving has been going on, although the relatively short history of such technology also limits the programs fans can trade.

While the necessity of access to home VCRs certainly narrows the timespan for the materials fans can offer to researchers, some fans take the role of archivist quite seriously, making a concerted effort to preserve and share even material that precedes the era of the home VCR. The best example I have found of this kind of fan archivist is the *World of Soap Themes* (WoST) website (wost.org). This site began as an America Online page in 1999, when founder Brian Puckett sought to put his childhood collection of audio recordings of soap opera theme music on the web. He included a co-worker's collection of promotional reels for daytime dramas and these two types of rare archival material drew a number of soap fans to the site. Soon, other collectors began to offer Puckett portions of their own archives, leading him to post video as well as audio clips and eventually some full episodes. When he ran out of space on his AOL page, Puckett moved the site around, eventually getting his own domain name in 2002. Meanwhile, soap collectors continued to donate material (Puckett 2007). WoST would soon include 1970s episodes of *The Young and the Restless*, *Guiding Light*, and *The Edge of Night*, clips from long-defunct soaps such as *Somerset* and *Love of Life*, and credit sequences from innumerable US soaps such as 1954's *The Road to Life* as well as British soaps such as *Coronation Street* in its 1960 debut year.

As unusual as the access WoST provides is, the site also demonstrates the ways in which even those archival practices that avoid traditional, institutionalized settings have their limits and exclusions. In addition to the fact that the site's collection is unavoidably partial, its availability is also short-lived. Puckett has announced that he will be taking WoST offline in August 2009, and he ceased adding new material as of Spring 2007. He points to the time involvement and costs of the site as barriers to its continuation but also to the unceasing demands the site's users have made of him to provide them with downloadable or recorded copies of the material he presents (the clips run on the site as streaming audio and video only). Honoring the wishes of his donors, Puckett refuses such requests, but they present a consistent burden. Ironically, it is the value of the material WoST provides to its users that has invited the site's imminent disappearance—the materials are coveted so intensely that it becomes near impossible to satisfy the desire for them, and thus they will be unavailable to all.

Even when WoST was seemingly thriving, however, the site's particular orientation toward soaps guided its offerings in ways that shaped the evidence of soap opera history which it offered. For example, Puckett and all members of the WoST Board are men, and, as their podcast and other offerings suggest, their interest in soaps is primarily that of an artistic appreciation of an extinct form. This is evident in their celebration of revered writers of concluded soaps, such as playwright and *Another World* writer Harding Lemay, and of revered serials of yesteryear, such as the mystery-oriented and thus not particularly "soap-y" *Edge of Night*. At the same time, these men express disdain for newer soaps with young target audiences, such as *Passions*, as well as with such contemporary storylines as that of *All My Children*'s transgendered character, Zoe. WoST's efforts to elevate culturally soaps of the past help to legitimate an interest in such a feminized genre by men, as if the "soap opera" that concerns WoST's membership is of a different caliber than that obsessed over by today's pre-teen girls and middle-aged housewives.[8] This results in an emphasis on certain kinds of soaps on the site and an overall discourse of soap opera that isolates the genre from the feminized associations it has always held. My point here is not to discount the valuable resources that WoST provides, but rather to examine the ways in which the concerns and agendas of those who engage in it in the present shape all processes of historicization. The ways such sensibilities shape the archive may be particularly prominent for soap opera, given the genre's denigrated, feminized cultural positioning and the challenge of justifying historical preservation in spite of it.

It is clear that soap opera historiography repeats and amplifies many of the challenges of media history more generally, and the histories of denigrated media in particular. Yet soap opera historiography also includes opportunities not necessarily available in all media history projects—in particular the resources and passions of the long-standing fan networks built around soaps. Soap opera history, like all history, is necessarily partial and incomplete, but the challenges that accompany it need not impede its progress. Instead, the active pursuit of soap opera history can help in the discovery not only of the soaps' past but also in scholarly inquiry into the histories of media genres more generally and into the histories of all feminized cultural forms. Perhaps the challenges of doing soap opera history can help to put into perspective the challenges faced by all attempts to historicize media genres—highlighting the value of dismantling the universalist claims so common to genre criticism and offering a template for what is and is not possible within such an historiographic effort.

Notes

1. Among the feminist media scholarship that analyzes the soap genre are Kuhn (1984), Modleski (1984), and Mumford (1995).
2. See e.g. Newcomb 1974; Allen 1985.
3. Some examples of this sort of genre scholarship include Carroll (1990) and Mumford (1995).
4. Brunsdon (1995) provides an overview of the role of soap opera in feminist television scholarship.
5. Among these revisionist takes on genre are Altman (1999) and Mittell (2004).
6. The UCLA archivists make every effort to accommodate researcher requests, as I have discovered in my own work, but they must do so in the face of economic and technological constraints.
7. See e.g. Schemering 1985; Warner 1995.
8. While men have always watched daytime soaps in greater numbers than either popular or scholarly discourse on the genre has allowed, WoST nonetheless represents a small, marginal community of soap fans and should not be taken as representative of contemporary soap opera viewership.

Works Cited

Adams, Maryjo. 1980. *An American Soap Opera: As the World Turns, 1956–1978*. Diss: University of Michigan.

Allen, Robert C. 1985. *Speaking of Soap Operas*. Chapel Hill: University of North Carolina Press.

Altman, Rick. 1999. *Film / Genre*. London: BFI Publishing.

Brunsdon, Charlotte. 1995. "The Role of Soap Opera in the Development of Feminist Television Scholarship." *To Be Continued...*, ed. Robert C. Allen. London: Routledge, 49–65.

Carroll, Noël. 1990. *The Philosophy of Horror or Paradoxes of the Heart*. New York: Routledge.

Feuer, Jane. 1992. "Genre Study and Television." *Channels of Discourse, Reassembled* (2nd edn), ed. Robert C. Allen. Chapel Hill: University of North Carolina Press, 138–159.

Kuhn, Annette. 1984. "Women's Genres: Melodrama, Soap Opera, and Theory." *Screen* 25.1: 18–28.

Levine, Elana. 2007. *Wallowing in Sex: The New Sexual Culture of 1970s American Television*. Durham, NC: Duke University Press.

Mittell, Jason. 2004. *Genre and Television*. New York: Routledge.

Modleski, Tania. 1979. "The Search for Tomorrow in Today's Soap Operas." *Film Quarterly* 33.1: 31–47.

———. 1984. *Loving with a Vengeance*. London: Routledge.

Mumford, Laura Stempel. 1995. *Love and Ideology in the Afternoon: Soap Opera, Women, and Television Genre*. Bloomington: Indiana University Press.

Newcomb, Horace. 1974. *TV: The Most Popular Art*. Garden City, NY: Anchor Press/Doubleday.

Puckett, Brian D. 2007. Personal Interview 21 September.

Schemering, Christopher. 1985. *The Soap Opera Encyclopedia*. New York: Ballantine Books.

Warner, Gary. 1995. *General Hospital: The Complete Scrapbook*. Santa Monica, CA: General Publishing Group.

Chapter 17

Stalking the Wild Evidence

Capturing Media History Through Elusive and Ephemeral Archives

Pamela Wilson

Researching media history is a slippery endeavor, a veritable treasure hunt to track down sources and to keep them from disappearing into the dustbin of history. Bringing to mind images of khaki-covered and pith-helmeted antiquities seekers, private archivist Rick Prelinger has bestowed the moniker of *media archaeology* on "the protracted sifting through of accumulated media detritus that so often gets swept under the historical rug" (Lewis-Kraus 2007, 55). Media texts themselves are scarce, with archives hard to locate and often difficult to access through the institutional or corporate channels that guard them. Even more challenges face the historians of digital media since their sources come and go, websites disappear from existence, and key texts are constantly changing, refusing to be frozen in time. We live with the enigma of the disappearing referent: by the time our histories see print, our indexical references may no longer point to anything that still exists. For archivists in the midst of a massive paradigm shift between print and digital culture, the looming task is to catalog—and digitize—more than a century's-worth of media images. As journalist Scott Carlson (2005) has noted, "Without organization, any history of moving images will be a cacophonous mass."

Archives today stand at a significant crossroads in terms of making historic media texts and documents accessible not only to academic researchers but also to new audiences who are consuming historic media in new ways, as well as consumers-turned-producers (e.g. amateur videomakers posting their work on YouTube). Beyond the massive paradigm shift leading to the digitization of historic and contemporary media documents, a shift is happening in the attitude of corporate producers and owners regarding proprietary ownership and the potential benefits of sharing archival texts. Cultural attitudes are changing from a concept of archives as public domain to an ideology of archives-for-profit.

The First Problem: Defining the Shifting Object of Study

As historians of media, what are our primary sources, our media history texts? While traditionally we think of films, broadcast television, and radio programs, media historians also need the supporting documents beyond the finished texts: the rough footage, the scripts, interview notes, production papers, corporate memos, and economic data, as well as related industry or consumer discourses (e.g. trade and fan publications and discourses, political or cultural controversies engendered by the media text and its process).

Moving beyond the traditional media texts of the 1920s to 1970s that have so far been the focus of most academic media history leads us into areas less well defined and for which the mechanisms for archiving, preservation, and research access are even more patchy or limited. Beyond the Hollywood feature film, social documentary, or corporate television news and entertainment programs lie thousands of ephemeral moving images such as home movies, amateur videos, social hygiene films, training films, trade films, infomercials, propaganda tracts, and more. The digital era has posed even more opportunities for media research as well as many challenges for archiving the constantly shifting flow of information and images: websites, blogs, listserv dialogues, emails, video games, even spam. All are ripe for study and, as cultural documents, need to be preserved and archived, yet the technological and philosophical challenges for doing so have not yet been overcome.

What Are "The Archives"?

Archives today are public and private, official and unofficial, non-commercial and commercial, institutional and individual, tangible or digital—and their holdings may range from a handful of items into the millions. Archival sites—and the ways in which we access them—are forever shifting, and the twenty-first-century media historian needs a different set of research skills and a different set of research questions than did our counterparts a few decades ago. Today's challenges may not be the same challenges that our students will face tomorrow, and so we must anticipate the shifting sands of media historiography and the changing trends that are shaping the future of this research endeavor.

Generally, "the archives" have been public, often governmentally funded, institutional collections such as, in the United States, the National Archives (NARA), the Library of Congress, various state archives, and those of university research libraries. The Library of Congress has recently opened a new repository for its more than 6.2 million holdings in its audiovisual collection, and its website (www.loc.gov/avconservation/) invites visitors to "Experi-ence the Collection." University-based archives are rich sources for finding a variety of materials and provide a range of types of collections that are perhaps the most accessible to scholars and students for local or regional research; yet—like the federal and state archives—they also provide many challenges to media historians in terms of accessibility.

In addition to official archives, museums—both public and private—have also served as repositories for creative and cultural works. However, the func-tions and missions of museums are in major transition as well as seeking to market to a new generation. Recently, board members of The Museum of Television and Radio (founded in New York as The Museum of Broadcasting in 1975) changed its name to the Paley Center for Media and, in doing so, rid itself of the mission of being a *museum*, since, according to President/CEO Pat Mitchell, " 'Museum' was not a word that tests really well with the under-30 and 40-year-olds," especially in the context of radio and television (Jensen 2007). The new Paley Center website (www.paleycenter.org) is less about history and more about contemporary media issues and programs, promi-nently featuring celebrity-centered seminar series, festivals, and programs. A prominent link to a blog by the Paley Center curators on the social networking site MySpace.com invites: "We're on MySpace. Join as a friend."

The word *archives* is nowhere to be found on the Paley Center site, and the only evidence that historic programs are available for viewing or study is in a link to "lost" programs, soliciting donations by private collectors. In contrast, the web page for Chicago's Museum of Broadcast Communications, a non-profit organization founded in 1987, prominently features a "From the Archives" frame on its home page and also provides opportunities for online listening and viewing of an increasing number of digitized historic broadcast programs.

The most elusive archives for media historians may well be those associated with the media corporations that produce and distribute media. For television and radio historians, the major broadcasting networks have provided innumer-able challenges in terms of accessibility, copyright issues, and comprehensive-ness of available collections. For example, although the early NBC corporate papers are archived in the Wisconsin Center for Film and Theater Research—though quite patchy—finding copies of television and radio programs covering the same period can be quite challenging, and trying to access more con-temporary archival network materials can be a formidable experience.

Yet there are occasional and fortuitous partnerships between the corporate and public institutions. The Vanderbilt Television News Archives, for example, created as a non-profit organization and maintained through grants and fees, holds more than 30,000 individual network evening news broadcasts from ABC, CBS, NBC, and CNN since 1968 plus additional special news-related programming since 1989. For a fee, individuals may request videotape loans for reference, study, classroom instruction, and research, but they must stay within the restrictions of copyright law. Through educational institutions, one can now search the Vanderbilt database online, and, via subscription, one can view online video from the CNN collection.

Elusive Objects of Study

With all these archives, why is it still difficult to access the texts and documents we need? Media historians face a number of distinct situations: on the one hand, when we cannot find the texts and documents we need in any archives and, on the other hand, when we know that our primary sources are in collections, either public or private, but are not accessible—or when the process of accessing them becomes a quest for the proverbial holy grail.

The situation in which primary sources are not in official archives, or when value judgments are used to determine what is suitable and appropriate to archive and preserve, may reflect both financial priorities and ideological judgments. Decisions about culling—what to save and what to toss—reflect institutional priorities and sensitivities about the value of historical works as well as the existence of funding for storage, preservation, creating a system for cataloging, and staffing. Yet the age-old question of "quality" vs. "trash," "highbrow" vs. "lowbrow" reflects hierarchies of taste and judgment. While determining what is essential for archiving may often be a financial issue, it also frequently comes down to questions of moral or cultural politics. Many collections coming into archives have been purged either in full or in part based upon the personal judgment calls of archivists, and uncounted media texts and papers have selectively been tossed and deemed non-essential. Television historian Elana Levine (2007), who studies soap opera history, relates a frustrating story about "the precariousness of studying this kind of denigrated genre" when she discovered that a public library had recently discarded decades'-worth of soap opera fan magazines.

Many puzzle pieces of media history—ranging from films and television programs to so-called "ephemeral documents"—have not been deemed worthy of formal archival preservation. Some have been lost entirely, while many others are still floating around either privately stored or undiscovered. How do we find these sources if they are not in archival collections? Many of them may be stashed away in garages, attics, basements, or warehouses somewhere out there. One of the legends of film historiography was the accidental discovery in 1983 in a warehouse in a Texas town of thousands of 35 mm film canisters containing a significant collection of African-American-produced "race movies" from the 1930s and 1940s, forgotten and abandoned for over thirty years. Although perhaps less dramatic, in the early 1990s, while researching the cultural and political controversy surrounding a 1958 television documentary on Native American rights, *The American Stranger*, I located the key centerpiece—the original roll-in footage and perhaps the only existing kinescope of the hour-long television news documentary—in film canisters in the attic of the late director, Robert McCormick, thanks to his daughter's dusty searching. Neither NBC nor the Library of Congress had a copy.

Primary media documents, as well as ephemera related to media history—publicity stills and posters, fan magazines, correspondence, brochures—are often to be found at auctions, estate sales, flea markets, yard sales, second-hand bookstores, directly from fans who are collectors, and—for those who might realize the potential worth of a collection—online on eBay. Media historians are now venturing into the "lowbrow" free market to find the documents they seek since many of them are not circulating in the "highbrow" world of institutional archives.

Copyright and other legal issues often keep key historical texts and documents inaccessible (or make access challenging). Major corporations own and copyright some works that for legal and/or financial reasons cannot be restored or preserved (Joseph 2007). Corporate copyright holders are frequently reluctant to allow full and unlimited access, and therefore place many restrictions on access. This is true of public as well as private or corporate archives. Many libraries have explicitly closed stacks or require institutional affiliation for research.

Another situation is when collections are physically *in* archives of one kind or another but have not been organized, cataloged, or indexed. The first challenge is locating these collections of personal papers. Radio historian Susan Siegel (2007) points out the many imperfections of current search mechanisms and finding tools. These include contradictory spellings, incorrect date ranges, the frequent inability to search the "content" field by keyword, as well as the lack of finding aids, unavailability of unpublished finding aids, and/or limitations in existing finding aids.[1]

Yet for those perseverant sleuths who are indeed able to crack through these barriers, many stories of great discovery exist. Once archives are fortuitously located, a persistent media-historian-turned-treasure-hunter may come upon a staggering collection of cardboard boxes bursting with information—unorganized though they may be—that may seem like the proverbial pot of gold. While researching *The American Stranger*, I located not one but at least three significant but uncataloged archival collections that proved to be central to my research. An email tip from an archivist led me to Princeton University where the uncataloged papers of the American Association for Indian Affairs were literally sitting piled in boxes in a back corner of the stacks. Similarly, I discovered the uncataloged papers of an activist nun (a key advisory figure to director McCormick) stashed in the back hallway of the Sisters of Mercy Convent in Spokane, Washington.

My most amazing research experience, however, occurred when trying to find correspondence from 1958 to 1959 about the impact of the documentary upon the Blackfeet Tribe in Montana. Upon contacting the tribe, I learned that no official tribal archives existed. Crestfallen, I spoke to the son of one of the key Blackfeet leaders of the 1950s, who remembered that his widowed mother had kept all of her husband's papers in filing cabinets in their garage. When the garage door was opened, after clambering over boxes of old clothes, toys, and holiday ornaments, I came to the end of the rainbow in filing cabinets that held the entire Blackfeet tribal archives from the 1950s, under inches of dust. These types of experiences lead to questions of unofficial archives—stashes, to be exact—as distinct from both private archives and public ones, and shine a spotlight on the value and priority placed or not placed upon—and finances allocated to—collecting and preserving historical documents.

The conceptual shift of archives from large physical holding tanks or repositories of tangible paper-, film-, and tape-based documents to digital collections is a paradigm shift that also needs more exploration, since with it comes not only a huge technological paradigm shift but also a new paradigm in which the boundaries between public and private, commercial and non-commercial, scholar and consumer are quickly crumbling.

Archives Without Walls—and Sometimes for Profit

Recent movements have seen long-guarded programming—even network-owned footage and programs—being made available digitally, either for altruistic or commercial purposes. The ability to access archival material digitally and online has become a major need for twenty-first-century seekers of archival material. The movement to digitize moving image collections and other archival references has been afoot for a number of years by university, state, and national libraries. However, standards still need to be set, and the process of digital archiving presents many yet-to-be-resolved challenges, both technical and legal. Some of these challenges include the cost of high-quality digitizing, the race against time (as video and tape collections are rapidly deteriorating), and technical issues of converting various formats (Carlson 2005).

The US Library of Congress is in the process of digitally archiving its media holdings. In 2007, the Swedish National Archives of Recorded Sound and

Moving Images announced a program to digitize 1.5 million hours of audiovisual material. Since preservation services to digitize film and video are quite costly, these initiatives require a partnership of public and private efforts: public archivists, software developers, and corporate information companies like Google (Carlson 2005). Copyright stipulations also complicate the situation.

The National Archives and Library of Congress of the USA, along with national libraries in Egypt, Brazil, and Russia, in late 2007 presented a prototype of the new World Digital Library at the UNESCO General Conference in Paris with plans for a public launch in 2009. The mission of The World Digital Library is to

> make available on the Internet, free of charge and in multilingual format, significant primary materials from cultures around the world, including manuscripts, maps, rare books, musical scores, recordings, films, prints, photographs, architectural drawings, and other significant cultural materials. The objectives of the World Digital Library are to promote international and inter-cultural understanding and awareness, provide resources to educators, expand non-English and non-Western content on the Internet, and to contribute to scholarly research.
>
> (www.worlddigitallibrary.org)

Digitization is coming to the institutional archives in numerous ways and, as funding allows, often in partnership with commercial ventures. In conjunction with the Association of Moving Image Archivists (AMIA), the Library of Congress sponsors MIC: Moving Image Collections (mic.loc.gov), a collaborative venture in moving image archives, information technology, and digital education. MIC "documents moving image collections around the world through a catalog of titles and directory of repositories, providing a window to the world's moving image collections for discovery, access and preservation." From this site, one can search the MIC Union Catalog online, which includes several national US collections (such as the Smithsonian), several regional public and university archives, archives of non-profit organizations (such as Witness Video Archives, focusing on human rights violations), commercial archives such as Oddball Film and Video (a stock footage company), and corporate archives such as National Geographic and the CNN Library.

In a separate program announced in February 2006, about 100 historic movies and documentaries held by the US National Archives were to be available free to the public via Google Video (video.google.com/nara.html) as well as the National Archives website (www.archives.gov). "This is an important step for the National Archives to achieve its goal of becoming an archive without walls," said Archivist of the United States Allen Weinstein.

Our new strategic plan emphasizes the importance of providing access to records anytime, anywhere. This is one of many initiatives that we are launching to make our goal a reality. For the first time, the public will be able to view this collection of rare and unusual films on the Internet.

("National" 2006)

BBC Motion Gallery (www.bbcmotiongallery.com) now boasts online access to selected video clips from BBC, CBS News, CCTV (China Central Television), the Australian Broadcasting Corporation, and NHK Japan via their website. As the "exclusive global representative" for CBS News, the BBC Worldwide site contains 700,000 hours of CBS News content, including outtakes and other news footage. From a cursory examination of this site, however, it appears to be more of a stock footage site than an archive, and content is only available through searches (which often come up empty or with a page full of five-second footage clips for sale) rather than browsing for particular programs. A company called CustomFlix Labs will digitalize ABC News Classics and Specials, it was announced in July 2007, and will sell them to the public via Amazon.com through CustomFlix Lab's DVD on Demand program ("ABC News" 2007).

This impetus to turn archival holdings into profit-making ventures, however, is not limited to the commercial media corporations. These non-exclusive agreements are in contrast to the exclusive agreement that The Smithsonian Institution inked with Showtime in March 2006. Birthed from this marriage was The Smithsonian Channel (www.smithsonianchannel.com), offering branded, original content from the historical institution including high-definition television programming as well as online videos on demand. A fact sheet on the museum's website explains the need for such a revenue-producing program to generate funding for its "popular exhibitions and public programs." However, this partnership caused an uproar among filmmakers who feared that their access to historic film documents would be blocked by the Smithsonian Network's "first right of refusal" clause (Bangeman 2006). Since then, in June 2008, Smithsonian Networks, dubbing itself "America's Storyteller," signed an exclusive DVD distribution agreement with Infinity Entertainment Group. [2]

In July 2007, the US National Archives announced its own partnership with Amazon.com and CustomFlix Labs to reproduce and sell to the public copies of historic moving images—specifically, a series of Universal Newsreels from 1920 to 1967. The deal allows Amazon and its subsidiary CustomFlix to digitize the historic footage and sell it in DVD form via the Internet (Ruane 2007). The intent, while masked as a gesture to making archival images more available to the public, seems primarily to be about creating a self-sustaining financial mechanism for NARA, a government agency.

Archives of the Future

Yet beyond either the traditional public archives or the large centers that are hybrids of commercial and non-profit, when it comes down to it, the archives become wherever you can find what you need—whether it is for free or for a fee, through loan or purchase from private collectors, stock footage companies, or eBay. Today, there are new concepts of what the twenty-first-century archive or library might be, hold, and do in order to meet the changing public needs.

An example is the most fascinating Prelinger Empire: the Prelinger Library in San Francisco and the affiliated Internet Archives. Rick Prelinger may be one of the most innovative pioneers in reconceptualizing the twenty-first-century archive and especially in recognizing the value of "ephemeral" and non-mainstream moving images as well as books, periodicals, and other papers. In 2002, he sold his private collection of over 48,000 ephemeral films to the Library of Congress and turned his attention to the building of the Prelinger Library; he has also been instrumental in the development of the Internet Archive (www.archive.org), founded by Brewster Kahle, a digital library of Internet sites and other cultural artifacts in digital form that is based upon a premise of free access to researchers, historians, scholars, and the public (Lewis-Krauss 2007). The online archive contains archived "snapshots" of websites at different points in their history ("The Way Back Machine"), a sizable moving images collection, including nearly 2,000 of Prelinger's ephemeral films, a live music archive, an audio archive, digital texts, and other innovative forms including "speed runs" of video games.

Media scholars of the twenty-first century face very distinct challenges as we try to pursue an endeavor that requires us to fix a fleeting moment, to carve a slice out of a flowing stream in order to study it. Are there alternative ways to imagine doing such histories? What norms and conventions have been established, and how might they change in the coming decade? How might we better conceptualize, document, and display our historical "data" or evidence, be it visible or not?

In summary, let us reflect upon and anticipate what the next paradigm may be. It is not hard to imagine a future in which museums favor trendiness over historic collections and in which most if not all archives (or at least those believed to have commercial potential) are available digitally online or on DVD by Demand. The notion of the historian and the concept of the consumer may merge, and what may be left accessible for the serious researcher will only be what someone in a corporate office seems worthy of sharing (a.k.a. selling); the rest may face the shredder to make room for more recent and trendier fare. However, this vision reflects a loss that some may mourn, since it favors finished products (and in particular those finished products deemed to be commercially viable) over the evidence of the process and the supporting materials.

Notes

1. See also Siegel and Siegel (2006).
2. See www.si.edu/ondemand/pdfs/SOD_factsheet.pdf and www.smithsonianchannel.com/site/smithsonian/pdf/press/Infinity_Press_Release.pdf (June 11, 2008).

Works Cited

"ABC News and CustomFlix Labs Announce Deal to Bring Previously Unavailable Programming to ABC News and Amazon.com Customers With DVD on Demand." 2007. *TMCNet* (online), July 12. www.tmcnet.com/usubmit/2007/07/12/2778237.htm.

Bangeman, Eric. 2006. "Smithsonian Deal with Showtime Draws Fire." *Ars Technica* (online), April 4. Retrieved from http://arstechnica.com/news.ars/post/20060404-6523.html.

Carlson, Scott. 2005. "The Revolution Will Be Digitized." *Chronicle of Higher Education* 29 April.

Crupi, Anthony. 2006. "Showtime, Smithsonian Launch VOD." *Media Week* March 8. Retrieved September 30, 2007 from www.mediaweek.com/mw/news/cabletv/article_display.jsp?vnu_content_id=1002154831.

Jensen, Elizabeth. 2007. "New Name and Mission for Museum of Television." *New York Times* June 5. Retrieved September 30, 2007 from www.nytimes.com/2007/06/05/arts/design/05pale.html?_r=1&oref=slogin.

Joseph, Jeff. 2007. Discussion on AMIA-L listserv (the electronic discussion group of the Association of Moving Image Archivists), September 27.

Levine, Elana. 2007. Personal communication. June.

Lewis-Kraus, Gideon. 2007. "A World in Three Aisles: Browsing the Post-Digital Library." *Harpers* 314, May 1984: 47–57. www.harpers.org/archive/2007/05/0081511.

"National Archives and Google Launch Pilot Project to Digitize and Offer Historic Films Online." 2006. Press Release, National Archives February 24. Retrieved 30 September, 2007 from www.archives.gov/press/press-releases/2006/nr06–64.html.

Ruane, Michael E. 2007. "Amazon to Copy and Sell Archives' Footage First DVDs Already Available Under Non-Exclusive Deal." *Washington Post* July 30. Retrieved from www.washingtonpost.com/wp-dyn/content/article/2007/07/30/AR2007073001589_pf.html.

Siegel, Susan. 2007. Personal communication. June.

—— and David Siegel. 2006. *A Resource Guide to the Golden Age of Radio*. Yorktown Heights, NY: Book Hunter Press.

Chapter 18

Historicizing Web Design

Software, Style, and the Look of the Web

Megan Sapnar Ankerson

Most Internet histories typically trace key inventors, institutions, and technologies through the network's Cold War roots as ARPAnet to its final incarnation as the World Wide Web, developed at CERN by Tim Berners-Lee in the early 1990s. Rarely mentioned are the business and culture of making websites. Indeed, too often economists and Internet scholars alike have dismissed the volatile times of the dot-com boom as a moment that we would do best to recover from and not as a period worthy of further inquiry where we might take more seriously the cultural artifacts that emerged from the web's first decade. As the value of Internet stocks continued their exorbitant climb, the design and production of commercial websites became a specialized endeavor entrusted to creative workers at the core of a rapidly growing new media cultural industry. But the dynamics of this industry, and the reciprocal links between aesthetics and modes of production, have yet to be fully explored.

Why is there surprisingly little work that connects the social and economic context of the dot-com boom to an historical understanding of web style, production practices, and industrial logic? Similar questions have been occupying media historians for decades now. As a number of film and broadcast historians have noted, aesthetic decisions, narrative structures, and conceptual approaches are all intimately related to the organization of media industries, the relations of creative workers, the deployment of new technologies, and the numerous strategies employed to help manage the uncertainties of an industry marked by constant changes in popular taste.[1] One of the first and most influential projects to connect film style to the motion picture industry is *The Classical Hollywood Cinema*, which systematically demonstrates how aesthetic and narrative conventions were formalized and standardized between 1917 and 1960 (Bordwell et al. 1985). Likewise, Robert Allen and Douglas Gomery's reformulation of aesthetic film history eschews the "masterpiece tradition" and asks instead:

> How and why have the elements of film form (lighting, editing, camera movement) been used in particular films at particular points in film

history? How and why have some styles become normative for long periods of film history (the Hollywood "style," for example), while others have flourished for only brief periods?

(1985, 79)

Broadcast historians, meanwhile, have explored the various ways in which industry structures and network economics (along with other factors) have helped shape the types of programs that were made, their formal structures, and the formatting and scheduling practices employed (Gitlin 1984; Boddy 1990; Anderson 1994; Caldwell 1995). These histories help alert us to the multiple ways in which American media might be organized differently, reminding us repeatedly that it is by no means "natural" or "obvious" for television, radio, or film to work or look the ways they do.[2]

But new media historians have yet to tackle similar questions. Perhaps this is the result of the web's relative newness; barely fifteen years have passed since the Mosaic browser first introduced a larger audience to the web. But these gaps in scholarship also point to some of the problems of web historiography, an undertaking made particularly challenging given the difficulty of doing research in a realm where texts are evanescent. How can we study the web of the recent past when so much of what was produced was subsequently deleted, disabled, or amended? Dot-coms were born and buried in a matter of months. Domain names were vacated and resold, leaving little evidence of first-generation websites. These problems, of course, are familiar to media historians trying to investigate the cultural roots of film and broadcasting, who know all too well the difficulties in piecing together the past when so many films have been lost, damaged, and destroyed, and much of what was sent over the airwaves was broadcast live and unrecorded.

However, many new media scholars and computer historians have resisted comparing new media to old media texts and technologies. Lev Manovich, for example, points out that while new media have numerous historical precedents in earlier media, comparing computable cultural forms with old media "cannot address the fundamental quality of new media that has no historical precedent—programmability" (2001, 47). He advocates a shift from "media studies" to what he calls "software studies," which would examine "the new terms, categories, and operations that characterize media that has become programmable" (48). Since software is what is unique to new media, Manovich argues, comparing new media to print, photography, or television will never tell the whole story. But what kinds of stories might "old media" historians help new media historians tell? And how might software studies contribute in return to a critical web historiography? With these questions in mind, this chapter evaluates the problems and possibilities of applying methods developed for writing cultural histories of old media to the task of recovering and writing web histories.

The Rise of Software Studies

The gaps and erasures that media historians contend with have helped bring post-structural historiographical methods to the forefront of cultural histories of mass media. Rejecting "master narratives" about the past by recognizing multiple, over-lapping histories, this approach acknowledges the ways in which preserved traces of the past help shape the stories we purport to tell. But recognizing the multiplic-ity of histories and the often-contradictory nature of truth has not been a domi-nant tradition in the history-of-computing field. Paul Ceruzzi, for example, describes how the first generation of computer historians worked to "reconcile" the convergent stories of the stored-program digital computer in order to come up with a coherent narrative about computing and the past, and he urges histor-ians to apply this same narrative cohesion to the history of the personal computer (PC) (2001, 54–55). The problem with such cohesion, however, is that it tends to privilege "great men" or otherwise becomes occupied with the task of allocat-ing credit where credit is due. This may help explain how computers are bound up in a complex of engineering decisions and industry constraints, but as Paul Edwards puts it, "There is little place in such accounts for the influence of ideolo-gies, intersections with popular culture, or political power" (1996, xii).

Recent interest in the study of software and software histories is helping to make some of these intersections more palpable for scholars concerned with media and culture.[3] Matthew Fuller argues that software has been a "blind spot" in the cultural theorization of computational and networked digital media: "Software is seen as a tool, something that you do something with. It is neutral, grey, or optimistically blue ... This ostensive neutrality can be taken as its ideological layer, as deserving of critique as any such myth" (2008, 3).[4] So often elided in accounts of digital culture, software has become the "repressed" of new media studies. Its mutability and multidimensionality have caused some to mistakenly emphasize software's "immateriality," a contention that has been widely refuted (Mackenzie 2006, 2; Fuller 2008, 4; Kirschenbaum 2003). Software is "a seemingly amorphous object," notes software historian Michael Mahoney, "yet [it] produces visible and tangible effects in the world" (2000, 277). For Fuller, the materiality of software is operative at many scales: from the underlying code and interaction with hardware to the operational constraints of the interface and its thorough integration into patterns of work, play, and communication (2008, 4).

In this way, software extends outside the computer into social worlds; in return, cultural processes and discourses find their way back into code. Websites may come and go, but software leaves its mark on web practices (a set of widely held stylistic norms that constitute assumptions about how a website should behave, look, and function; how users should interact with it, and so on), and in modes of production (the economic organization, division of labor, and overall ways of conceiving the work of web production).[5] Software leaves traces when individual websites may not. As Matthew Kirschenbaum pointedly remarks:

> Software is the product of white papers, engineering specs, marketing reports, conversations and collaborations, intuitive insights and professionalized expertise, venture capital (in other words, money), late nights (in other words, labor) ... These are material circumstances that leave material traces—in corporate archives, in email folders, on whiteboards and legal pads, in countless iterations of alpha versions and beta versions and patches and upgrades, in focus groups and user communities, in expense accounts, in licensing agreements, in stock options and IPOs.
>
> (2003, 149)

The historical materialist studies of new media that Kirschenbaum advocates can also be a way to reflect on the process and consequences of writing histories based on the selective evidence and biased traces left behind. Is there not something about the very malleability of software that seems pertinent to an insistence on the partiality of truth?

Approaching web historiography through the lens of software studies, I offer the following brief history of the web animation software, Flash, as an example of how new media historians might engage the culture of software in constructing histories of the web.[6] This very partial account presents the discourses surrounding Flash as one entry point into some of the conflicting ways cyberspace was imagined and produced at the zenith of the dot-com bubble and in the aftermath of its collapse.

What is Flash?

Now an industry-standard multimedia authoring application used to create web content and applications, motion graphics, and games, Flash was first launched by FutureWave Software in the summer of 1996 as a simple animation program called FutureSplash. Soon after its release, the software received a huge boost when Microsoft deployed it in their MSN website in an attempt to create "the most television-like experience possible on the Internet" (Gay 2001, 4). Fox used FutureSplash in their 1996 website for *The Simpsons*, and Disney used it in their subscription-based online service, *Disney's Daily Blast*.

By December 1996, FutureSplash had generated so much attention that Macromedia acquired FutureWave and relaunched it as Macromedia Flash 1.0 in early 1997.

However, the ability to add animation to the web was only one of the draws of Flash. For web designers working in the heat of the Browser Wars, the competition between Netscape and Explorer meant that it was not unusual to create up to four different versions of the same website. Both companies were releasing browsers that incorporated their own proprietary tags for generating "dynamic" websites with multimedia elements. This opened the door to a radical shift in web aesthetics. As Jeffrey Zeldman (2000) explains

> No more static, print-like Web layouts! Images could move, buttons could beep, whole chunks of text could appear and disappear at the twitch of a hapless visitor's mouse. The problem . . . [was that] if it worked in Navigator, it would fail in Explorer, and vice versa.
>
> (2000)

Flash offered developers a way to solve the problem of "cross-browser compatibility" by creating a single website that displayed uniformly across multiple browser versions. Not only did this substantially reduce the cost of development, it also provided designers with a new skill-set they could use to negotiate higher salaries. Furthermore, Flash's vector format made fullscreen high-resolution graphics possible for a fraction of the filesize as a bitmapped image. But perhaps more than anything, Flash appealed to a whole new vision of the web, one that was vastly different from the static, silent, textual form that imitated the aesthetics of print. These possibilities captured the imaginations of independent designers who were navigating the huge industrial shifts impacting the organizational structure and creative work of web production by 1998.

Growth of the Web Media Industry

The first wave of "web service providers" (as web design start-ups were then called) exploded on the scene in 1995 amidst a huge demand for web design talent. Since ad agencies found it difficult to turn interactive projects into a major revenue stream, they were more than happy to subcontract the work to these startups (Wilder 1995), but only two years later, these once tight partnerships were becoming strained. Animosity between interactive shops and traditional ad agencies grew as agencies realized online media billings were growing faster at independent upstarts than at traditional media departments (Hodges 1997). In response, agencies bought stakes in web companies or started their own in-house interactive units. Many mid-size web shops, meanwhile, positioned themselves as marketing and branding consultants; they no longer wanted to be seen as web designers but as full-service interactive advertising agencies that specialized in Internet strategy (Voight 1997, IQ20).

As sites became more elaborate and required significant backend technical expertise to handle the demands of e-commerce, these industry restructurings culminated in a wave of mergers and acquisitions in 1998 that gave rise to mega-agencies (Butcher 1999).[7] However, while industry consolidation meant more consulting expertise and backend support, a pressing concern was that the mergers took a toll on creativity. Although e-commerce attracted significant buzz, shopping carts and secure servers did little to convey the sexiness and excitement that new media evoked. Small, specialized design firms thrived partly because they represented independent talent untouched by the corporatization of web design. Hip San Francisco boutiques and New York design shops were highly sought after due to the edgy, avant-garde, creative images they conveyed (Williamson 1999).

In this industrial climate, freelancers and boutique shops saw Flash as one way to gain an edge through creative technical expertise. In her study of web design workers in the 1990s, Nalini Kotamraju observes that the job insecurity of contract-based service work propagates a system in which workers must always be ready to update their skill-sets as soon as new software is introduced. This pressure of "keeping up" underlies key structures of the workplace, she argues, most notably in terms of pay, promotion, and hierarchy (2002, 2). Indeed, some of the first Flash websites were those of freelance designers using their personal studio sites to showcase their skills. These sites spoke directly of a "new era of web design," one that emphasized creativity, expression, and impact; websites were to no longer be used, but experienced.[8]

David Gary Studio's Flash website "Full Throttle" (launched in April 1999) is one such example. Full Throttle opens with a dedication ("For Lala") as howling winds and a barking dog give way to slick chrome graphics and the headline "an experiment in expression." Motion graphics mimic garage-style mechanics and a heavy soundtrack kicks in after the interface loads. Engine-revving sound effects and a lifelike exhaust flame are all designed to "wow" users with a memorable experience. The site received tremendous word-of-mouth attention within the web design community and was selected in 2006 as one of the Favourite Website Award's (FWA) most influential Flash sites of the decade. Personal studio sites like this served as calling cards for independent designers who presented Flash as a specialized skill to help clients deliver websites that "cut through the clutter." Because Flash websites looked so different from the web most users were accustomed to seeing, clients began

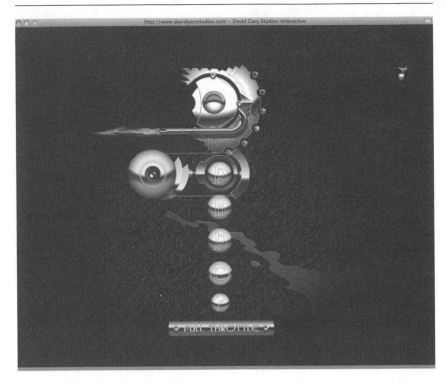

Figure 18.1 David Gary Studio's website, "Full Throttle," was built entirely in Flash and generated quite a stir among web designers when it was launched in 1999.

demanding Flash integration into commercial websites as a way to achieve "stickiness," another buzzword of the late 1990s that emphasized content compelling users to "stick around."

By 2000, Flash had become a multi-million dollar industry of not just software sales, but numerous Flash-related products: training videos, workshops, magazines, books for inspiration, books for learning code, and even books by design studios that analyze (in painstaking detail) the process of conceiving, building, and coding their websites. Popular events such as the semi-annual "Flash Forward" conference and Film Festival generated a massive interest in the software and in the practice of web design. As dot-com speculation moved to euphoria, the "hottest" designers and agencies became sought-after brand names commanding extraordinary sums for their involvement in a project.

But it was not long after the stock market reached its tipping point in March 2000 that the discourse surrounding Flash registered a noticeable chill. Critics like usability expert Jakob Nielson lambasted Flash as "99% Bad" in October 2000 for "encouraging design abuse" and "breaking with Web fundamentals," charges that expressed a biting exasperation with the bells, whistles, and lengthy animated intro sequences that were seen as part of the "look what I can do" bravado of the Flash aesthetic. After the crash, the mythos of the hot-shot designer and its visual expression in Flash came to signify everything that was wrong with irrational exuberance: the greed, the hubris, the renovated lofts, foosball tables, and twenty-something-year-old millionaires that would soon be regarded as extravagant relics of the dot-com bubble. As commentators reflected on the state of the industry after the bust, the links between web design and the indulgences of dot-com IPOs were framed as a "boys' club" atmosphere of "tech fetishism, aggression, and adolescent image-consciousness that quickly became the dominant culture of web media agencies" (Mahoney 2003). Flash was just one expression of this image, but it came to stand in for a host of critiques surrounding the hype and ego of the e-culture industry.

Once fashionable Flash introduction sequences soon became denigrated. A popular parody of the "skip intro" style, named after the obligatory button added to sites should users want to skip the animation and enter the website, was created in 1998 by Yacco Vijn; it circulated with viral ferocity after the bust. In it, viewers are forced to watch an endless array of orange balls while

Figure 18.2 Yacco Vijn's parody of Flash introductory sequences became a viral sensation after the dot-com bubble burst.

the site loads; underneath a message explains, "this may take forever, but hey it's an intro!" Once loaded, the site reveals fullscreen rotating spheres and welcome messages, accompanied by a score of "over-the-top science fiction sound samples ... [reminiscent of] the Gaborcop.com envy that was all the rage at the time" (Vijn 2008).

To combat the software's reputation for gratuitous animation, Macromedia went on damage control by heavily promoting the notion of "Flash usability," which involved educating the Flash community about the importance of "user-friendly" experiences. "Skip intro" became a lesson that designers were taught to avoid. Macromedia hired flash nemesis Nielsen to develop "best practice guidelines for creating usable rich Internet applications with Flash," and the software was revamped further in Macromedia MX, adding features designed to help Flash developers "to be more productive while ensuring their work is both usable and accessible" (Macromedia 2002).

Today, Flash is just as ubiquitous as it was at the height of the dot-com boom, but most casual web surfers are probably not even aware that the software mutated from an animation tool to an application-building program. Popular "Web 2.0" sites like YouTube and Flickr are built on Flash. Google's finance pages use Flash to generate stock graphs. Newspapers use it to illustrate maps and timelines. Far from the grandiose sound effects and "skip intro" buttons that were once a staple of Flash websites, the software has become so ordinary it is almost invisible. Indeed, it is this "everyday" aspect of software that intensifies the desire to make the study of it more visible, to challenge its peripheral status in the study of digital objects. But the story of Flash—its embrace by designers who wanted to see the web as a form of creative expression, its disparagement by those tired of dot-com exuberance, and its revamping by Macromedia (and later Adobe which bought it)—helps to illuminate a discursive web connecting aesthetics, ideologies, economies, and industries.

The challenge for a web historiography of Flash is that despite the abundance of commentary about the software's popularity (and notoriety), finding remains of early Flash websites now is like looking for dinosaur bones. Some are out there, but in pieces, and they are hard to find and hard to recover. Web archive sites like the WayBack Machine have received much attention for their ability to recover the past and pull up old versions of now dead websites.[9] But unlike HTML pages—which allow viewers to "Save Page As"—the Flash sites that once commanded so much attention, admiration, and scorn remain mostly inaccessible. A critical web historiography must acknowledge how the traces left behind shape the stories we tell about the past. But here, it is precisely the erasure of so many Flash sites that is equally worth noting.[10] Many of the most extravagant Flash sites produced between 1998 and 2001 have been removed or modified precisely because the dominant web practice underwent a massive revision after the bubble burst. The post-crash pursuit of "user-friendly" design should not be seen as a simple case of web designers "coming to their senses" at long last. Instead, it is a register of a new dominant discourse that gained momentum in response to shifts in the larger socio-economic context. Software is remade again and again, and the new upgrades, tutorials, and help files reveal ideologies as well as bug-fixes. If we hope to track cultural histories of the web, we should recognize the ways in which software can reveal contested sites of web practice where dominant discourses find their way into material and symbolic forms.

Notes

1. See e.g. Schatz (1993) and Wyatt (1994) on the connections between economics and aesthetics in post-classical cinema.
2. Comparing the British and American broadcasting models, Raymond Williams (1974) challenged Marshall McLuhan's dictum "the media is the message" as a case of technological determinism which neglects the social, political, and economic choices that have shaped the experience of television in different national contexts.
3. See e.g. Fuller 2003, 2008; Mackenzie 2006; Manovich 2001; Lovink 2003; Kirschenbaum 2003.
4. Gillespie (2003) offers one such critique of Macromedia Dreamweaver.
5. This notion of a web practice owes much to Bordwell, Staiger, and Thompson's description of classical Hollywood film practice (1985).
6. Kirschenbaum offers another example with his account of VRML but does not engage with the stylistic questions that interest me here.
7. For example, interactive group Modem Media merged with ad agency Poppe Tyson; Internet technology firm USWeb merged with interactive marketing agency CKS; Razorfish acquired six other interactive agencies in the USA and made substantial acquisitions overseas.
8. The first website to receive significant attention for this was Gabo Mendoza's site Gaborcorp.com www.thefwa.com/flash10/gabo.html (30 July 2008).
9. Available online at www.archive.org.
10. See Trouillot (1995) for a reflection on the role of silences and erasures in the writing of history.

Works Cited

Allen, Robert and Douglas Gomery. 1985. *Film History, Theory and Practice*. New York: McGraw-Hill.

Anderson, Christopher. 1994. *Hollywood TV: The Studio System in the 1950s*. Austin: University of Texas Press.

Boddy, William. 1990. *Fifties Television: The Industry and Its Critics*. Urbana: University of Illinois Press.

Bordwell, David, Janet Staiger, and Kristin Thompson. 1985. *The Classical Hollywood Cinema: Film Style and Mode of Production to 1960*. New York: Columbia University Press.

Butcher, Mike. 1999. "Net Ready; 1998 was a Tumultuous Year for Web Groups." *Design Week* 29 Jan.

Caldwell, John. 1995. *Televisuality: Style, Crisis, and Authority in American Television*. New Brunswick, NJ: Rutgers University Press.

Ceruzzi, Paul. 2001. "A View from Twenty Years as a Historian of Computing." *IEEE Annals of the History of Computing* 23.4: 49–55.

Edwards, Paul. 1996. *The Closed World: Computers and the Politics of Discourse in Cold War America*. Cambridge, MA: MIT Press.

Fuller, Matthew. 2003. *Behind the Blip: Essays on the Culture of Software*. New York: Autonomedia.

———. 2008. *Software Studies: A Lexicon*. Cambridge, MA: MIT Press.

Gary, David. 1999. "Full Throttle." Website. David Gary Studios, 30 July 2008. www. davidgarystudios.com/v1/.

Gay, Jonathan. 2001. "The History of Flash." *Adobe* 30 July (2008). www.adobe.com/ macromedia/events/john_gay/.

Gillespie, Tarleton. 2003. "The Stories Digital Tools Tell." *New Media: Theories and Practices of Digitextuality*, ed. John Caldwell and Anna Everett. New York: Routledge, 107–126.

Gitlin, Todd. 1983. *Inside Prime Time*. New York: Pantheon.

Hodges, Jane. 1997. "Media Buying & Planning: Online Work Leaves Media Department, Goes To Specialists." *Advertising Age* 4 August: S20.

Kirschenbaum, Matthew. 2003. "Virtuality and VRML: Software Studies After Manovich." *The Politics of Information: The Electronic Mediation of Social Change*, ed. Mark Bousquet and Katherine Wills. Alt-X Press eBook, 30 July 2008. www.altx.com/ ebooks/infopol.html.

Kotamraju, Nalini P. 2002. "Keeping Up: Web Design Skill and the Reinvented Worker." *Information, Communication, and Society* 5.1: 1–26.

Lovink, Geert. 2003. *My First Recession: Critical Internet Culture in Transition*. Rotterdam: V2 Publishing/NA; Publishers.

Mackenzie, Adrian. 2006. *Cutting Code: Software and Sociality*. New York: Peter Lang.

Macromedia. 2002. "Macromedia And Usability Guru Jakob Nielsen Work Together To Improve Web Usability." Press Release 3 June, 30 July 2008. www.adobe.com/mac-romedia/proom/pr/2002/macromedia_nielsen.html.

Mahoney, Karen. 2003. "Bubble or Extinction Burst?" *LOOP: AIGA Journal of Interactive Design Education*. June: 7, 30 July 2008. http://loop1.aiga.org/content.cfm?Alias =bubbleessay.

Mahoney, Michael. 2000. "Probing the Elephant: How Do the Parts Fit Together?" *History of Computing: Software Issues*, ed. Ulf Hashagen, Reinhard Keil-Slawik, and Arthur L. Norberg. Berlin: Springer Verlag, 277–283.

Manovich, Lev. 2001. *The Language of New Media*. Cambridge, MA: MIT Press.

Nielsen, Jakob. 2000. "Flash: 99% Bad." *Alertbox* 29 October, 30 July 2008. www.useit. com/alertbox/20001029.html.

Schatz, Thomas. 1993. "The New Hollywood." *Film Theory Goes to the Movies*, ed. Jim Collins, Hilary Radner, and Ava Preacher Collins. New York: Routledge, 8–36.

Trouillot, Michel-Rolph. 1995. *Silencing the Past: Power and the Production of History*. Boston, MA: Beacon Press.

Vijn, Yacco. 1997. "Skip Intro." Web animation. 30 July 2008 www.skipintros.com/.

———. 2008. "Re: Skip Intro." E-mail to Megan Sapnar 29 July.

Voight, Joan. 1997. "IQ's Leading Agencies." *Mediaweek* 17 November: 11–30.

Wilder, Clinton. 1995. "Plugging In to The Web—A Whole New Industry of Consultants is Springing up to Help Major Companies Set Up Shop on the World Wide Web." *Information Week* 3 April.

Williams, Raymond. 1974. *Television: Technology and Cultural Form*. London: Fontana.

Williamson, Deborah Aho. 1999. "Agencies Left In Cold As Marketers Expand Online." *Advertising Age* 26 July: S26.

Wyatt, Justin. 1994. *High Concept: Movies and Marketing in Hollywood*. Austin: University of Texas Press.

Zeldman, Jeffrey. 2000. "Creative Revolution on the Web II: Counterrevolution." *Adobe* 17 July, 30 July 2008. http://web.archive.org/web/20000815061549/www.adobe.com/web/columns/zeldman/20000717/main.html.

Bibliography on Media Historiography

Allen, Robert C. 1982. "The Archeology of Film History." *Wide Angle* 5. 2: 4–12.

—— and Douglas Gomery. 1985. *Film History: Theory and Practice*. New York: Knopf.

Altman, Charles F. 1977. "Towards a Historiography of American Film." *Cinema Journal* 16. 2 (Spring): 1–25.

Alvarado, M. 1981. "Authorship, Organization and Production." *Australian Journal of Screen Theory* 9/10: 11–35.

Beck, Philip. 1985. "Historicism and Historicism in Recent Film Historiography." *Journal of Film and Video* 37. 1 (Winter): 5–20.

Benjamin, Louise M. 1996. "Communication for the Love of It." *Journal of Broadcasting & Electronic Media* 40. 4 (Fall): 558–562.

Bordwell, David. 1981/1982. "Textual Analysis, Etc." *enclitic* 5, 1/6. 1 (Fall/Spring): 125–136. See also responses by Lawrence Crawford. 1983. *enclitic* 7.1 (Spring): 87–91, and Bordwell, 92–95.

——. 1985. "Lowering the Stakes: Prospects for a Historical Poetics of Cinema." *Iris* 1. 2: 5–18.

—— and Kristin Thompson. 1983. "Linearity, Materialism, and the Study of Early American Cinema." *Wide Angle* 5. 3: 4–15.

Branigan, Edward. 1979. "Color and Cinema: Problems in the Writing of History." *Film Reader* 4: 16–34.

Brennen, Bonnie. 1995. "Newsworkers During the Interwar Era: A Critique of Traditional Media History." *Communication Quarterly* 43. 2 (Spring): 197–209.

Browne, Nick. 1994. "On the Historiography of American Film." *History of Moving Images: Reports from a Norwegian Project*, ed. Jostein Gripsrud and Kathrine Skretting. Oslo, Norway: The Research Council of Norway, 9–15.

Buscombe, Edward. 1977. "A New Approach to Film History." *Film: Historical-Theoretical Speculations: 1977 Film Studies Annual, Pt. 2*, ed. Ben Lawton and Janet Staiger. Pleasantville, NY: Redgrave Publishing Co., 1–8.

——. 1979. "Introduction: Metahistory of Film." *Film Reader* 4: 11–15.

Comolli, Jean-Louis. 1971–1972. "Technique et Ideologie" [6 parts], *Cahiers du cinema* 229, 230, 231, 233, 234–235, 241 (May).

Corner, John. 2003. "Finding Data, Reading Patterns, Telling Stories: Issues in the Historiography of Television." *Media, Culture & Society* 25. 2: 273–280.

Dahl, Hans Fredrik. 1994. "The Pursuit of Media History." *Media, Culture & Society* 16. 4: 551–563.

Dhoest, Alexander. 2004. "Breaking Boundaries in Television Historiography: Historical Research and the Television Archive, University of Reading, 9 January 2004." *Screen* 45. 3 (Autumn): 245–259.

Ellis, John. 1977. "The Institution of Cinema." *Edinburgh '77 Magazine* 2: 56–66.

Elsaesser, Thomas. 1986. "The New Film History." *Sight and Sound* 55. 4 (Autumn): 246–251.

Film History. 1994. *Film History* 6. 1 (Spring). Special issue on historiography.

Gomery, Douglas. 1982. "The Economics of Film: What is the Method?" *Film / Culture: Explorations of Cinema in its Social Context*, ed. Sari Thompson. Metuchen, NJ: Scarecrow Press, 81–94.

———. 1983a. "Historical Method and Data Acquisition." *Cinema Journal* 22. 4 (Summer): 58–60. See also Charles Musser, "Response," 61–64.

———. 1983b. "Rewriting the History of Film in the United States: Theory and Method." *Wide Angle* 5. 4: 75–79.

Gunning, Tom. 1990. "Film History and Film Analysis: The Individual Film in the Course of Time." *Wide Angle* 12. 3: 4–19.

Hamm, Charles. 2004. "Popular Music and Historiography." *Popular Music History* 1. 1 (April): 9–14.

Heath, Stephen. 1977. "Contexts." *Edinburgh '77 Magazine* 2: 37–43.

"In Focus." 2004. *Cinema Journal* 44. 2 (Fall). Special issue on historiography.

Iris. 1984. *Iris* 2. 2. Special issue on theory of film history.

Lounsbury, Myron O. 1980. "'The Gathered Light': History, Criticism and The Rise of the American Film." *Quarterly Review of Film Studies* 5. 1 (Winter): 49–85.

Mast, Gerald. 1976. "Film History and Film Histories." *Quarterly Review of Film Studies* 1. 3 (August): 297–813.

McChesney, Robert W. 1996. "Communication for the Hell of It: The Triviality of U.S. Broadcasting History." *Journal of Broadcasting & Electronic Media* 40. 4 (Fall): 540–552.

Metz, Christian. 1979. "The Cinematic Apparatus as Social Institution: An Interview with Christian Metz." *Discourse* 1: 7–37.

Mittell, Jason S. 1997. "Invisible Footage: 'Industry on Parade' and Television Historiography." *Film History* 9. 2: 200–218.

Mottram, Ron. 1980. "Fact and Affirmation: Some Thoughts on the Methodology of Film History and the Relation of Theory to Historiography." *Quarterly Review of Film Studies* 5. 3 (Summer): 335–347.

Nowell-Smith, Geoffrey. 1976. "Facts about Films and Facts of Films." *Quarterly Review of Film Studies* 1. 3 (August): 272–275.

———. 1977. "On the Writing of the History of the Cinema: Some Problems." *Edinburgh '77 Magazine* 2: 8–13.

———. 1990. "On History and the Cinema." *Screen* 31. 2: 160–172.

O'Connor, John E., ed. 1990. *Image as Artifact: The Historical Analysis of Film and Television*. Malabar, FL: Robert E. Krieger Publishing Co.

Palmer, William J. 1993. "Introduction." *The Films of the Eighties: A Social History*. Carbondale, IL: Southern Illinois University Press, 1–15.

Perry, Stephen D. and Keith Massie. 2007. "A Historiographic Look at Online Selling: Opening the World of the Private Collection." *Convergence: The Journal of Research into New Media Technologies* 13. 1 (February): 93–103.

Petro, Patrice. 1990. "Feminism and Film History." *camera obscura* 22 (January): 9–26.

Popple, Simon. 1998. "'Cinema Wasn't Invented, It Growed': Technological Film Historiography before 1913." *Celebrating 1895: The Centenary of Cinema*, ed. John Fullerton. Sydney, Australia: Libbey, 19–26.

Pryluck, Calvin. 1976. "The Aesthetic Relevance of the Organization of Film Production." *Cinema Journal* 15. 2 (Spring): 1–6.

Rentschler, Eric. 1981. "Expanding Film Historical Discourse: Reception Theory's Use Value for Cinema Studies." *Ciné-tracts* 13 (Spring): 57–68.

Rosen, Philip. 2001. *Change Mummified: Cinema, Historicity, Theory*. Minneapolis: University of Minnesota Press.

Rosenstone, Robert. 1988. "History in Images/History in Words: Reflections on the Possibility of Really Putting History Onto Film." *American Historical Review* 93. 5 (December): 1173–1185.

Scannell, Paddy. 2004. "Broadcasting Historiography and Historicality." *Screen* 45. 2 (Summer): 130–141.

Scherer, Paul H. 1983. "New Approaches to the Teaching of Film History." *The History Teacher* 16. 3 (May): 371–382.

Schudson, Michael. 1991. "Media Contexts: Historical Approaches to Communication Studies." *Handbook of Qualitative Methodologies for Mass Communication Research*, ed. Klaus Bruhn Jensen. London: Routledge, 175–189.

Sklar, Robert. 1988. "Oh, Althusser!': Historiography and the Rise of Cinema Studies." *Radical History Review* 41: 10–35.

Sobchack, Vivian, ed. 1996. *The Persistence of History: Cinema, Television, and the Modern Event*. New York: Routledge.

Staiger, Janet. 1985. "The Politics of Film Canons." *Cinema Journal* 24. 3 (Spring): 4–23. See responses by Dudley Andrew, Gerald Mast, and Staiger, *Cinema Journal* 25. 1 (Fall): 55–64.

——. 1990. "This Moving Image I Have Before Me." *Image as Artifact: The Historical Analysis of Film and Television*, ed. John E. O'Connor. Malabar, FL: Robert E. Krieger Publishing Company, 247–275.

——. 1992. *Interpreting Films: Studies in the Historical Reception of American Cinema*. Princeton, NJ: Princeton University Press, 154–177.

——. 1995. "The Pleasures and Profits of a Postmodern Film Historiography." *Norsk Medietidsskrift* [Oslo, Norway] 2. 2: 7–17.

Stenzl, Jurg. 1995. "In Search of a History of Musical Interpretation." *Musical Quarterly* 79. 4 (Winter): 683–699.

Straw, Will. 1980. "The Myth of Total Cinema History." *Ciné-Tracts* 9 (Winter): 8–16.

Streeter, Thomas. 1996. "The 'New Historicism' in Media Studies." *Journal of Broadcasting & Electronic Media* 40. 4 (Fall): 553–558.

Sundholm, John. 2003. "Narrative Machines, or, From 'Bottom to Top'." *Nordicom Review* 24. 1 (January): 107–114.

Tomasulo, Frank P. 2001. "What Kind of Film History Do We Teach? The Introductory Survey Course as a Pedagogical Opportunity." *Cinema Journal* 41. 1 (Fall): 110–114.

White, Hayden. 1988. "Historiography and Historiophoty." *American Historical Review* 93. 5 (December): 1193–1199.

Yeh, Yueh-yu. 2002. "Historiography and Sinification: Music in Chinese Cinema of the 1930s." *Cinema Journal* 41. 3 (Spring): 78–97.

Zhang, Yingjin. 2000. "A Typography of Chinese Film Historiography." *Asian Cinema* 11. 1 (Spring/Summer): 16–32.

Contributors

Megan Sapnar Ankerson is a Ph.D. candidate in Media and Cultural Studies at the University of Wisconsin, Madison. She is currently finishing her dissertation, which examines the cultural industry of web production during the dot-com boom. Her work has been published in *NMEDIAC: The Journal of New Media and Culture* and *The Electronic Literature Collection Vol. 1* (2006). She also co-founded and edited the online literary journal *Poems that Go* (2000–2004).

Kyle S. Barnett is an Assistant Professor of Media Studies in the Department of Communication at Bellarmine University and a Fellow in the university's Institute for Media, Culture, and Ethics. His publications include "Furniture Music: The Phonograph as Furniture, 1900–1930" in the *Journal of Popular Music Studies*. He co-edited *The Velvet Light Trap* #51, "Sounding Off: Film Sound/Film Music." His current research focuses on cultural production and genre formation in the US recording industry.

Richard Butsch is Professor of Sociology, American Studies, and Film and Media Studies at Rider University. His book, *The Making of American Audiences* (2000), won the International Communication Association Best Book Award and the American Culture Association Cawelti Prize, and has been translated into Chinese. His most recent book, *The Citizen Audience: Crowds, Publics and Individuals* (2008), links media and politics by exploring how entertainment audiences have been represented and evaluated as citizens. He also edited *Media and Public Spheres* (2008), an international collection of studies. In 2008 he was the Fulbright Distinguished Chair in the History of Communication at Vercelli, Italy.

Chris Cagle is a visiting Assistant Professor of Film History and Theory in the Film and Media Arts Department at Temple University. His research interests include postwar Hollywood cinema, social theory, and documentary studies. His article, "Two Modes of Prestige Film," was the 2006/2007 winner of the *Screen* journal award, and he has forthcoming essays in *Star Decades: 1970s* (2009) and *American Cinema and the Southern Imaginary* (2009). He is currently working on a book-length study on Hollywood liberalism and the social problem film, tracing the genre's industrial economics, public sphere aspirations, and sociology of taste.

Marsha F. Cassidy teaches Media Studies in the Departments of English and the Honors College at the University of Illinois at Chicago. She is an award-winning teacher and feminist scholar whose essays have appeared in a number of journals and books since 1980. Her book, *What Women Watched: Daytime Television in the 1950s* (2005), offers a critical appraisal of popular women's genres before the prominence of soap opera.

Sue Collins recently completed her dissertation from the Department of Media, Culture, and Communication at New York University. Her dissertation examines the US government's recruitment of film stardom as a source of political authority during the World War I bond drives. Her recent publications include "Making the Most Out of 15 Minutes; Reality TV's Dispensable Celebrity," *Television & New Media*; "Traversing Authenticities: President Bartlet and Activist Sheen," *Politico-Entertainment: Television's Take on the Real* (2007); and "Celebrity Activism and 9/11: 'A Simple Show of Unity,'" *War Isn't Hell, It's Entertainment: War in Modern Culture and Visual Media* (forthcoming, 2009).

Harper Cossar is a Visiting Instructor at Georgia State University. His publications have appeared in *Flow, Quarterly Review of Film and Video, Journal of New Media and Culture, Film and History: An Interdisciplinary Journal of Film and Television Studies* and *Journal of Film and Video* (forthcoming). He is currently at work on a book-length project about widescreen film style, genre, and authorship. He has previously written about golf narrative in "Televised Golf and the Creation of Narrative" in the anthology *All-Stars and Movie Stars: Sports in Film and History* (2008).

Ken Feil is Scholar-in-Residence in the Department of Visual and Media Arts at Emerson College. He earned his Ph.D. in Radio-Television-Film at The University of Texas at Austin. He is the author of *Dying for a Laugh: Disaster Movies and the Camp Imagination* (2005) and " 'Esthetically As Well As Morally Repulsive': *Kiss Me, Stupid*, 'Bilious' Billy, and Middlebrow Taste" (forthcoming). He is currently at work on a book about "bad" taste in American mainstream film and television comedy of the 1960s and 1970s.

Kathryn H. Fuller-Seeley is an Associate Professor of Moving Image Studies at Georgia State University, whose research specializations are early US film exhibition and historical audience reception studies. Recent publications include: *Hollywood in the Neighborhood: Historical Case Studies of Local Moviegoing* (ed.) (2008); "Learning to Live with Television: Technology, Gender and America's Early TV Audiences" in *The Columbia History of Television* (2007); "Dish Night at the Movies: Exhibitor Promotions and Female Audiences during the Great Depression" in *Looking Past the Screen* (2007); and " 'What the Picture Did for Me': Small Town Exhibitors' Strategies for Surviving the Great Depression" in *Hollywood in the Neighborhood* (2008).

Derek Johnson is a Ph.D. candidate in Media and Cultural Studies at the University of Wisconsin, Madison, where his dissertation examines entertainment franchises as an historical nexus of economic, creative, and democratic cultural practices. His prior publications include "Inviting Audiences In: The Spatial Reorganization of Production and Consumption in 'TVIII'" in *New Review of Film and Television* and "A Knight of the Realm vs. The Master of Magnetism: Sexuality, Stardom, and Character Branding" in *Popular Communication*. He has also published anthology chapters in *Fandom: Identities and Communities in a Mediated World* (2007) and *Film and Comic Books* (2007).

Dan Leopard is an Assistant Professor of Media Studies at Saint Mary's College in the San Francisco Bay Area. He has a Ph.D. from the School of Cinema-Television at the University of Southern California in Los Angeles and an MFA from the School of the Art Institute of Chicago. His essays have been published in *Cinema Journal*, *Television and New Media*, and *Flow*. He is completing a book on the interplay between pedagogical agents and teaching machines across the screens of media culture.

Elana Levine is Associate Professor in the Department of Journalism and Mass Communication at the University of Wisconsin-Milwaukee. She is the author of *Wallowing in Sex: The New Sexual Culture of 1970s American Television* (2007) and the co-editor of *Undead TV: Essays on Buffy the Vampire Slayer* (2007). She has also published articles in such journals as *Critical Studies in Media Communication*, *Television and New Media*, *Media, Culture and Society*, and *Feminist Media Studies* (forthcoming).

Hamid Naficy is the John Evans Professor of Communication, teaching screen cultures courses in the Department of Radio, Television, and Film, Northwestern University. His areas of research and teaching include documentary and ethnographic films; cultural studies of diaspora, exile, and postcolonial media; and Iranian and Middle Eastern cinemas. Among his English language books are: *An Accented Cinema* (2001), *Home, Exile, Homeland* (1999), *The Making of Exile Cultures* (1993), and *Otherness and the Media* (1993). His forthcoming multi-volume book, *Cinema, Modernity, and National Identity: A Social History of a Century of Iranian Cinema*, will be published by Duke University Press.

Alisa Perren is Assistant Professor in the Department of Communication at Georgia State University. Her research interests include television studies, media industry studies, and US film and television history. She has published on the development of niche markets in contemporary Hollywood as well as on the formation of US broadcast and cable networks in the 1990s. Her essays have appeared in *Film Quarterly*, *Journal of Film and Video*, *The Television History Book* (2003), and *The SAGE Handbook of Media Studies* (2004), and she is co-editor of *Media Industries: History, Theory, and Method* (2009).

Karl Schoonover is Assistant Professor of Film Studies in the Department of English at Michigan State University. He is completing a book that examines how the international success of Italian Neorealism endorsed the idea of a global film culture after World War II, refashioning the practice and politics of filmgoing. He is also co-editing an anthology on art cinema for Oxford University Press. In addition to his published work on Italian cinema, classical film theory, and the history of photography, he has essays in *European Film Theory, An AFI Reader* (2008) and *Screen Stars of the Seventies* (2009).

Laura Isabel Serna is finishing a manuscript on the cultural reception of American films in Greater Mexico during the Silent Era, *Making Cinelandia: American Films and Mexican Film Culture before the Golden Age*. She is currently an Assistant Professor at Florida State University where she teaches courses on cultural history and film.

Mark Williams is Associate Professor of Film and Media Studies at Dartmouth College. He has published in a variety of journals and anthologies, including *New Media: Theories and Practices of Digitextuality*; *Collecting Visible Evidence*; *Television, History, and American Culture*; and *Living Color: Race, Feminism, and Television*. He is the founding editor *of The Journal of e-Media Studies* (http://journals.dartmouth.edu/joems/), and co-edits the book series *Interfaces: Studies in Visual Culture*. His book *Remote Possibilities: A History of Early Television in Los Angeles* is forthcoming.

Pamela Wilson is Associate Professor and Chair of Communication at Reinhardt College. Her interdisciplinary interest in indigenous cultural advocacy through both new and traditional media is reflected in *Global Indigenous Media* (2008), co-edited with Michelle Stewart. Wilson's writing on various aspects of media, cultural politics, television history and popular culture has been published in *Television and New Media*; *Quarterly Review of Film and Video*; *Historical Journal of Film, Radio and Television*; *Camera Obscura*; and *South Atlantic Quarterly*, as well as a number of anthologies.

Also from Routledge

Beyond Prime Time: Television Programming in the Post-Network Era

Edited by Amanda D. Lotz

Daytime soap operas. Evening news. Late-night talk shows. Television has long been defined by its daily schedule, and the viewing habits that develop around it. Technologies like DVRs, iPods, and online video have freed audiences from rigid time constraints—we no longer have to wait for a program to be "on" to watch it—but scheduling still plays a major role in the production of television.

Prime-time series programming between 8:00 and 11:00 p.m. has dominated most critical discussion about television since its beginnings, but *Beyond Prime Time* brings together leading television scholars to explore how shifts in television's industrial practices and new media convergence have affected the other 80% of the viewing day. The contributors explore a broad range of non-prime-time forms including talk shows, soap operas, news, syndication, and children's programs, non-series forms such as sports and made-for-television movies, as well as entities such as local affiliate stations and public television.

Importantly, all of these forms rely on norms of production, financing, and viewer habits that distinguish them from the practices common among prime-time series and often from each other. Each of the chapters examines how the production practices and textual strategies of a particular programming form have shifted in response to sweeping industry changes, together telling the story of a medium in transition at the beginning of the twenty-first century.

Contributors: Sarah Banet-Weiser, Victoria E. Johnson, Jeffrey P. Jones, Derek Kompare, Elana Levine, Amanda D. Lotz, Jonathan Nichols-Pethick, Laurie Ouellette, Erin Copple Smith

Amanda D. Lotz is Associate Professor of Communication Studies at the University of Michigan. She is author of *Redesigning Women: Television after the Network Era* and *The Television Will Be Revolutionized*.

ISBN 10: 0-415-99669-4 (pbk)
ISBN 10: 0-415-99668-6 (hbk)

ISBN 13: 978-0-415-99669-3 (pbk)
ISBN 13: 978-0-415-99668-6 (hbk)

Available at all good bookshops
For ordering and further information please visit:
www.routledge.com